Ada® in Industry

The Ada Companion Series

There are currently no better candidates for a co-ordinated, low risk, and synergetic approach to software development than the Ada programming language. Integrated into a support environment, Ada promises to give a solid standards-orientated foundation for higher professionalism in software engineering.

This definitive series aims to be the guide to the Ada software industry for managers, implementors, software producers and users. It will deal with all aspects of the emerging industry: adopting an Ada strategy, conversion issues, style and portability issues, and management.

Some current titles:

Life cycle support in the Ada environment
Edited by J. McDermid and K. Ripken

Portability and style in Ada
Edited by J.C.D. Nissen and P.J.L. Wallis

Ada: Languages, compilers and bibliography
Edited by M.W. Rogers

Ada for multi-microprocessors
Edited by M. Tedd, S. Crespi-Reghizzi and A. Natali

Proceedings of the Third Joint Ada Europe/Ada Tec Conference
Edited by J. Teller

Proceedings of the 1985 Ada International Conference
Edited by J.G.P. Barnes and G.A. Fisher

Ada for specification: possibilities and limitations
Edited by S.J. Goldsack

Concurrent programming in Ada
A. Burns

Ada: Managing the transition
Proceedings of the 1986 Ada-Europe International Conference
Edited by P.J.L. Wallis

Selecting an Ada environment
Edited by T.G.L. Lyons and J.C.D. Nissen

Scientific Ada
Edited by B. Ford, J. Kok and M.W. Rogers

Ada components: Libraries and tools
Proceedings of the 1987 Ada-Europe International Conference
Edited by S. Tafvelin

Programming Distributed Systems in Ada
Edited by C. Atkinson, T. Moreton and A. Natali

Ada in Industry

Proceedings of the Ada-Europe International Conference
Munich 7-9 June 1988

Edited by

STEPHAN HEILBRUNNER

Industrieanlagen-Betriebsgesellschaft mbH
Ottobrunn, Fed. Rep. of Germany

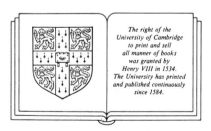

The right of the
University of Cambridge
to print and sell
all manner of books
was granted by
Henry VIII in 1534.
The University has printed
and published continuously
since 1584.

CAMBRIDGE UNIVERSITY PRESS

Cambridge

New York   New Rochelle   Melbourne   Sydney

Published by the Press Syndicate of the University of Cambridge
The Pitt Building, Trumpington Street, Cambridge CB2 1RP
32 East 57th Street, New York, NY 10022, USA
10 Stamford Road, Oakleigh, Melbourne 3166, Australia

First published 1988

Printed in Great Britain at the University Press, Cambridge

Library of Congress Cataloging in Publication data available

British Library Cataloguing in Publication data

Ada-Europe International Conference
(*1988 : Munich, Germany*)
Ada in industry : proceedings of the Ada-Europe International Conference,
Munich, 7-9 June 1988. --- (The Ada Companion series).
1. Industries. Application of computer systems.
Programming languages. Ada language.
I. Title II. Heilbrunner, Stephan
III. Series
338'.06

ISBN 0 521 36347 0

CONTENTS

PREFACE

The theme of this seventh Ada Europe conference is most appropriate for the Ada programming language. The language was designed for applications in technical systems manufacture and it was inspired by the time honoured principles of good engineering which form the basis of the industrial process. It blends convincingly state of the art language features with novel software engineering techniques and refrains from leaving the platform of established rules of programming. It is our hope that this conference will once more prove correct the claim that the Ada language is fit for industry.

In selecting the technical contributions to this conference our endeavour was to achieve a fair balance of reports from industrial applications and presentations of enhancements to the Ada programming environment. The abstracts answering the call for papers were reviewed by a large international panel of referees. The final choice was made on the basis of referee reports by the programme committee consisting of

A. Alvarez
H. Davis
S. Heilbrunner
M. Mac an Airchinnigh
J.-P. Rosen

The programme Committee is most grateful to the referees and to the sponsoring organisations as well as to the many unnamed individuals who made this conference possible. Special mention should be made of J. and E. Teller who organised the local arrangements and of Cambridge University Press for their co-operation in publishing these proceedings in their Ada Companion Series.

Stephan Heilbrunner
Programme Chairman

Part 1 The Ada Workbench

NASA SOFTWARE SUPPORT ENVIRONMENT: CONFIGURING AN ENVIRONMENT FOR ADA DESIGN

F. Blumberg

J. Kantor

M. McNickle
Planning Research Corporation, 1150 Gemini Dr., Houston, TX 77085

A. Reedy
Planning Research Corporation,1500 Planning Research Dr., McLean, VA 22102

Abstract. The NASA Space Station Program Software Support Environment (SSE) is the standard software engineering environment that will be used for the development, integration, and maintenance of the operational Space Station Program software. This paper reports on the Ada design approach chosen for the SSE and on the configuration of the SSE Interim System to support this design approach. The Interim System provides an example of current Ada design techniques and an environment that can be configured to support these techniques for a large project.

Introduction

The National Aeronautics and Space Administration (NASA) Space Station Program Software Support Environment (SSE) is the standard software engineering environment that will be used for the development, integration, and maintenance of all Space Station Program software. As NASA has mandated Ada for all operational Space Station Program software, the SSE will be developed in Ada and will support the use of Ada. The first phase in the development of the SSE is the Interim System, which is currently operational at Johnson Space Center (JSC) in Houston, Texas. The Interim System is supporting work on the early phases of the lifecycle for NASA Space Station Work Package centers and contractors. The Interim System also supports the development of the Initial SSE System, scheduled for release in October of 1988. The Interim System is an operational prototype for later releases of the SSE and embodies the kernel concepts that will be used as the basis for later SSE design. This paper reports on the Ada design approach chosen for the SSE and on the configuration of the Interim System to support this design approach.

The Interim SSE is based on a portable, distributable framework that allows integration of third party software tools. The tools supply the "active" components of the environment and create or modify products including design or program components. The framework supplies the "passive" logistics support for the environment, including the Project Object Base, configuration control and management, and standards and testing enforcement. The framework is configurable to project needs: by lifecycle methodology; by project products; and by project organization. The environment as a whole is configurable to the methods selected for each lifecycle phase by integrating tools that support the selected methods. The impact of Ada on configuration management and standards and testing enforcement is outside the scope of this report and is discussed in Blumberg, et al. (1987). This paper focuses on those aspects of the environment configuration affected by the Ada design approach selected.

The design approach for the SSE is object oriented and has evolved from past experience on Ada contracts and on internal projects, both Ada and non-Ada. The approach has grown from the integration of techniques for the design of asynchronous data-coupled processes and of Ada specific techniques. The Ada specific techniques were first used on the design of a small information system (see McNickle & Reedy, (1986)) where an Ada specific diagramming technique proved extremely useful. The asynchronous process techniques have been used in the design of a variety of highly successful information systems. Each set of techniques complements the other, and the synthesis provides a solid design approach that can be further refined through experience. The approach is also consistent with other design approaches that are emerging in the Ada industry.

The following paragraphs will provide background on the SSE and address the lifecycle methodology required for SSE development, the methods chosen for the design phases of the lifecycle, and the tools selected to support the chosen methods and their integration into the Interim System framework.

Background

According to the definition in NASA (1987), the SSE is the software, procedures, standards, hardware specifications, documentation, policy, and training materials which, when implemented on SSE System hardware, provides the environment to be used for the lifecycle management of all Space Station Program operational software. The SSE is to be developed and maintained in a specialized SSE System facility called the SSE Development Facility (SSEDF). The NASA Work Package centers and contractors will perform software development at SSE System facilities called Software Production Facilities (SPFs) which will support the subset of the full SSE capabilities needed for the Work Package mission. The SSE subsets for the SPFs will be generated and managed by the SSEDF. The SSEDF will support the full SSE.

The Interim System consists of the Interim SSE supported at an interim SSEDF plus a network with workstations located at NASA centers and Work Package contractor sites. Until their own SPFs can be set up, the Work Package centers and contractors will use the facilities at the SSEDF. The Initial System will consist of the Interim System plus an additional mainframe from a different vendor architecture. Additional tools for that mainframe will also be added to the overall tool set. The Initial System SSEDF will be moved to a permanent building at JSC.

The Interim SSE contains both commercially available and proprietary software. The SSE will evolve towards a combination of NASA owned and commercially available software. The framework for the Interim SSE, the Automated Product Control Environment, is proprietary software from Planning Research Corporation (PRC). It will be replaced by NASA owned software as the SSE is developed. The proprietary software tools that are being employed in the Interim SSE will be replaced by NASA owned tools or by commercially available software.

The contract for the design and development of the SSE was won by a team headed by Lockheed Missles and Space Corporation. PRC is the major subcontractor on that team with responsibilities in the areas of system architecture and software development.

Lifecycle Methodology

The software lifecycle methodology required for the SSE project is similar to DOD-STD 2167 (1985). The phases relevant to Ada design are software requirements analysis, software preliminary design, and software detailed design. The corresponding reviews are the Software Specification Review, the Preliminary Design Review, and the Critical Design Review, respectively. Prototyping will be used for verification and validation of concepts in the Requirements Analysis and Preliminary Design phases.

The SSE framework requires testing of the products generated during each phase of the lifecycle as an integral part of the phase. This testing can be configured by product, but a minimal level must be defined and performed before a product can be released. This minimal testing must consist of one level each of component, integration, and system level testing for each product. Reviews are considered a "system" level test for a document product. Prototyping activities can also be configured as system level tests for requirements analysis and design documents. Requirements analysis prototyping should consist of prototypes for testing external interfaces, especially user interfaces (if present). Preliminary design prototypes should test the basic features of the architecture, implementing the critical functionality and using the proposed protocols and communications to test the performance and capacity assumptions of the design.

The SSE will be developed in a series of incremental deliveries, where each delivery provides enhanced automation of functions. Each delivery corresponds to a complete pass through the lifecycle, with each pass producing an enhancement to features of the previous delivery. Each new delivery will be developed using the previous delivery.

Methods

Specific development methods have been chosen to support each phase of the SSE lifecycle. In general, the design methods were chosen based on Lockheed team experience and on analysis of industry trends in Ada software engineering. The chosen set of lifecycle methods had to fit together to provide smooth transitions between phases. Also, methods were chosen which involved notations and processes that were well suited for automated support.

The selected methods are expected to evolve and change over the life of the SSE project. A new method can replace an old one provided that the new method supports the transformations between both the prior and subsequent phases of the lifecycle and that the new method can be supported adequately with software tools available on the SSE hardware configuration. The tool integration concept of the framework allows the environment to be retooled easily to adapt to software technology changes, as discussed below.

The methods chosen for those phases most relevant to Ada design, Preliminary Design and Detailed Design, are discussed below.

Preliminary Design. The method used in the Preliminary Design phase is called Structured Object Oriented Design (SOOD). It is similar in some respects to other emerging object oriented approaches but is integrated with a Structured Analysis approach and focuses on identifying asynchronous processes at a high level.

Data Flow Diagrams (DFDs) with associated Data Dictionary information and the software CSCI and CSC hierarchy with the allocated requirements are the major inputs to the Ada design portion of Preliminary Design from the Requirements Analysis phase. The DFDs are used to extract the relevant objects to begin object oriented design. This selection of objects is a non-trivial process. On a high level, the asynchronous process objects (i.e., active objects) and major data manager objects (i.e., passive objects through which the asynchronous process objects interact) are identified. The relationship among the process objects and the system states, as represented by the data in the data manager objects, is recorded. For example, two of the asynchronous process objects for the SSE framework might be the process to develop a software component and the process to test a softwware component or group of components. The test process can execute only when the components in question are ready for testing; i.e.,when the development process is complete for those components.

Once identified, the high level objects are allocated to a CSC. In SOOD, the CSCI and CSC structure is used for the management of the software and related documentation. CSCs are not assumed to relate to a single Ada unit. Refinement and object oriented decomposition progresses until individual library units, for some appropriate level of detail, are identified.

The notation used for Ada Preliminary Design is Buhr style diagrams, based on the diagrams introduced in Buhr (1984), with added data dictionary entries, and state transition diagrams. The diagramming technique is an extension of that presented in Buhr. At the high level, a new symbol has been introduced to represent asynchronous processes (see Figure 1a) since these process objects may not be implemented as Ada tasks. (In fact, each asynchronous process may be implemented as a separate Ada program that communicates only through information in a database.) The diagramming technique is used at the higher levels to present a picture of a part of the system based on Ada concepts, but without implying a specific implementation. This approach is consistent with Buhr's approach. Data Dictionary entry formats have been defined for each diagram entity. These entries include such items as: the name of the entity; its purpose and function; information on parameters, exceptions, and/or generic instantiations; and design rationale.

The SOOD diagramming approach emphasizes flexibility in the amount of detail visible on any given diagram. The rule is to practice abstraction and only show the details of interest for the design concept that the diagram is illustrating. For example, if an entity (symbol representing an Ada unit or a subpart thereof) is placed on a drawing for the purpose of displaying a dependency, a "specification" style version of that entity should be used as illustrated in Figure 1b. Such a version of the entity symbol shows only the sockets (callable subparts of the entity such as subprograms for packages or entries for tasks) as details. If there are many sockets for this entity, only the ones that are called are shown. If this level of detail is still too high, the calls and sockets can be collapsed. There should also be "body" level diagrams of entities where all the sockets are shown along with any dependencies and internal structures of interest as illustrated in Figure 1c. For example, a generic package is always illustrated by a "body" style diagram, but its instances are represented by "specification" style diagrams since there is no need to repeat the detail.

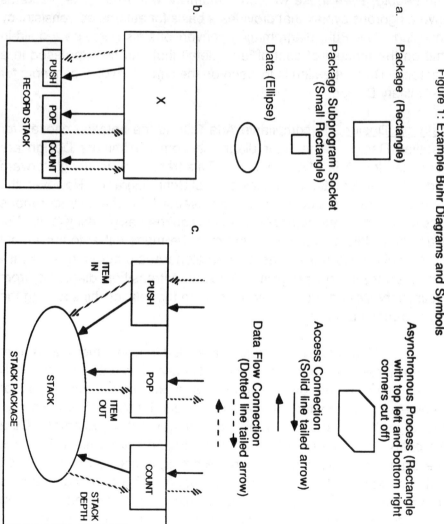

Figure 1: Example Buhr Diagrams and Symbols

SOOD was developed to integrate the object oriented approaches emerging in industry with the Structured Analysis method and asynchronous process analysis that has worked very well in previous experience. Both the notation and the method processes are similar in many ways to those presented in Booch (1987) and NASA (1986). The Buhr style diagrams were selected because they provide a graphic presentation that is reasonably compact and has a clear relationship to Ada. The graphic format promotes good communication with people, even those who are unfamiliar with Ada. The diagrams have a rigorous syntax that provides a basis for automated consistency checking. The Buhr diagramming conventions also provide a build-in limit on the amount of control level detail that can be expressed in a diagram. Thus, attention is focused on the correct level of concepts for Preliminary Design.

Detailed Design. A compilable Ada PDL is the notation chosen for Detailed Design. The Buhr diagrams from Preliminary Design are translated into Ada PDL skeletons. This translation is straightforward and can be automated for the lower level Buhr diagrams. However, the translation of the components represented by the asynchronous processes and data manager objects requires design decisions. For example, at this point the decision must be made either to implement the asynchronous process as a stand alone Ada program or as a task within a larger Ada program. The state transition diagrams from Preliminary Design provide information on the relationships among the asynchronous processes.

The Ada PDL skeletons are filled in using information from the Preliminary Design phase Data Dictionary. The data Dictionary will contain information on exceptions and the mode and types of parameters, commentary on the purpose and function of components, and algorithmic and performance requirements. Example Data Dictionary entries for two of the entities in Figure 1 are given in Figure 2. The Data Dictionary contents and the prologue comments of the Ada PDL are standardized so that the transfer of information can be automated. Refinement proceeds by filling in more detail, first to complete the specifications, and then, where necessary, to fill in algorithmic information for some of the bodies. Object oriented decomposition is performed as required. The approach chosen allows flexibility so that more detail can be supplied for those units that are the most difficult and unclear. Units that can be supplied from a reuseable library, or that are well understood and require only straightforward coding, require only a complete specification.

Figure 2: Example Data Dictionary Entries

Entity Type: Package   Name: RECORD STACK

Generic Instance of:
    STACK PACKAGE   Library Unit: Yes

Description: RECORD STACK is an instantiation
of STACK PACKAGE with Item Type RECORD. It is
intended for import by units that require LIFO
storge of RECORDs.

Entity Type: Package Socket   Name: PUSH

In Package: STACK PACKAGE

Description: Procedure PUSH has one input parameter
of type ITEM. PUSH places the value of the input
parameter on the top of the stack. If the stack is
full, PUSH raises an exception.

Compilable Ada PDL was chosen because it has worked well in past experience and is rapidly becoming the Ada industry standard for Detailed Design. There is a smooth transition from the Buhr diagrams of Preliminary Design into the Ada PDL and a trivial transition into Ada code for implementation. Minimal automated support is supplied by Ada compilers, and more sophisticated support tools are becoming widely available due to industry demand. The major problem with the use of Ada PDL is the development and enforcement of standards to prevent premature coding.

Tools

Given the selection of design methods, the selection of tools to support the given methods was a process of evaluating a variety of trade-offs. The emphasis for the Interim System configuration was on the acquisition of available commercial tools, not on the development or even the transporting of tools. There were no fixed hardware requirements for the SSE Interim System when tool selection began, so there was relative freedom to select tools. There were sets of criteria that were applied to individual tools and to the tool set as a whole. The goal of the combined tool/hardware selection process was to select a mainframe and a set of workstations and tools such that equivalent functionality was available to any type of user through any workstation.

One criteria for the tool set as a whole (i.e., the tool set for the entire lifecycle) was the constraint that each tool in the set run on one or more pieces of hardware in the same mainframe/terminal set configuration. There were pragmatic constraints on the mainframe and terminals selected. They had to be commercially supported, widely accepted by industry, and had to have a wide range of software products available. Emphasis was placed on selecting a tool set with as much functionality as possible residing on the workstations. The goal was to reduce user dependence on the network and to insulate the user from the mainframe operating system. With both framework processes and tools resident on the workstations, the users can interact with the Project Object Base while remaining in complete ignorance of its location. This latter feature will become more important when the Initial System becomes available and the Project Object Base may reside on either of two different mainframes.

The criteria applied to individual tools fell into three major categories: method support criteria; framework integration criteria; and large project support criteria. In the area of method support, the trade-offs were among features such as flexibility or customizability and interactive standards enforcement. Ideally, a tool should offer integrated support for method notation and transformations with interactive enforcement of standards and, at the same time, be readily customizable. In the area of framework integration support, tools need to support the import and export of individual product components: individual diagrams and related data dictionary information or units of Ada PDL, in the case of design products. Ideally, the tools should produce export files that are formatted according to industry wide or hardware vendor supported standards (e.g., ASCII or Postscript). In the area of large project support, tools need to be able to integrate design components from large numbers of designers so that consistency checking could take place. If the tools do not meet the criteria in the last two areas, then the cost of providing software to make the tool meet minimum requirements must be measured against the benefits of using the tool.

The design tool and hardware configuration selected for the Interim System is shown in Figure 3. In some cases, the workstations must access tools on the mainframe in terminal mode. The Rational system has been included as an optional piece of special purpose hardware for Ada support. (That is, the Rational is included in the Interim System SSEDF but will not be required for SPFs.) PLEXUS is a Lockheed proprietary tool; all others are commercially available. The remaining paragraphs in this section present and discuss as examples the major tradeoffs considered for some of the tools that were selected.

Figure 3: SSE Interim System Hardware and Ada Design Support Tools

	Preliminary Design	Detailed Design
Macintosh II	Power Tools	DEC LSE
IBM PC AT Compatible	Customized Excelerator	DEC LSE
APOLLO	PLEXUS	Rational PDL DEC LSE
Rational	N/A	Rational PDL

Mainframe: DEC VAX 8700

 Shading indicates use in workstation terminal mode

The tool chosen to support Preliminary Design on the IBM PS2 was Excelerator. This tool is customizable and allowed the introduction of the Buhr diagramming techniques and the coupling of these to new data dictionary forms. In addition, reports were programmed to identify violations of many of the design consistency rules. This tool allows the needed flexibility in an design notation that is still evolving, although it does so at the cost of making many standards and consistency checks after the fact instead of interactively. The tool allows export and import so that design segments (both graphics and data dictionary information) from several designers can be integrated for consistency checking. This import/export feature also makes it easier to integrate Excelerator into the Interim System framework. Excelerator has the added advantages that it supports Data Flow Diagrams (used in the Requirements Analysis phase) and state transition diagrams and that it may be available on other workstations in the future.

The tool chosen to support Detailed Design was the integrated PDL support feature of the Rational system. Here, the highly interactive nature of the tool was its chief advantage. The tool enforced most of the standards interactively and further customizing features are expected in future releases. Import and export of compilable Ada PDL as Ada source is straightforward, and the Rational system offers good facilities for integrating Ada (PDL) units into libraries, which of course, is a primary method for consistency checking for Ada PDL.

Use of the Rational system and its specialized hardware is not required, however. Users can also access the mainframe in terminal emulation mode to use the DEC VAX Language Sensitive Editor (LSE) for PDL support. The LSE is customizable for standards enforcement and can be run with the DEC Ada compiler in an integrated mode. However, the degree of integration and interactive standards enforcement is not as high as with the Rational system. Again, import and export of Ada PDL is treated in the same way as ordinary source code. The DEC Ada compiler system will also allow the integration of the PDL units into libraries but offers less automated support for this process than the Rational.

Tool Integration

The major form of designer interaction with the environment framework is very straightforward. After receiving management approval to begin a work task, the designer checks out the designated design component for work, and the current baseline version (null for new work) is delivered to his local workstation (if he is working in distributed mode) or host workspace (if he is working in terminal mode). The designer then uses the available workstation or network based tools to create or modify the design component. When he is satisfied with his work, he checks in the component, and the framework marks the new version for formal testing. Only the designer who checked out the component may check it back in. No further changes can be made to the baseline version (contained in the Project Object Base) unless new changes (as the result of change requests) are authorized by management or the component is returned from formal testing for corrections. Designers can get "read only" copies of any design component or a component from a previous lifecycle phase at any time.

Thus, the tools are loosely coupled to the Interim System framework. Integration consists of establishing the procedures necessary to pass product parts to the framework, in and out of the tool-independent Project Object Base. Product parts are kept in a standard internal form within the Project Object Base. These standard formats has been developed to support the translation between tool specific formats. The goal is to support the processing of product parts by any tool of the appropriate functionally equivalent set, regardless of the tool or workstation that was first used to create the part. For example, a design drawing with the associated data dictionary information, first created by a designer using Excelerator on the IBM PS2, should be modifiable by a designer using Power Tools on the Macintosh II. This translation is already available for the different word processors selected for the Interim System.

The loose coupling of tools allows easy replacement of tools with new or upgraded tools. However, new tools must be qualified for use by the same process that was used to select the original tools. This loose coupling of tools is necessary to allow flexibility for adapting to the rapidly changing technology in the software industry and for adapting an environment for the diverse needs of an organization like NASA. The approach does not preclude the use of an integrated tool set or of tools that require specialized hardware as shown by the inclusion of the Rational system in the Interim System. Loose coupling provides support for changes in the lifecycle methodology and methods, as well as in individual tools or sets of tools. Further, the amount of technology insertion is under the control of the project manager.

Summary

The SSE Interim System provides an example of current Ada design techniques and an environment that can be configured to support these techniques in a large project environment. All the technology discussed is currently in use, although some of the software is proprietary and not commercially available. The SSE Interim System framework allows the flexibility to refine the methods during a long project and to incorporate new and improved tools as they become available. The criteria for selecting methods and support tools are being carefully recorded so that this process can be assisted by an expert system in the future. This case study shows the extent to which automated support can currently be applied to Ada design.

References

ANSI/MIL-STD 1815A (1983). Ada Programming Language.
Blumberg, F., McNickle, M., Reedy, A., and Stephenson, D. (1987). A Compiler Independent Approach to Test and Configuration Management for Ada. In Proceedings of the Joint Ada Conference, Arlington, VA, March 16-19, pp.205-212. Springfield, VA: U. S. Department of Commerce.
Booch, G. (1987). Software Components with Ada. Menlo Park, CA: Benjamin/Cummings.
Buhr, R. (1984). System Design with Ada. Englewood Cliffs, N.J.: Prentice-Hall.
DOD-STD 2167 (1985). Defense Systems Software Development.
McNickle, M. & Reedy, A. (1986). Experiences in Using Ada with DBMS Applications. Ada User, 7 , no. 3, 54-61.
NASA (1986). General Object-Oriented Software Development. NASA Software Engineering Laboratory Series, SEL-86-002.
NASA (1987). Space Station Software Support Environment Functional Requirements Specification. JSC 30500, Draft 4.0.

Configuration Management and Version Control in the Rational Programming Environment

Thomas M. Morgan

Rational
1501 Salado Drive
Mt. View, California 94043
U.S.A.

1. Introduction

The Rational Programming Environment has been designed to provide full lifecycle support for Ada[1] software systems. Early releases of the Environment concentrated on tools to support the coding and debugging phases of the lifecycle. These tools included a syntax directed editor, a validated Ada compiler with incremental capabilities, a symbolic debugger, interactive cross reference facilities, and an Ada specific command interface. All tools were integrated under a common interactive editor-based interface.

Recent releases have extended the Environment by adding tools for design support, compilation for multiple targets, and configuration management and version control. This paper describes the Configuration Management and Version Control System (CMVC). CMVC provides methods for system decomposition, library management, configuration management, source control and project management. CMVC is designed to enhance the modularity, abstraction, and reusability features of the Ada programming language [9]. Special importance is placed on integration between CMVC and the underlying programming environment.

2. Goals

CMVC was designed with several goals in mind. These goals have been derived from Rational's experience in developing large Ada systems [1]. This experience has shown, for example, that conventional schemes separating configuration management from library management are impractical for large systems developed using Ada and modern software engineering principles. The goals of CMVC are:

1. Provide support for the decomposition of systems into smaller component subsystems that can be developed, tested, and released independently. Decomposition into subsystems implies that the interfaces and connectivity of the subsystems must be managed.

2. Support flexible system construction from diverse components. In order to support recombinant testing and release strategies it must be possible to combine subsystems into system configurations without an inordinate amount of effort. For example, system construction should not require recompilation of the entire system.

3. Track the history of versions and configurations. During the development of large systems it is important to be able to track the history of individual versions and the configurations that those versions participate in. This is especially important when multiple developers are working on the same versions and configurations.

4. Coordinate multiple developers and multiple development activities. In large development projects,

---

[1]Ada is a registered trademark of the U.S. Government Ada Joint Program Office

multiple developers will need to work on the same objects and thus must be coordinated to prevent conflicts. Furthermore, since developers will often be working on many activities it should be possible to track the progress and effects of each individual activity.

5.   Integrate configuration management and library management. CMVC should prevent the confusion that can arise when program libraries become out of date with respect to source configurations.

6.   Integrate configuration management and version control with the underlying programming environment to prevent subversion of CMVC policies. Furthermore, the configuration management policies that are provided should be well suited to the software engineering principles embodied in Ada.

The following sections will show how CMVC has attempted to satisfy its design goals and how it compares to similar systems.

3. Subsystems

As was mentioned above, it is important in the development of a large system to be able to decompose it into a set of subsystems that can be developed, tested, and released independently. CMVC supports the creation of subsystems and controls the interfaces and interconnections among them.

3.1. Basic Subsystem Concepts

A subsystem is composed of a set of *elements*. Elements may be Ada program units, documents, test data, or other types of objects. Each element may have multiple *generations*, that reflect different states of the element. For example, the generations of an Ada program unit contain the source code for the unit at different points in its development history.

The mechanism used to select a generation for elements in the subsystem is called a *view*. Views are source configurations in the sense that they specify a generation of the source for elements in the subsystem. Views are also program libraries in the sense that they enforce Ada semantic consistency on the generations selected by the view. Generations in the view that are not semantically consistent appear in an "uncompiled" state. Each view maintains a distinct copy of the source for the generations that it selects. The copy is used for compilation into the program library of the view and for use by the interactive cross-reference tools that operate on compiled objects. The source control tools described later ensure that if two views select the same generation then they have identical copies of the source.

In the same way that subsystems are used to group together sets of logically related elements, views are used to group together and compile together sets of logically related generations. For example, a single subsystem might contain all of the source code necessary to implement a set of device drivers. Different views in the subsystem can represent alternative implementations as new operations are added or bugs are fixed.

Compilation in a view is accomplished by basic mechanisms in the Environment. Compilation dependencies are computed automatically from the text of the generations. The dependencies are used to correctly compile individual units or entire views according to Ada language semantics. All compilation occurs in the program library associated with the view. Incremental compilation at the declaration and statement level for units in views is also supported.

Figure 3.1 displays the structure of a sample subsystem. The subsystem contains two views. Each view selects a generation for the two elements in the subsystem. Both views select the same generation for the first element, but a different generation is selected for the second element. Since the views are also program libraries, the views contain the compiled code for the selected generations.

Subsystem

Figure 3.1. - A Simple Subsystem

3.2. Subsystem Interfaces

In order to control the interfaces between subsystems and reduce compilation requirements, subsystems have the equivalent of visible parts and bodies. *Spec views* contain the Ada specifications that are exported by subsystems. *Load views*[2] contain the complete ada units (specifications and bodies) for the subsystem, and thus represent complete implementations. Spec views need only contain Ada specifications because these views are only used for compilation by other subsystems. Load views contain complete Ada units because the code in these views is actually executed.

A *client view* is a view containing Ada units that require Ada visibility to the units in another subsystem in order to compile. A *supplier view* is a spec view that contains Ada specifications that views in other subsystems may compile against. Client views *import* supplier views. Importing by a client view provides the client with Ada visibility to the Ada specifications compiled into the program library of the supplier view. For example, assume a low level subsystem contains packages that define basic types. If other subsystems contain views that wish to use the basic types then two things must occur. First, a supplier spec view must be created which contains the package defining the basic types. Second, client views in other subsystems must import the supplier spec view in order to get Ada visibility to the package containing the basic types.

Importing allows the Ada units in a client view to be compiled against the units in a supplier view. Since only spec views can be imported there are never any cross-subsystem compilation dependencies on Ada units in load views. This provides an important boundary on recompilation effects. In particular, load views may be changed and recompiled without causing recompilation in any other subsystems. This boundary on recompilation is important in large system development to decrease turn-around time and improve the interactive nature of development activities.

Importing establishes a one-way *import relationship* between the supplier and client views. The import relationships between views are useful in imposing a hierarchical structure on the overall system. In the same way that Ada specifications are prevented from having circularities in their context closure, supplier spec views are prevented from having such circularities by CMVC. Such a restriction is useful in enforcing hierarchical design rules.

---

[2]Load views are so named because they are referenced by the linker-loader.

Subsystem spec and load views are a natural structuring mechanism for Ada programs. Ada makes an important distinction between specification and implementation. Subsystems extend this distinction beyond the unit level to groups of related units that should be developed, tested, and released as a group.

3.3. System Construction

Subsystems generally contain multiple load views. Each load view represents an alternative implementation of the subsystem. The construction of a system for execution requires the selection of a single load view for each subsystem. An *activity* is a data structure that selects a load view for each subsystem. Activities are used by the linker-loader to resolve the references that were created when a client view was compiled against Ada units in a supplier spec view.

Figure 3.2 presents the structure of a system with two subsystems. Subsystem Device_Drivers implements low level mechanisms for reading and writing physical devices. Subsystem Files implements a file system on top of Device_Drivers.

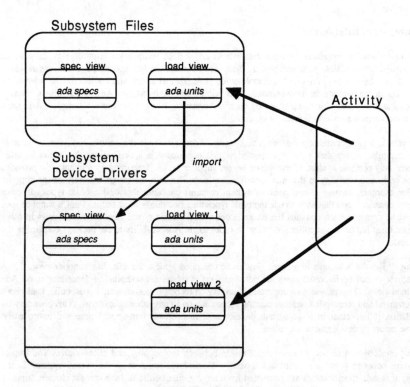

Figure 3.2. - Multiple Subsystems

The load view in the Files subsystem imports the spec view from Device_Drivers to get access to the operations for reading and writing devices. The entire system is specified by the activity which selects one load view from each of the component subsystems.

Execution of programs containing multiple subsystems is possible as long as the load views of a subsystem are *compatible* with the spec views that have been exported by the subsystem. A load view is compatible with a spec view if the load view implements all of the declarations specified in the spec view. For example, assume that Device_Drivers exports an operation Buffered_Read with a specific parameter profile and that a view of the client subsystem Files is compiled against that specification. Correct execution will only occur if Buffered_Read is actually implemented in the load view that is executed. Thus, compatibility means that the operations promised by the spec view are satisfied by the load view.

Operations exist in CMVC to determine compatibility when multiple subsystem programs are constructed. It is important to note that checking compatibility for a large system is significantly less expensive, by several orders of magnitude, than actually recompiling the entire system together in a single library. Thus, the division of subsystems into spec and load views supports all of the compile-time interface checking that is one of the strengths of Ada, but also allows much easier system construction than would be possible in a conventional library system.

It was stated above that execution is possible as long as spec views and load views in a subsystem are compatible. Compatibility is a weaker, but more useful, condition than absolute equality between spec and load views. Compatibility requires that load views implement the Ada specifications in spec views, however load views may also contain additional Ada units, and packages in load views may contain additional declarations. This allows a spec view to be compatible with a set of *upward compatible* load views all of which satisfy the requirements of the spec view.

Activities are integrated with the execution and debugging facilities of the Environment to allow straightforward testing and debugging of systems specified by activities. Developers are able to specify default activities that are to be used whenever any execution or debugging operation is performed.

The use of subsystems and activities supports a recombinant testing strategy that allows views to be combined in a flexible way. Since no recompilation is required to insert a load view into an activity, testing environments can quickly be constructed. For example, a new view can be debugged by testing it within an activity that specifies well tested views for the other subsystems of the system. No compilation is required in order to test in the new environment.

3.4. Programming Environment Integration

The subsystem mechanisms are fully integrated with the Rational Environment. All facilities of the Environment are available for programs developed as subsystems, including:

- Automatic dependency analysis and compilation facility. Semantic dependencies between Ada units (even in other subsystems) are computed automatically and thus cannot become obsolete. The compilation facilities are designed to use the dependency information to compile entire views or systems.

- A symbolic debugger that is integrated with the activity mechanism to allow debugging of multi-subsystem systems.

- Incremental compilation facilities that reduce compilation requirements. This is especially important in large systems to promote interactive development.

- Interactive cross-reference capabilities that deal with cross subsystem dependencies.

- Security for objects provided by the access list mechanism of the Environment.

4. Source Control

The source control functions of CMVC have been designed to track the history of the elements in a subsystem and to coordinate the activity of multiple developers. Source control is built around the concepts of subsystems, elements, views, and generations.

As was mentioned earlier, an element may have multiple generations. The generations form a time-ordered linear sequence of the different states of the element. The development history of each element is represented by the sequence of its generations.

In order to produce a new generation, an element must be *reserved* by a view. A reservation establishes an exclusive right to produce a new generation for an element in the view holding the reservation. Reservations are used to coordinate the activities of multiple developers by prohibiting the creation of conflicting generations in different views.

A reservation is established when an element is *checked-out* by a user into a view. The check-out operation causes the view to select a new generation of the element that is an exact copy of the previous generation. The new generation may be edited in the view holding the reservation. While the reservation is in effect no other view may check-out the same element. The *check-in* operation releases the reservation on the element and makes the new generation permanent.

Operations exist in CMVC to cause a view to select a different generation of an element. Since views are Ada libraries, changing the generation of an element will normally cause recompilation of the element and its Ada dependents in the view. CMVC has been integrated with the compilation system of the Environment to reduce the recompilation requirements whenever possible in such cases. CMVC will attempt to copy compiled state from one view to another to reduce the required recompilation.

CMVC retains the complete history for each element in a subsystem. Generations that are not included in any view are stored in the CMVC Database in a compact differential form. Retention of the complete history is important for maintenance since it may be necessary to determine at a later time exactly what changes were made. All generations of an element may be displayed through the editor interface of the Environment. Furthermore, the differences between successive generations may be displayed.

An interactive note pad is available that allows a developer to associate comments with each generation. Note pads and all other CMVC information are accessible through the common editor-based interface of the Rational Environment. For example, reservation information can be displayed and manipulated through the editor interface.

Figure 4.1 shows a sample display for a view of the Device_Drivers subsystem. The view contains visible parts and bodies for four different Ada compilation units. Each element is named twice to represent each Ada package visible part and body.

```
!Device Drivers.Main Working
    Buffered_Read'G(1)      :   In  87/12/09 13:07:03 MARY
    Buffered_Read'G(2)      :   Out 87/12/09 13:09:48 JOHN
    Disk_Interface'G(3/4)   : * In  87/12/13 11:08:15 JOHN
    Disk_Interface'G(5/8)   : * In  87/12/14 09:05:32 JOHN
    Network_Interface'G(1)  :   In  87/12/09 13:07:16 MARY
    Network_Interface'G(1)  :   In  87/12/09 13:07:16 MARY
    Tape_Interface'G(1)     :   In  87/12/09 13:07:17 MARY
    Tape_Interface'G(1)     :   In  87/12/09 13:07:17 MARY
```

Figure 4.1 - Source Control Display

Each line in figure 4.1 displays source control information for the designated element. The "G'(n)" attribute following each name is used to designate the generation that the view selects for the element. The current reservation state and the time of the last reservation operation follow the name. The body of `Buffered_Read` is checked-out while all other elements are currently checked-in. All generations are up-to-date except for `Disk_Interface` which has undergone development in another view. The view selects the third of four possible generations for the visible part of `Disk_Interface` and the fifth of eight possible generations for the body. The name of the developer who performed the last reservation operation follows the date on each line. The editor-based interface of the Environment allows lines of the display in figure 4.1 to be selected and operated on.

In the previous discussions, each element has a single sequence of generations that represents the development history of the element. CMVC also supports multiple generation sequences that can be used when parallel development is required for an element. When multiple generation sequences are used, each view selects a generation sequence and a generation in that sequence for each element. Reservations are applied to a particular generation sequence. Development can proceed on each generation sequence independently. Generation sequences can be merged together at a later time if desired. The use of multiple generation sequences will be covered in more detail in the next section.

To summarize the source control properties of CMVC:

•   A reservation policy exists that prevents conflicting changes by acquiring exclusive access to elements.

•   Consistency between the source structure and the library structure of a subsystem is guaranteed since views are both source configurations and Ada libraries.

•   Independent or parallel development on a generation can be managed by CMVC through the use of multiple generation sequences that can be reserved independently.

5.   Development Paths

In the previous section generations, generation sequences, views, and reservations were discussed as the mechanisms for source control. CMVC also provides higher level facilities that make use of those mechanisms to provide a model of the development process for subsystems. As the source control mechanisms provide a way to track the history of individual elements, the following mechanisms provide a way to track the history of entire views.

5.1. Coordinated Development

A *development path* is a time-ordered sequence of views representing the development history of a subsystem. A distinguished view, called the *working view*, is always at the head of the sequence. The other views in the sequence are called *releases*. The working view is the view that is used for ongoing development. Releases are snapshots of previous states of the working view which are now frozen and cannot be changed.

CMVC supports multiple lines of coordinated development through *development subpaths*. A subpath is also a sequence of views headed by a working view. However, a subpath is rooted in a parent path in the sense that the subpath was initially created as an exact copy of the path. A subpath shares reservations on all of its elements with its parent. Development is coordinated between a path and its subpaths through the reservations on the elements.

A typical usage of paths and subpaths might include creation of a path for each major development effort on a particular subsystem. A subpath could then be created for each individual developer. Shared reservations on the elements in the subsystem coordinate the developers as they make progress and test code in their subpaths. Changes from several developers are integrated in the main path by using CMVC to update the generations selected by the working view of the path. Once changes have been integrated and tested in the path, a new release can be created.

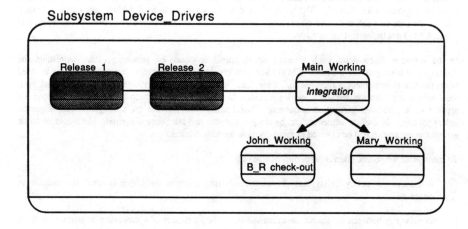

Figure 5.1. - Path Structure

Figure 5.1 presents the path structure for the development of a new `Device_Drivers` product. The main path is called `Main` and has working view `Main_Working`. The view `Main_Working` is used for integration and for the creation of new releases. There have been two releases from the path. The releases are called `Release_1` and `Release_2`. `Release_2` was the last release.

The path in figure 5.1 has a subpath for each developer. The subpaths have working views `John_Working` and `Mary_Working`. New development is carried out in the working views for the subpaths. Currently, the package `Buffered_Read` is checked-out to the view `John_Working` where it is undergoing a major revision. Since it is checked-out, `Buffered_Read` cannot be modified in any other view of the path. When development is finished on `Buffered_Read`, the package will be checked-in and then the view `Main_Working` will be updated to include the new generation of `Buffered_Read`. After testing, a new release of `Main_Working` will be created that includes the updated `Buffered_Read` package.

5.2. Parallel and Multi-Target Development

In the previous sections the emphasis has been on coordinating development activities so that each element in a subsystem develops in an orderly manner. However, it is sometimes the case that an element must develop simultaneously in several different directions. For example, in order to support installed systems it may be necessary to fix bugs, while at the same time a totally new implementation is being developed for the next product. For such circumstances CMVC supports parallel development paths.

Parallel development paths have distinct generation sequences for all of the elements. Development in each path is independent for all elements and no reservations are shared between parallel paths. Elements in parallel paths are checked-out independently, and changes in one path may not be accepted into another path. Parallel paths may also be customized to share reservations on some elements, but remain independent on others.

Parallel development paths provide an effective way to manage the demands of multi-target development. A different target compiler can be associated with each path. For program units that are to be common across targets, the working views of the different target paths can share reservations, and thus have their development coordinated. For program units that need to be distinct for each target the elements can have different reservations and generation sequences and therefore be developed independently.

5.3. Subsystem Releases

In a development path, releases represent previous states of the path. CMVC supports three kinds of releases for use in different situations. All capture the state of the path at the point of release, however, they differ in their execution and debugging characteristics as well as the space required for storage of the release.

- A *released view* is a view that is an exact copy of the path's working view at the time of release. A released view can be executed, the source can be displayed, and the cross reference facilities of the Environment can be run on the view. Furthermore, when executing released views the symbolic debugger of the Environment has full capabilities.

- A *released configuration* is a source configuration that contains all of the generations of the working view. However, released configurations have no program library associated with them and thus cannot be compiled or executed. The source for generations in a released configuration is stored compactly in the CMVC Database. Released configurations are most useful when a previous configuration is to be retained for historical reasons only. Released views can be created from released configurations if a view is later required for execution or debugging.

- A *code-only view* contains executable code in a binary form. Code-only views may be executed, but debugging is limited. The source code that was used to create the code-only view is stored in the CMVC Database and may be displayed but may not be compiled. Code-only views are useful for system releases when source code is not to be revealed or when space usage needs to be minimized.

6. Project Management

Any software development project involves multiple activities each of which may involve the modification of multiple objects. For example, each activity to fix a bug may involve the coordinated changing of several Ada units. In order to track the progress of development activities and the objects they affect, CMVC supports work orders, work order lists, and ventures.

A *work order* is used to keep track of all objects that are modified during a particular development activity. Work orders also record user commentary and status that is entered during the development activity. Work orders automatically collect information about CMVC operations performed under the auspices of the work order. For example, whenever an element is checked-out, that fact is noted automatically in the appropriate work order.

The automatic record keeping abilities of work orders provide a way of tracking the progress of individual development activities and for keeping a permanent record of how development goals are accomplished. The state of a work order can be examined at any time in order to determine what progress has been made toward accomplishing the desired development goal. Also, because work orders are permanent it is possible to review a work order to determine how a development task was accomplished.

Work order lists are used to group work orders together. For example, each developer might have a work order list of work orders that are currently in progress. Similarly, a project manager might have a work order list of work orders that have been created but have not yet been assigned to a developer.

The format and characteristics of the information in a work order are specified by a *venture*. Ventures provide templates for work orders and each work order is associated with exactly one venture. Ventures can be customized to record information specific to a given project. For example, a venture might contain fields specifying which test suites have been run and their results. Ventures may also specify certain policies that must be followed by developers working on the work order of a particular venture. For example, a venture policy may require a developer to provide comments when an object is checked-in.

7. Comparison With Other Systems

A number of systems provide facilities for source control, configuration management and project management. This section will compare and contrast three widely available systems with CMVC. The three systems are:

- The Code Management System/Module Management System (CMS/MMS) [4,5] which is available on DEC VAX/VMS systems. CMS provides source control while MMS constructs systems from VMS files or source structure managed by CMS. CMS/MMS is the VMS equivalent to SCCS [3] and MAKE [6] which are available on UNIX systems.

- The DOMAIN Software Engineering Environment (DSEE) [2,8] which supports software development on Apollo workstations.

- VM/Software Engineering (VM/SE) [7] which runs under VM on IBM System 370 architectures. VM/SE is implemented on top of the SQL/DS relational database system.

The systems will be analyzed along four dimensions: 1) basic source control mechanisms, 2) facilities for system structuring, 3) mechanisms for system construction, and 4) ability to monitor project activities.

7.1. Basic Source Control

All of the systems provide synchronization mechanisms to coordinate the development of source objects by multiple developers. CMS and DSEE support operations similar to check-out and check-in in CMVC. All the systems except VM/SE store generations as incremental changes to conserve space.

DSEE and CMVC explicitly support parallel lines of development that can be merged together at a later time. Also, both DSEE and CMVC support multi-target development by allowing different compiler switches to be explicitly associated with each line of development.

7.2. System Structuring

Most systems provide some facilities for structuring systems along logical boundaries. CMVC supports subsystems for grouping elements and views for gathering together generations. CMS provides *groups* and *classes* for creating collections of elements and sets of generations. VM/SE implements *projects* and *domains* for the same purpose. DSEE has a naming mechanism that can be applied to generations which allows all generations with the same name to be manipulated as a group.

CMVC spec views and import operations provide explicit user control over the relationships between views. Of the other systems, only VM/SE provides any support for managing system connectivity. In VM/SE one domain can reference another only if a *domain relation* has been created. However, unlike CMVC there is no finer control, access to a domain provides access to all objects in the domain. Neither DSEE nor CMS/MMS provide any control over system connectivity.

7.3. System Construction

Constructing systems requires generation selection criteria and compilation rules. Generation selection criteria specifies which generations are to be included in the system. Compilation rules describe how a compiler is to be invoked on the selected generations and what the compilation dependencies are between the generations in the system. Compilation dependencies are used to determine a correct compilation order when building the system.

DSEE provides a flexible mechanism for generation selection by allowing generations to be selected on the basis of name, reservation status, specific generation, or other criteria. MMS supports generation selection based on CMS class or actual generation number. CMVC takes a more structured approach to generation selection at the view level, but a flexible approach at the system level. Because views are both source configurations and program libraries, only the generations that are selected by a view may be compiled together. However, arbitrary views may be combined together into systems through the activity mechanism. Thus, CMVC promotes a tight coupling of generations at the view level but a loose coupling of views into systems.

MMS captures compilation rules in *description files*, while DSEE uses *system models* for the same purpose. Both description files and system models are created and maintained by the system developer, although DSEE does provide a tool to analyze "include" dependencies which are created when one object contains a copy of another object. The problem with system models and description files is that they may contain errors or become obsolete as the structure of the system changes. A more subtle problem is that compilation dependencies may be correct for one set of generations, but incorrect for another. Correct maintenance of compilation dependencies is especially important in Ada due to the complex nature of Ada context dependencies. CMVC computes all compilation dependencies automatically for the actual generations included in a view.

7.4. Project Management

It was mentioner earlier that CMVC provides work orders, work order lists, and ventures to monitor the progress of development activities. DSEE provides similar mechanisms in *tasks* and *task lists*. Both work orders and tasks allow development activities to be monitored by automatically recording objects that have changed, collecting commentary, and maintaining the status of each activity. VM/SE provides a data structure, also called a *task*, for monitoring the status of development activities, but does not automatically record the objects that were changed. CMS has no mechanism for tracking development activity or recording objects that have been updated.

8. Conclusion

Ada supports the development of systems by providing mechanisms for abstraction, modularity, interface checking, and separate compilation. CMVC enhances the mechanisms of Ada by extending them to subsystems which can be used to effectively manage the development of large systems. CMVC supports decomposition and flexible system construction from diverse components. CMVC allows the interfaces between components to be managed. CMVC tracks the history of units and subsystems. CMVC coordinates the activities of multiple developers and tracks their progress. CMVC minimizes compilation costs that can become prohibitive as the size of a system grows. Finally, integration between CMVC and the underlying programming environment produces an implementation that is reliable and straightforward to use.

CMVC is currently being used to manage large software development projects in both the United States and Europe. The Rational Environment itself involves more than one million lines of Ada source code in forty subsystems and is managed by CMVC. The need for CMVC will grow as increasingly ambitious software projects are attempted.

9. Acknowledgments

CMVC is the result of work by a number of people, too numerous to mention individually, who have designed and built the tools described in this paper. CMVC would not be possible without the underlying facilities of the Rational Programming Environment which have been developed over the last seven years by the product development team at Rational.

10. References

1. J.E. Archer Jr. and M.T. Devlin, "Rational's Experience Using Ada for Very Large Systems", *Proceedings of the First International Conference on Ada Programming Language Applications for the NASA Space Station*, (June 1986).

2. "DOMAIN Software Engineering Environment (DSEE) Reference", Apollo Computer Inc., Chelmsford, MA. (July 1985).

3. "Source Code Control System User's Guide", *UNIX System III Programmer's Manual*, Bell Telephone Labs, (October, 1981).

4. "Guide to VAX DEC/Code Management System", Digital Equipment Corporation, (April 1987).

5. "Guide to VAX DEC/Module Management System", Digital Equipment Corporation, (April 1987).

6. S.I. Feldman, "Make - A Program for Maintaining Computer Programs", *Software Practice and Experience*, (April, 1979).

7. "VM/Software Engineering Program Description/Operation Manual", IBM, SH21-0011-0, (November, 1986).

8. D.B. Leblang and R.P. Chase Jr., "Computer-Aided Software Engineering in a Distributed Workstation Environment", *Proceedings of the ACM SIGSOFT/SIGPLAN Software Engineering Symposium on Practical Software Development Environments*, (April 1984).

9. *Reference Manual for the Ada Programming Language*, United States Department of Defense, Washington, D.C., (1983).

A Graphic Workstation for Ada

Helmut Dipper, Roland Klebe
Siemens AG
Communication and Information Systems

Otto-Hahn-Ring 6
D-8000 Muenchen 83

1. Introduction

Just in time for the 1987 Ada-EUROPE conference Siemens
completed the validation of its Ada compiler for the host and
target configuration being operating system BS2000 on 7.500
mainframes. Basing on this compiler an R&D project has been
started aiming to build an Ada Programming Environment
(Ada-PE) on decentralized graphic workstations. Its key
features are: support of all development phases, an
object oriented user interface, and the use of graphics both
for visualizing program and library structures and for
coding.

2. Application area

The Ada-PE allows development of Ada programs for the BS2000
target. The development system itself is located on a
combination of BS2000 mainframe and SINIX (*) PC. The
system's distribution over these two machines allows the user
to fully explore the computational power of the mainframe and
the local workstation's power on window system, graphics and
fast terminal interaction.

The functional domain of the developer's PC is the Ada-PE's
command handling, editing, and documenting; the domain of the
BS2000 mainframe is compiling, linking, debugging, and
running of Ada programs.

Ada-PE is designed to support the development steps design
specification, component specification, coding, component
test, documenting, integration test, and shipping.

In a first step towards the goal of supporting all these
project phases, Ada-PE is being built as a framework with the
necessary tools for Ada coding and with investigation into
some selected fancy tools exploring the graphic capabilities.

3. Methodology

The programming environment must not be tied to a particular
SW development method (top down, bottom up, outside in) or
support only a given method of software-engineering (SWE).
Ada-PE is open by allowing the user to define or select his
own SWE-method. The framework may be extended by tools for
such methods. Restrictions or methodology are at most
reflected in the functionality presented.

4. Architecture

The separation of functional domains between local and remote
systems is echoed in the distribution of components:
Following language requirements the validated Ada compiler
must handle the Ada library. For the Siemens Ada compiler
this is realized by a multilibrary system which preserves
source code and intermediate representations (similar to
DIANA [DIA83]) for correctly compiled Ada programs and which
allows the definition and management of variants and
versions.

This multilibrary system is the heart of the Siemens Ada
System (AS) located on the BS2000 mainframe computer [DIE87
and DIE88]. It is a stand alone compiler's 'operating system'
including a symbolic debugger and has its own command
interpreter.

On the PC side the AS is extended to a programming
environment by supporting the editing and handling of all Ada
texts under development, as well as the management of test
data, testing protocols, and documentation. By Ada texts we
mean both correctly compiled source code and fragments, i.e.
source text which is (still) incomplete or incorrect Ada or
not yet submitted to a compiler.

The system architecture as shown in figure 1 is embedded in
the Siemens DOMINO (*) concept which provides the framework
of distributed environments, linking the machines via remote
call handlers and file transfer. On the SINIX side we make
use of DOMINO's application monitor and of its window manager
COLLAGE (*). Ada-PE runs as an application within DOMINO and
works as a submonitor.

According to the decentralized working model all user action
originates from the SINIX PC side. The user performs his
dialog on the PC primarily with the graphical user interface
(PE-PC-UIF) using functions of COLLAGE. The user interface is
object oriented and menu driven.

Exclusively for the purpose of testing the Ada-PE system
during development there is a command handler in parallel,
providing the same interface language to PE-PC-FRAME.

Similarly on the BS2000 side, commands to the PE-HOST-FRAME

flow from the SINIX side through the REMOTE-CALL-HANDLER. But again, there is a possibility to issue PE-HOST commands directly to the interface, testing via the parallel PE-HOST-COMMAND-HANDLER.

The frames on PC and host guarantee consistent integration of the component tools and subsystems, handling of the interface, and access to the database.

Figure 1.   Architecture of Ada-PE

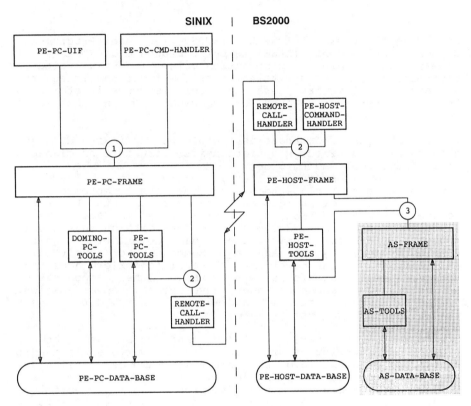

On the SINIX side the DOMINO-PC-TOOLS provide standard components for editing, graphics, and documentation. PE-PC-TOOLS refer to the Ada specific components.

Communication between the SINIX and BS2000 sides supported by the REMOTE-CALL-HANDLER are both synchronous and asynchronous.

The AS is embodied into the PE-HOST-FRAME as a black box via its functional interface. The interior of the AS is shown to demonstrate its structural similarity to the enclosing system.

For functions and data required on the BS2000 mainframe but not handled in AS the architecture must provide additional PE-HOST-TOOLS and a PE-HOST-DATA-BASE. These might cover the handling of executable programs, central test evaluation and statistics, and the master-site administration of database transaction and consistency.

Distribution of data across the databases is according to operational needs.

5. Database

Following the view of STONEMAN [STO80] an Ada Programming Support Environment (APSE) is built around a database whose primary objects are Ada compilation units. In our distributed environment with the splitting up of the functionalities the database is likewise separated: compiled code is stored in the AS; currently developed Ada fragments are in the local PC.

Viewing the Ada-PE database as a whole the primary database objects are organized in a hierarchical structure of classes. These are in descending order:
        Ada-PE-System, project, library, unit.
Top are objects of class Ada-PE-system; they represent the starting point for navigation to database objects. Libraries relate to the definition of program library in Ada [LRM83, ch.10.1], extended by documents and test data on this level. Objects of class unit are Ada compilation units, distinguishable by an Ada name. Components of a unit which are relevant for the compiler in AS are: (compiler accepted) source, intermediate forms, symbol table. Other components of a unit are fragments under development, specification, design, and maintenance documents, test data, test statistics, error listings, etc..

The objects may have attributes and relations between themselves. Attributes bear meta-information (e.g. last edit date) and content (e.g. source text). Examples of relations are configuration dependencies, relations from user definitions (design - specification - implementation, program - documentation), language relations (specification - body, with, elaboration order), and technical dependencies between development variants of programs.

This complexity is best described by an abstract entity-relationship (ER) model. The model for the Ada-PE database is viewed as a union of the ER models for the three partitions, the local PE-PC-DATA-BASE, the PE-HOST-DATA-BASE, and the AS-DATA-BASE. The latter two are also referred to as the BS2000 host database. Taking compilation units as the primary objects we combine the database partitions by installing for every unit, Ada-library and project a representative (object) in every partition. The database partitions are then connected over a 1-1 mapping of project names, Ada-library names (unique within project), and Ada compilation unit names (unique within library).

The AS-DATA-BASE contains Ada libraries, compiled Ada sources and intermediate representations as required by Ada's separate compilation. The compiler works with and guarantees consistency of this data base.

The PE-HOST-DATA-BASE contains global system information and executable programs.

The PE-PC-DATA-BASE is the primary working database. Here the meta-information is kept for navigation as well as the Ada fragments for local development. Documents, test data, etc. may appear here as components of units or related to main programs if they apply more generally. For consistency fragments on the PC will always have a correctly compiled program companion in the AS-DATA-BASE.

Objects are stored in the database partition of their current use: on the PC during development and on the BS2000 host when released. The migration of data between the database partitions follows transaction protocols.

To provide parallel access to the database for many users the 'long transactions' of 'get-a-unit / work-on-it / release-it' must be monitored for the complete database. A transaction monitor has to guarantee the consistency of the database partitions and consistent update of their similar structures.

The Ada-PE should allow decentralized development by several users working with one or more graphical workstations on the same Ada project. Since the primary working data is stored on the PC, and the host database is only a subsystem, we have an uncommon consistency problem:

"n users on m master sites with 1 slave site".

For the realization of a pilot version of Ada-PE we first assume m=1, permitting development of a project on a single workstation, only. Extending to m>1, thus to a multi-workstation system, will later be achieved by transparent data distribution over a local area network (LAN). A necessary condition for this step is to connect project data to a single, central project node. This node may be held central on a workstation (as in figure 2) or later on a single net wide node located on any LAN workstation or on the PE-HOST-DATA-BASE.

This connection of project data also solves the multi-user problem: In the realization not the name of the user matters but the user's access path in SINIX. A user may start an Ada-PE-system at any node of his access range within the SINIX file system (/user/<user>/.../*.ada). If he creates a project at this point he becomes registered as owner with the sole right of deleting the project - while no other users are

noted. If he wishes to connect to an existing project he has
to know its name and access keys. Then he is catalogued as
secondary user and is linked to the same unique project node.
Thus, within an Ada project the n users are organized by the
schema "1 master -- (n-1) slaves". Therefore, an user views
only the projects he explicitly creates or connects to.

Figure 2. Data Structure of Ada-PE

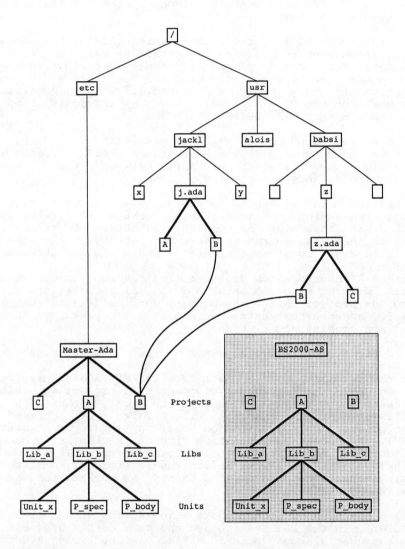

With password mechanisms the database objects are protected
against misuse, disallowing direct access to the host
database other than by Ada-PE's functionalities.

6. User interface

For the user interface an object oriented approach is selected as it is implied by the object related structure of the database and favored in the design of modern man-machine-interfaces. The set of objects is hierarchical structured in a quite natural way. There are some projects, each composing a number of libraries. The libraries finally contain the units. Units in this sense are the entities of the database: compilation units, documents, programs, related test data, etc..

6.1 Principals of navigation

Logical base for the command language of Ada-PE's kernel and object oriented user interface is the following sequence of navigation levels in the object hierarchy:

PROJECTS	projects to which access is possible
PROJECT	selected project
LIBRARIES	libraries belonging to the selected project
LIBRARY	selected library
UNITS	units contained in the selected library
UNIT	selected unit

Characteristical for this logical structure is the alteration between plural levels and singular levels in the sequence of navigation levels. Related navigation steps are:

- "select"/"generalize" : from plural level to singular level of the same hierarchic level and vice versa

- "open"/"close" : from singular level to plural level of different hierarchic levels and vice versa

The set of navigation steps is completed by the pair "create" "delete". The semantics of this pair include the navigation steps "select"/"generalize". That means, creation starts at plural level and after execution the new object is considered to be selected; deletion starts at singular level and after execution no object is selected.

In a multilibrary system the set of libraries itself may be structured too, distinguishing main- and sub-libraries. Respecting the principals of object navigation this fact is taken into account in the way that the navigation levels LIBRARIES/LIBRARY succeed one another several times.

For the association of methods to objects the hierarchic levels are considered as the object classes.

In the following the verbs "generalize" and "deselect" will be used synonymously.

Figure 3 shows the principals of the object navigation and figure 4 the navigation steps in particular.

Figure 3   Figure 4

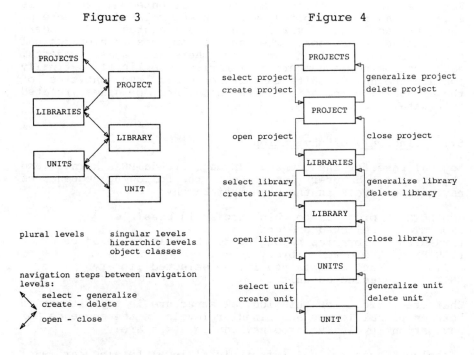

6.2 Functionality of user interface

All functions of the Ada-PE's user interface can be separated into three groups:

- object bound methods
  The group consists of all functions that as methods may be applied to a specified object. That is the union of the sets of methods associated with each object class.
- navigation methods
  The group consists of all functions concerning management of object hierarchy, navigation herein as well as selection and execution of an object bound method.
- monitoring and global functions

The object bound methods are realized by functions of the kernel of the Ada-PE. The user never is concerned whether a function is performed locally on PC side or is supported by the functionality of the AS located on the mainframe.

Most of the monitoring and navigation facilities of the user interface will be realized by use of COLLAGE, an application monitor with integrated window manager, including a functional interface, for the graphical SINIX-PC.

6.3 Object tied methods

The method selection to a specified object is decided not only by the class but also by other attributes of the object:

- For a project or library the protection of the object (read-write or read-only) has to be regarded.
- For a unit there is a first distinction about the kind of unit (Ada-text, Ada-program, document, etc.).
  If an Ada-text is at hand further criterions are
  - type of Ada-text (package spec, package body, etc.)
  - state of Ada-text (compiled, obsolete, fragment, etc.)

Thus, for the method selection to the object specified, only permissible methods are presented. So the user cannot apply inadequate methods to an object.

6.4 Navigation methods

The pairs of navigation steps mentioned above built the kernel of the group of navigation methods. The principals of the object navigation are applied also to the selection of an object bound method: Transition from plural to singular level and vice versa is realized by the pair "select"/"generalize". To accomplish the group some other navigation methods must be introduced; the users view thereon is described by quotation marked verb-noun combinations:

- transition from object navigation to method selection
  "apply method"
- transition from method selection back to object navigation
  "break method selection" or "change object"
- explicit execution of the selected method
  "execute method"
  After selection of a method the user has the choice to execute the selected method, to select another method or to continue with object navigation. So an explicit user action to execute a method is required.

Abbreviations for two sequences of two navigation steps, "close and deselect" or else "deselect and close", complete the group of navigation methods.

The situations of the navigation dialog considered as states and the navigation methods considered as state transitions form a finite state machine called "navigation automaton".

From the user's point of view the navigation automaton works in the following way:

- The information displayed to the user at each state of the navigation dialog consists of two parts:
  - The object part indicates the objects of the actual hierarchic level or the object bound methods to the specified object.

- The meta-method part indicates the applicable navigation
  methods.
To distinguish the singular from the plural level, the
selected entry in the object part is highlighted. Because
at each state it is obvious, which selection method
(select/deselect) may be executed, in the meta-method part
only additional applicable navigation methods must be
presented explicitly.

- To perform one step in the state transitions, the user may
  execute either a selection method or one of the explicitly
  presented navigation methods, always using the pointing
  device of his PC in the usual way.

- The navigation method "execute method" completes the cycle
  of applying methods to a selected object. After execution
  of the method the user can continue with the selection of a
  method or turn back to object navigation.

Figure 5.   Navigation Automaton

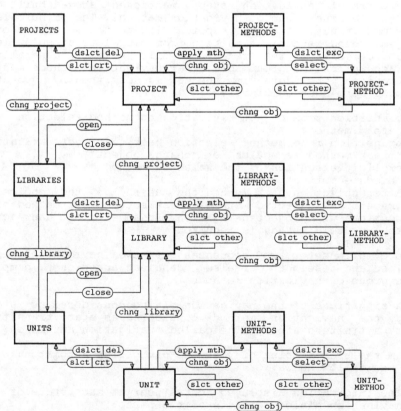

The state transition diagram of the navigation automaton can
be seen in figure 5 as a directed graph.

6.5 Monitoring facilities

The navigation automaton has a special feature: There is neither a particular state to start nor a particular state to stop. In other words: Each state may be the start state or the stop state. Therefore interruption and continuation at each state is possible. The current state of the automaton is determined by the names of the selected objects given in a form similar to path-names for a tree-structured file system.

Based upon this feature we do a further step of abstraction and call the description of the current state of a navigation automaton a "navigation path", consider it as an object, assign an attribute (active/passive) and apply following methods to it:

- create (start a new navigation at highest level)
- delete (forget the navigation path)
- copy (copy the active navigation path)
- activate (continue the dialog with this navigation path)

The state of a session with the Ada-PE then is described by a set of navigation paths, to which the following two functions belong to:

- store (retain the state of the session)
- load (rebuilt the state of a session)

These functions, together with 'help' and 'end', built the group of the monitoring functions. A suitable realization for presentation of and access to members of these group are pull-down menus.

7. Functionalities

As the functionalities of Ada-PE are offered to the user object oriented, they are grouped according to the hierarchy of classes. Global monitoring functions have already been described above as well as functionalities on every level for creation, deletion, and selection of the objects of the particular class. So we concentrate here on selecting other interesting functionalities for a single object:

On project level functions will present the content, i.e. the list of libraries including attributes in two forms, a text form and a graphical one. The latter may show library interconnections and allow browsing.

Functionalities for libraries likewise include the presentation of the contained units in table and graphic forms. Subsets of units may be selected according to its development status or by restriction to units in dependency relation to a single main program. Another function useful for a quick overview would show the subset of main programs or - when successfully bound - of executable programs in the library. A function 'elaborate' has the same effect as 'pragma ELABORATE' [LRM83, ch.10.5] for program binding but avoids recompilation - provided it does not conflict with a language defined elaboration order.

Most functionalities concern Ada units. For organizing versions and variants with the multilibrary system units may be copied or fetched from another library avoiding recompilation. Fetching implies the creation of a pseudo-unit as a representative with a standing reference to the original unit in the other library.

Units in a library may be barrowed from a released and compiled version into a fragment. This fragment is edited by the DOMINO editor which may be applied to Ada text or to documents. The compile function transfers fragments to the mainframe AS and compiles there, changing the status to 'compiled' when successful. This function also allows the automatic recompilation of dependent units according to Ada's compilation order. For incorrect compilations error listings may be inspected and integrated with the fragment source when editing for corrections.

The list of attributes of a unit and its components - source text, design document, etc. - can be shown. Parts of the Ada text of units may be drawn in a graphic form. This includes the possibility to edit graphically and generate new code as explained in detail below. When all dependent units are compiled, a main program may be bound producing an executable program for the BS2000 mainframe. The units belonging to this executable program can be listed or shown in a diagram. A list of all executable programs which make use of the given unit will allow to assess the effect of modification and recompilation.

Finally a program may be executed on the BS2000 mainframe testing with the debugger of the AS. To complete the development or update transaction a correct unit must be released, ending its fragment status.

8. Graphic features

The graphic tools of the Ada-PE make usage of the language independent graphic system GRAPES(*) adapting it for Ada language features. GRAPES supports representations of trees and nets in structured diagrams and allows graphic coding.

The most important tool for huge Ada libraries seems to be the visualization of unit dependencies [HOY84]. The drawing function will show the units in a forest of trees. The trees are built from units connected by the specification - body and the body - separate_body relations. Variations of this function draw diagrams of the WITH relations, compilation and elaboration order. The diagrams may be examined with usual editor functions selecting regions on the screen and zooming into detail, enlarging the information on relations and units. Similarly, the dependencies and import - export relations between libraries of the multilibrary system are presented.

Another visualization tool will present single compilation units in a flow-of-control block diagram. The diagram has graphic elements for control structures while the expression level is simply taken as text. A lexical and syntactic analysis of Ada programs produces a graphic interface language then transformed by the graphic editor. Only correct Ada programs are accepted for this representation. On the level of graphical representation the semantics of the control structures may be debugged by simulation.

The inversion of this process is supplied by a tool which generates code from the flow-of-control block diagrams. As well as Ada text, the user may edit the graphic representation of programs. The generator part of GRAPES will be enlarged to produce Ada control structures, leaving the semantic correctness of expressions to the user.

Currently GRAPES is being extended to systems and software modeling [GRA86]. The interactive diagrams for communication and parallelism, interfaces, modularization and data as defined in the GRAPES-86 modeling language will be incorporated into the Ada-PE step by step. Resulting tools will support graphic design of systems and programs and their transformation into Ada code.

9. Perspectives

The system is currently developed with the scope described. For enhancements of the novel graphic capabilities the acceptance of graphical components should be evaluated. Further tools should be integrated into the decentralized framework. We envisage design tools for the early phases of the life cycle and test and maintenance support for the late ones. Enriching the programming environment by integrating a syntax oriented editor and semantic checkers - combined with graphics - the dependency on the mainframe based compiler could be reduced to code generation.

References:

[DIA83] Goos,G.; Wulf,W.A. (ed.): DIANA Reference Manual. Institut fuer Informatik II, Universitaet Karlsruhe, Bericht 1/81. Revision 3, Technical Report TL-83-4, Tartan Laboratories Inc., Pittsburgh, PA, Feb.1983

[DIE87] Diessl,G.; Koehler,W.; Schlueter,P.: Das Siemens-Ada-
        System; in: Scheibl,H.-J., ed.: Software-Entwick-
        lungs-Systeme und -Werkzeuge. Technische Akademie
        Esslingen, Esslingen, Sep.1987

[DIE88] Diessl,G.; et al.: Benutzerbeschreibung fuer eine Ada
        Programmierumgebung. Siemens AG, ZTI SOF, Interner
        Bericht, Muenchen, 1988

[GRA86] GRAPES-86, Einfuehrung in die Modellierungssprache;
        Siemens AG, K D AP 4, Muenchen, Nov.1987

[HOY84] Hoyer,W.; Raffler,H.; Stadel,M.; Wehrum,R.P.: Imple-
        mentierungsaspekte der getrennten Uebersetzbarkeit in
        Ada; in: Programmierumgebungen: Entwicklungswerkzeuge
        und Programmiersprachen, p.131-166, Informatik-
        Fachberichte Band 79, Springer Verlag, Berlin,
        Heidelberg, New York, 1984

[LRM83] Reference Manual for the Ada Programming Language,
        ANSI/MIL-STD 1815 A, United States Department of
        Defense, Washington D.C., Jan.1983

[STO80] Requirements for Ada Programming and Support
        Environments STONEMAN; United States Department of
        Defense, Washington D.C., Feb.1980

Programming-in-the-Large with the System-Oriented Editor

Dick Schefstrom

TeleLOGIC, Laboratoriegrand 11, 951 64 Lulea, Sweden

Abstract. In this paper, the functionaliy and philosopy of a programming environment for Ada is discussed. The characteristic property is *integration*, where support for different tasks have been tightly integrated into a single homogeneous framework. Finally, we report on the practical usage experience and point out directions of future work.

1. Programming: in-the-small and in-the-large

The tasks performed in producing software can be categorized in many different ways. One such categorization, which will be used in this paper, is to distinguish between programming-in-the-small and programming-in-the-large. Those aspects are usually supported by different and not integrated tools, implying different user interfaces, different concepts, and low degree of information exchange between the areas.

But what do we exactly mean with those terms? For the purpose of this paper, we relate them to the *size of the typical object of concern,* leading to the following definitions:

With programming-in-the-small, we understand all tasks whose main focus of interest is at the level of statements, procedures, and detailed datastructures. We most of the time stay inside a single module, and the typical tool used is the editor.

With programming-in-the-large, we understand the tasks, and the level of thinking about a system, where the module is the atomic entity. This level is important since it is the level of granularity at which we distribute repsonsibility and assign individual work. This is also the level at which we do version control and configuration management. Finally, many people like to think about the architecture of a system in terms of which modules there are and how they relate to each other in different ways.

The emphasis of the work presented here is on integrating support for both those aspects into a single well integrated whole. Thinking of it in an editor evolution context, we have proposed the term *System-Oriented Editor,* (Schefstrom 1987), to emphasize the path from text-orientation, over language-orientation, into what might be a next step: system-orientation.

The new aspects about this environment, which we call *Arcs,* are mainly in programming-in-the-large, and in its approach to integration. However, to point out the the feeling of continuity between the two levels of granularity we describe the system bottom-up, starting within the single module/compilation unit.

2. Programming-in-the-Small

The Arcs editor allows the text of a single module to be structured hierarchically, and provides operations for creating, modifying, and traversing that hierarchy. This feature is not language dependent in any way, and typical usages are structuring of a document and decomposition of a program text into convenient pieces. This property has previously been called *Structure-Orientation,* (Stromfors 1981, Stromfors 1986), and the system described here is in this aspect based on the *ED3* editor, (which is the subject of the referenced documents). This structure-orientation provides good means for creating an overview of the internals of a module.

In addition, the editor has an integrated Ada syntax and pretty-printing capability. Since these services are provided as integrated parts of the editor, they are easy and fast to use. The parser is just a procedure within the editor, working directly on the internal buffers. Furthermore, since the hierarchical structuring provides a natural limited scope for such operations, response time is often decreased to level where it is almost not noticable. We believe that this approach is a good and practical alternative to the more "pure" language directed editors.

3. Programming-in-the-Large

Just as we have a model within which we think about the small issues, (characters, sections, procedures, statements and declarations), we need a model in terms of which to think about the larger granularity. A suitable such model seems to be that of an attributed directed graph with typed edges, as is supported by many of todays environment database proposals, (PCTE 1986, Programmin Environment Workshop 1986).

This model is also the one supported in Arcs, where it is used to represent the Ada program at the package level as well as other information such as subsystem decomposition, non-Ada software, documents, etc.

Permanent storage is managed by the TeleSoft Ada program library, which is open-ended and supports the graph-oriented data model discussed above, (Narfelt & Schefstrom 1984, Narfelt & Schefstrom 1985).

3.1. A User Oriented View

When viewing the top level internal structuring of a module, which in the Arcs editor appears like the "contents" page of a book, one often feel a strong need for taking a further step "up", investigating the current modules role in the surrounding system. Infact, a number of questions relating to the programmin-in-the-large level are very natural in this context:

* Which modules are used by this module, and what do their interfaces look like?

* Which modules are using this module? What do those modules look like, and why are they using the first module?

* What is the state of the system? Are there missing parts, or inconsistent relationships?

* What is the current "project state"? Who is working with what? Are changes going on?

Arcs provides the desired next level and allows the above questions to be answered promptly without leaving the editing context.

To be very concrete, the user can with a single keystroke move from spec to body, or the other way, point at with statements and have the corresponding module retrieved, possibly in another window. For increased overview, he may also start the module level browser in another window, (showing the system structure at a package level), point at any module, and have the source retrieved into the editor. In short, the system-oriented editor makes it easy, fast, and very natural, to change between different levels of abstraction.

3.2. Module Manipulation

The above questions are just some examples out of a large space of potential programmin-in-the-large level queries. This feeling of special case when considering questions like the above led us to the conclusion that there should be a sufficiently general language available, making it possible to meet unforeseen usages, and increasing the degree of programmability.

This general module manipulation is provided by a small and simple yet powerful language, based on an extended relational algebra. The two basic relations are as follows:

Edge(Tail, Edge_Type_Name, Edge_Status, Head)
Node(Name)

Program graphs, describing for example package interconnections, are represented as sets of four-tuples of the first format. The *Tail* and *Head* components represent nodes, connected by edges with type *Edge_Type_Name*. Edges also have an attribute *Edge_Status*, which has different values depending on whether the *Head* node is missing or has changed. This is a built in mechanism for certain consistency checking.

Over this relation scheme, the traditional relational algebra operations are provided...

* Selection
* Projection
* Union
* Difference

...but also a couple of special graph-oriented operations:

* Topological Sort
* Reachable Graph

Since the nodes, (head and tail), may have arbitrary attributes, selections may also refer to those, extending the otherwise static relation scheme. Expressed differently, the head and tail fields are composite structures, containing an unlimited set of sub-attributes.

Selection is the most central command and has the most options. It provides selection with respect to head or tail name, timestamp, sublibrary membership, node type, edge typename, status, attributes, nodes with changed sources, reserved nodes, etc, etc. Projection is the only operation producing objects of the unary relation "Node(Name)" kind.

As will be described later, the (fragments) of graphs produced by using these operations may be viewed and presented in different ways, and arbitrary operations may be performed over its nodes or edges. In doing so, there is a need for "sorting" the node and edges with respect to different criteria, such as:

* Depth first order
* Alphabetic with respect to node name
* Modification time order
* Sublibrary membership order
* Etc, etc.

Just like text-editors usually can manage multiple files and buffers, the system-oriented editor allows for multiple "system graphs".

Infact, the operations above are included in a framework where the results may be assigned to "graph" or "node list" objects. Those objects may then be further manipulated and used as the parameters of other commands, whenever meaningful. Examples of such commands includes, besides the extended relational algebra commands above, copying, compilation, graphical presentation, editing or printing of associated text, and anything else that might be done with a compilation unit, (or whatever the nodes represent).

4. Examples of Integration

The key aspect of this effort is *integration*, an issue we believe to be most important in the production of effective programming environments. The different parts of a programming environment must be easy to access, and must know about each other.

If, for example, using the programming-in-the-large level facilities implies leaving the editor and starting up another program which don't know about the prtevious context, it will not be used very much. This is our experience. Leaving one program for another is inefficient not only from a computational point of view, but is also inefficient from a human engineering standpoint. The context gets lost, meaning that the user forgets and feels disturbed.

The word integration currently lacks a precise commonly agreed upon definition, a problem which will not be solved here. However, by providing some examples, some light might be shed on the issue:

4.1. Automatic maintenance of database contents.

As was described above, the relationships between separately compiled units are represented by nodes and edges using the underlying datamodel. This provides a unification in the way we perceive and manipulate software relative to other information within the underlying database. A crucial point is however how the information got there: if the information has to be maintained by hand, we probably create more problems than we solve. We also believe the same is true for all kinds of attempts to maintain the database by updates from another representation held in parallel, such as in (Pierce 1987).

In this case, the most obvious information generator is the Ada compiler, which therefore should manitain the database to reflect immediatelly changes as the user compiles. In Arcs, this is the case, and all tools work directly on exactly the same single representation as the compiler. This guarentees that what is manipulated by the tools in Arcs is a consistent picture of the system under development. In this sense, Arcs is very well integrated with the Ada compiler.

4.2. Recompilation Support

The module manipulation language described previously is complete, and in some senses general enough to allow for the expression of most things we'd like to do with or know about systems. This does, of course, not exclude the inclusion of a set of precanned services, even though these could be expressed using the basic facilities. As an example, lets consider one of the 'most obvious of those services: the computation of recompilation orderings.

Recompilation could always be done using the module manipulation language as follows:

(1) *Select* edges having a non-ok status.

(2)   *Reach backwards*, starting at the tails of those edges.

(3)   *Topologically sort* the resulting graph.

The *Compile* command is just a nice packaging of this, but could be worth discussing as a prototype for other commands.

First of all, since compile just takes a graph as a parameter, the "scope" of the check is self-evident and independent of the compile command. If only the units necessary for the *compilation* of a given unit should be considered, we just provide the corresponding graph. On the other hand, if all units necessary for *execution* should be considered, another, bigger graph is used. This idea immediately generalizes into the ability to recompile *arbitrary subsets* of program systems, subsets that may have been produced by other commands, or sequences of commands. The user has full control.

The second point we should recognize is the usage of "graph objects" as a communication medium between different commands. We have already seen that the input graph of Compile may be the result of other commands. With this in mind, it should be no surprise that the result of compile also is reported in "graph objects". There may be several such objects generated:

*   The edges having non-ok status,

*   Edges pointing to a missing node,

*   Nodes having changed sources, and finally

*   A list of nodes, in correct order, needing recompilation.

Those objects may be viewed and traversed using the *Navigate* or *List* command, or used as the parameter in arbitrary further investigations. The graph objects, and the common operations for their manipulation, acts in this way as an important integrating force.

4.3. Browsing and Structure Presentation

A central component of the user interface is the *Navigate* tool, which allows the user to view graph objects, to "walk around" among the nodes, and to perform operations relative to the current node.

Our initial attempt was to present complete graphs, presented on the screen using a depth first ordering of units. This is sometimes useful, but is often just too complex, showing too much. The depth-first view is, however, just one among several possible views, and the problem of finding those "right" views is an important and interesting problem.

One possible alternative is the *center view*, where not the complete system is presented, but only the edges pointing into and out from a given node. We say that we *center around* that node. Given a centered view, the cursor could be moved to any of the input or output nodes, and centering be requested around this one instead. In this way the user can *navigate* among the modules, seeing limited and understandable but important subsets of a complex system.

Another special case is the *Ada-visible* units. This view includes the neighbouring nodes together with, depending on the type of the starting node, units imported by ancestor compilation units.

Yet another example is the nodes reachable, forward or converse, starting at a given node, and the "Ada tree". The most basic view, "raw mode", is used for presenting graph fragments for which we know nothing, and for which no suitable structure is found. In this mode, a list of triples, "Head -- Edge_type --> Tail" appear on the screen.

Finally we'd like to point out the relationship between graphically oriented design methods and tools, and the viewing facility presented here. The approach taken in the Arcs Editor has an important strength in that it requires no representation of the program/design besides what is actually in the program library. This guarantees that the picture-oriented overviews are consistent with the actual program. If a separately maintained representation is used for graphic overviews, there is always a significant risk this picture of the system gets obsolete, and is therefore not used. Since the Browser works on graph objects, as are produced by many other commands, and are manipulated by the same basic query language, it is very well integrated with the rest of the system.

4.4. Non-Ada Entities

Since the underlying program library is open ended, the user is free to introduce arbitrary other nodes and edges. One example of this is the inclusion non-Ada software, and introduction of "vertical" relationships, showing subsystem decompositions.

Those features were also used during the development of the Arcs Editor, where certain parts were written in other languages than Ada. Usually such parts are not visible when viewing an Ada program library, and it will therefore not act as a true description of a piece of software under development. However, the inclusion of such foreign software was easy in this case, by just introducing new types of edges, linking Ada-nodes to non-Ada nodes.

Another service integrated in this framework is compilation unit revision control, allowing units to be reserved and relased, providing information on who is working with what, avoiding conflicting changes, etc. This feature has been reported in detail in another paper, (Schefstrom 1986a), and is not developed further here. Examples of how to introduce and use "vertical" relationships is included in (Schefstrom 1986b).

Since those information structures discussed above, edges and nodes, are "equal right citizens", they are automatically included when viewing, copying, querying, etc. There is no unnecessary difference between such structures and the Ada program stored in the same database. Because of this, such non-Ada structures are well integrated with the rest of Arcs.

5. Project Organization and the Program Library Database

In practice we seldom work alone, but are members of a team working on the same system. The parallell work we are thereby confronted with has of course implications for the management of separate compilation, since the compilation unit *is* the unit of independent manipulation.

The environment component keeping track of all those compilation units is the program library, and its design is a key issue in making it practical to work with Ada. To meet those needs, our program library is built up out of a set of *sublibraries*, each of which may contain an arbitrary set of compilation units. The *sublibrary* is the unit of sharing between different programmers.

Since the sublibrary scheme provides big freedom - program libraries are built up from arbitrary combinations of sublibraries - it deserves discussing some particular usage patterns, taken out of more than two years of actual usage experience.

So, one way of using those sublibraries is by establishing a *project baseline* held in one or more sublibraries. Those baseline-sublibraries are intended to show the most recent stable state of the evolving system, and acts in some senses as a communication media between programmers.

All programmers then include those sublibraries in their libraries. However, each individual also has a private sublibrary, holding the units he is currently modifying and testing. A simple program library for an individual called "X" would then typically look like the following:

    X_Private
    Product_Baseline
    Standard_Sublib

Another individual, "Y", working on the same project, uses a similar library, but with an own private sublibrary:

    Y_Private
    Product_Baseline
    Standard_Sublib

Work now proceeds by programmers copying units from the common baseline into the private area, where they modify and test usits. Finally, after necessary testing, changed or created units are delivered back to the baseline sublibrary.

Since modules are *checked out* from the baseline sublibrary, using the revision control commands of Arcs, conflicting changes are avoided, and we automatically maintain a description of who is working with what.

This way of working with baseline sublibraries is the most basic one, and still leaves two problems to be solved:

(1) Access rights. We maybe don't want programmers to be able to modify the baseline in arbitrary ways. Still people must be able to signal finished results and making them available.

(2) Spec modifications. Especially the modification of Ada specifications may have big impacts, and we probably want to control when to take that impact.

Therefore, we extend the above working model to make use of two baseline sublibraries, one which is the real baseline, and to which only the Configuration Manager has write access, and another sublibrary, which we call *prerelease*, to which everyone has write access. We return changed units to the prerelase sublibrary, therebye making them avaliable for the one wanting it. The Configuration Manager then decides on the time for inclusion into the real baseline.

This latter task turns out to be very easy, and highly automatic due to the way the program library works. To create a new baseline, the configuration manager just creates a new library, consisting of the old_baseline, the prerelease sublibrary, and a newly created sublibrary intended to hold the new baseline:

    New_Baseline
    Prerelease
    Old_Baseline

All that is needed is now to use the Copy command of the System-Oriented Editor, and copy the system to the New_Baseline sublibrary. Due to the visiblity rules of the program library, where a package in Prerelease hides a module with the same name in the Old_Baseline, the New_Baseline will at the end consist of the Old_Baseline plus the changes and additions produced into the Prerelease. So, work proceeds by the programmer team doing successive updates to a common baseline.

6. Further Work

Ada compilers have this far suffered from a relatively poor performance when it comes to compilation speed, at least when compared to simpler languages. The situation is however improving rapidly.

As the next step in the development of Arcs, we are currently addressing this problem by once again applying integration: by integrating the compiler in the same very tight way as with the editor, we expect to produce significant increses in compilation speed.

The traditional way of programming, in combination with current operating system technology, has some obvious inherent inefficiencies. The typical cycle, repeated by programmers many times a day, is as follows:

(1) Loading the editing program, loading files, exiting the editor.

(2) Loading the compiler. "Exiting" compiler.

(3) Loading the linker, or...

(4) Loading the editor, and probably the same files again.

The inefficiencies of this cycle have been pointed out many times. However, there are good reasons believing that the waste is unusually big in the case of Ada, due to the cost of separate compilation, which requires a program library to be opened and read, over and over again. Instead of repeatedly opening and closing the program library, which is a significant overhead in any Ada compilation system, we call the compiler, as a procedure, allowing it to refer to existing datastructures and already open program libraries. The benefit is significant, especially for small compilation units.

Such integration is also efficient from a user interface point of view, since the user can keep his context, and call the compiler with a single keystroke directly from within the editor, getting detailed and fast respeonse on different kinds of error conditions.

7. Relationship to Other Work

The programming-in-the-large level facilities as described in this paper lead the thoughts to the work on "programming environments databases", important proposals of which are CAIS, (CAIS 1985, Carr et al 1987), and PCTE, (PCTE 1986, Gallo, Minot & Thomas 1986, PACT 1986). And infact, the underlying model of those databases shows many similarities with what we have presented here, graph oriented as they are. Some of what was presented here could therefore be viewed as a simple example of a query language for programming environment databases, and the basic ideas should be just as applicable in that context.

8. Acknowledgements

Mikael Beckman, Johnny Widen, Hans Ohman, and Nils Livingstone are all part of the Ada environments group at TeleLOGIC/Lulea. Possibly good ideas in this paper originates from them just as much as from the author.

9. References

ACM (1984),
> *Proceedings of the ACM SIGSOFT/SIGPLAN Software Engineering Symposium on Practical Software Development Environments*, Peter Henderson, ed., Pittsburgh Pennsylvania, April 1984.

CAIS (1985),
> *Military Standard Common APSE Interface Set (CAIS)*. Proposed Military Standard, US Dep of Defense.

Carr et al (1987),
> *Implementation of a Prototype CAIS Environment*, in ACM Ada Letters, Volume VII, number 2, March,April 1987.

Gallo, Minot, & Thomas (1986),
> *The Object Management System of PCTE as a Software Engineering Database Management System*, in Proceedings of the ACM SIGSOFT/SIGPLAN Software Engineering Symposium on Practical Software Development Environments, Palo Alto, Cal, Dec 1986.

Programming Environment Workshop, (1986),
> *Proceedings from International Workshop on Advanced Programming Environments*, Trondheim, Norway, June 1986.

PCTE (1986),
> *A Basis for a Portable Common Tool Environment*, Functional Specification. European Strategic Programme for Research and Development in Information Technology.

PACT (1986),
> *PACT General Description*, Bull etc, 1986.

Pierce (1987)
> *ECLIPSE - An APSE Based on PCTE*, in Proceedings of the Ada-Europe International Conference, Stockholm, May 1987.

Stromfors (1986),
> *Editing Large Programs Using a Structure-Oriented Text-Editor*, Ola Stromfors, Linkoping University. In (Programming Environment Workshop, 1986).

Stromfors (1981),
> *The Implementation and Experiences of a Structure-Oriented Text Editor*, in Proceedings of ACM SIGPLAN/SIGOA Symposium on Text Manipulation, SIGPLAN Notices, vol 19, no 6, 1981.

Narfelt & Schefstrom (1984),
> *Towards a KAPSE Database*, in Proceedings of the 1984 IEEE Conference on Ada Applications and Environments, StPaul, Minnesota 1984.

Narfelt & Schefstrom (1984),
> *Extending the Scope of the Program Library*, in 1985 International ACM Ada Conference, Paris 1985.

Schefstrom (1986a),
> *Integrating Ada in an Existing Environment - the Arcs Example*, 1986 ACM Ada Conference, Edinburgh, May 1986.

Schefstrom (1986b),
> *Project Support Building on the Ada Program Library*, in Proceedings of MILCOMP-86,

London, September 1986.

Schefstrom (1987),
The System-Oriented Editor - A Tool for Managing Large Software Systems, in Proceedings of the 1987 ACM International Ada Conference, Boston, MA, Dec 1987.

IDEFIX: DEBUGGING ADA TASKS WITH USER-DEFINED TIMING CONSTRAINTS

J.F. Caillet, C. Bonnet, B. Raither, P. de Seze
GSI-Tecsi
6, cours Michelet
92064 Paris La Défense, Cedex 52, France

Abstract. Many tools suitable for sequential programs are not adequate for the development of concurrent and real-time embedded applications. The tool described here helps debug the tasking activities of an Ada program. By performing a static analysis of the source code and a dynamic analysis of an execution, the tool determines which control paths of the program the execution could have followed. The user can specify timing constraints on the behaviour of tasks, and the tool reports if these constraints were violated during the execution.

1 INTRODUCTION

Concurrent and real-time programs create new problems in the specification, design, and debugging of software. Debugging methods and tools suitable for sequential programs are therefore not applicable to Ada. One of the software tools produced by the DESCARTES Project (Debugging and Specification of Ada Real-Time Embedded Systems) is a program that supplies the user with information about a program's tasking activities without disturbing the real-time environment: IDEFIX (Improving Debugging From Interpretation of Executions).

The problems of testing and debugging real-time concurrent software fall into three main stages. The first one, testing and debugging on a host computer, has the greatest variety of tools available, but there are differences between the host environment and the target environment which necessitate further testing and debugging in a less artificial environment (Taylor 1984). The second stage, using emulators, involves either emulating the target machine on the host, or the target computer is used to interact with an emulated external real-time environment. In the final state, testing and debugging in the final application situation, the target machine interacts with the real external environment. IDEFIX addresses the final stage, where an actual target execution is analysed.

The main difficulties of creating and integrating a real-time system written in Ada are:

- the errors related to tasking
- the verification of the conformity between the program and its real-time specification
- the production and analysis of execution traces.

The principle errors related to tasking are (LeDoux 1986):

- the incompatibility of the program with the compiler-specific run-time algorithm
- sequencing errors, in particular deadlock and shared data access
- recovery from task exceptions
- the influence of the package elaboration order on the access of tasks.

In addition, it is necessary to verify that a program respects constraints in time and entry queue length and to localize and correct the portions that do not.

One of the functions of IDEFIX is to show the user all of the possible control paths of a program that a particular execution could have followed. This is done by collecting traces of the execution during a dynamic analysis of the program. After a static analysis of the program's tasking activities, a diagram of the paths of the program's concurrency states is created to determine which paths the execution could have taken (Caillet et al. 1987). Another function of the tool is to allow the user to specify certain constraints on the timing behaviour of tasks (e.g. task A never waits more than 30 ms for a rendezvous with task B) and to report if these constraints were violated during the execution.

2 ANALYSING CONCURRENT PROGRAMS

Static and dynamic analysis each have their particular advantages which provide useful information about the behaviour of a program. However, their respective disadvantages make them each unsuitable to be the sole means of analysing real-time or concurrent programs. By combining the two methods, IDEFIX capitalises on the strong points of both while reducing their disadvantages.

Dynamic analysis consists of executing a program and recording a trace of its behaviour. Although it results in an accurate picture of a program's execution through one particular control path, it has the disadvantage of not giving any information about what the program would have done had it followed any other path. A program can be analysed dynamically by using either software or hardware methods. The software method consists of instrumenting the source program with additional code in critical places which leaves a trace of the execution (German 1984; Helmbold & Luckham 1985). The advantages of this method are that the program can be executed on the host system and it can be instrumented automatically by a preprocessor. One disadvantage is that these supplemental statements disturb the real-time environment of the execution. Another is that not every case possible within the semantics of the language can be traced, for example the termination of a task (German et al. 1982). To avoid these problems, the hardware method can be used, which records events on the target machine as they occur. However, the machinery can monitor only a limited number of events in a given time interval which makes the interpretation of the trace more difficult.

Static analysis examines the source code of a program in order to make certain deductions about its behaviour without executing it (Osterweil 1976; Taylor 1980; Taylor 1983a). The advantage of this method is that is covers all possible control paths to create graphs which give a simulation of certain actions. The disadvantage is that the more detailed the information in the graphs, the more time and memory the analysis takes (Taylor 1983b). It also wastefully analyses unexecutable paths.

A combination of these two methods of analysis is used in IDEFIX. The dynamic analysis is carried out by a hardware method which does not modify the source code or disturb the real-time environment. Only a subset of the total run-time events are recorded, but they are sufficient to create a history of the tasking activities which occurred during the execution. The approach to the static analysis differs from traditional methods in several ways. One is that instead of analysing the source code directly, the intermediate DIANA representation of the program (Evans et al. 1983) is traversed. Another difference is that only sections of the program which concern tasking are analysed. Moreover, the diagrams created record the control flow of only the concurrency states of tasks. Actions which do not concern tasking are ignored.

3 DESCRIBING CONCURRENT PROGRAMS

The structure which describes a concurrent program in IDEFIX is a Program Concurrency State Diagram (PCSD), a directed graph representing the states of all live tasks at any given moment. Each node of the PCSD is a part of a Task Concurrency State Diagram (TCSD), which is a directed graph that can contain cycles representing the concurrency state of an individual task.

In a traditional control flow graph of a program, a node represents a statement or basis block, and all branches are represented. However, a TCSD is a graph that represents the flow of only tasking activity for a single task, a task type, or a procedure containing tasking activity. A node in a TCSD represents a task state, and an edge shows the flow of control. The task states are:

> *created*
> *activated*
> *elaborating task body*
> *task activating its created tasks*
> *executing*
> *wait delay*
> *waiting for callee*
> *caller rendezvous*
> *abnormal rendezvous*
> *creating and activating subtask*
> *waiting for caller*
> *waiting for caller or terminate*

> *callee rendezvous*
> *waiting for termination*
> *elaborating block declaration*
> *unit activation its created tasks*
> *leaving block*
> *end of rendezvous*
> *terminated*

Each statement concerning tasking results in one or more nodes in the diagram. Statements which do not concern tasking are ignored, and branches are noted only if at least one path contains a tasking statement.

Since any number of tasks can be running simultaneously in a concurrent program, all live tasks must be taken into consideration in order to describe a program. Thus the state of a program at a given moment is a collection of the states of each of its live tasks. A PCSD is a graph in which a node is a collection of task states and an edge is a control flow path. A PCSD can contain cycles, and it always starts with a single node in which the main task is in the state *created* and all other tasks are inactive.

In order to create the PCSD, the tool first records the history of an execution through dynamic analysis and creates all the TCSD's of the program through static analysis. Then the PCSD is progressively built by consulting the TCSD's to see which state each task could have been in at a certain time and creating a node for each possibility. However, at each step of this process the history is consulted, and if a program state is discovered which the history could not have followed, this branch is no longer pursued and eliminated from the diagram. In an ambiguous case, all paths are noted. Thus the resulting PCSD shows all the possible paths to program states that are compatible with the execution history.

The results of this process are presented by a user-friendly, multi-window graphical interface. The user can scroll through various displays such as a call graph of the program, a classic control flow graph, the execution history, the PCSD, and the underlying source code. A more detailed description of this function of the tool is presented in Caillet et al. (1987).

4 USER-DEFINED CONSTRAINTS

IDEFIX provides the developer of a real-time system with a means of monitoring the size and timing of a program to make sure it satisfies the demands and limitations placed on it by its environment. An example is a protocol system with the requirement that the data transmission speed must be 48 kb sec. Such a global requirement can have repercussions on design decisions during refinement and coding stages of development of individual modules. Thus the limitation on the transmission speed can in turn create a requirement on a module that if a certain server task is called, the caller must never wait more than x ms for a rendezvous.

The user can make a list of all the constraints the program should obey. Then each time the program is executed, IDEFIX compares the execution history to the list and notifies the user if the constraints were violated. Moreover, it points out all possible troublesome sections of the program by displaying their source code, the execution history, and the PCSD in different windows.

A constraint is one or more limitations placed on certain program behaviour. For each constraint, the domain and resulting actions must be specified. The domain is the time during which the constraint is valid. The actions specify what should be done in the event that the constraint is violated. In the previous example of the task call, the constraint is the maximum duration of the state *waiting for rendezvous,* the domain is TOTAL (the duration of the entire program execution), and the action is a user-defined error message.

The following list notes the types of behaviour that can be monitored by constraints and gives an example of each:

- the sequence of occurrence of states and events: task A calls task B after task B has finished a rendezvous with task C
- entry queue length: there is an error if there are more than 3 tasks waiting for a rendezvous with task D at entry E
- frequency: task A calls entry E of task B at least once every 60 ms
- duration of states: task A is in state *waiting for rendezvous* for no more than 40 ms
- cyclic deadlock: there is no cyclic deadlock in the execution history.

The specification of constraints is based on the notion of time and intervals as described in Allen (1983), Allen (1984), and Ladkin (1986). Prolog II is used to write the timing constraints. The user is provided with predefined predicates that give him not only a general methodology and framework for writing the constraints, but also specific primitives for describing operations, objects, and relations. This method is sufficiently powerful to permit the expression of constraints based on temporal logic and interval logic (LeDoux 1986). Several aspects of the system make it particularly expandable: access to the translator's tool box, the use of run-time or logical events instead of states for object definition, and the user's ability to define new primitives or modify existing ones.

Once the list of constraints for a program is prepared, it can be applied to any number of executions of the program. The results of each application are saved for the user to examine and compare, giving him vital information on the tasking behaviour of the program which allows him to find and correct sections which do not work properly.

4.1 Domain

A domain is defined by a set of time intervals. A time interval is defined by a beginning and an end time, with a time point being an interval with identical beginning and end times. A domain is expressed by set operations on intervals (intersection, union, etc.). It is possible to have a domain that is a single interval, two obvious ones of this type being the *null* domain (never during the entire execution history) and the *total* domain (continuously throughout the execution). It must be specified whether a constraint applies sometimes or always to a domain. In the first case, if a constraint is violated at least once during the domain, an error has occurred. In the second, the constraint is valid for the entire domain.

An interval can be expressed by a key word, by absolute time, or by relation to specific events and task states. For example, a total domain can be expressed by the key word TOTAL, by the absolute interval <StartProgram, EndProgram>, or by the union of the intervals related to the states of certain tasks <main-*created,* main-*activated, . . . >*.

4.2 Constraints

A constraint has three parts: the temporal predicates, the objects involved, and the relations between these objects. The temporal predicates specify if the constraint has to be respected at least one time or each time it is possible during the domain. The objects define the tasks, their states, and their occurrences that must appear at least once during the domain. The relations between the objects describe the temporal relations between the objects.

Temporal predicates are implemented by two Prolog II predicates: *test-all* and *not*. *Test-all* searches for a particular object in a domain, and verifies that at least one instantiation exists, and for each instantiation tests the relations for constraint violations. *Not* is used to verify that at least one instantiation of an object exists and that its relations are respected.

Objects are defined by four attributes: the executing tasks, their states, the time intervals of those states, and the occurrences of those tasks and their states. A task can be identified by using its stack context, by counting the number of occurrences of its creation, or by using wild cards or variables. States are identified by their name (such as *waiting for callee*), and by their entries or other concerned tasks. A task can be created, terminate, and be recreated with the exactly the same context. Thus the user can specify to which occurrence of the task the constraint refers. During lifetime of a task, it can re-enter a particular state any number of times, so the user can also specify to which occurrence of the task the constraint refers.

Relations between objects are composed of the atomic relations between the value of their attributes, especially in the realm of time points and time intervals. The definition of these relations is found in the Appendix.

4.3 Actions

The actions taken when a constraint error occurs always include the appearance of a multi-window graphical display of the trouble spot in the program showing the task, the statements, the states, and the events which contributed to the error. In addition, the user can define specific error messages for a constraint which appear when it is violated.

4.4 Variables and Reports

In the specification of constraints, Prolog variables can be used to designate the values of object attributes. The unification of these variables with objects of the trace depends on the temporal predicate used in the constraints. When a constraint is violated, the default function of the tool is to display the source code of the suspect sections of the program. However when variables are used, the values with which they are unified are reported to the user.

5 ARCHITECTURE AND IMPLEMENTATION

The static and dynamic analysis are implemented on a VAX 785 using the Ada compiler of SYSTEAM (Schmidt et al. 1987). The compiler creates the DIANA representation of the program and the executable code. DIANA is traversed by a program written in Ada to do the static analysis which produces a file containing the TCSD's. The dynamic analysis carried out by the IDAS System ® (Muenier & Dencker 1987) which spies the run-time and leaves a trace of the execution in a file in hexadecimal form.

Figure 1. Static and Dynamic Analysis.

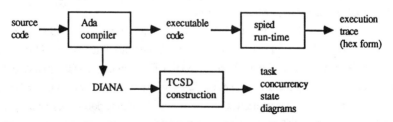

The results of the static and dynamic analysis are analysed by a Prolog II program (PrologIA 1985). It first creates a history of the execution by translating the execution trace into symbolic form. It then compares the history to the TCSD's to create the PCSD, which determines the control paths the execution could have followed, and by means of a graphical interface displays the results. It also compares the history to the user-defined timing constraints and informs the user if the constraints were violated.

Figure 2. Analysis of Execution History.

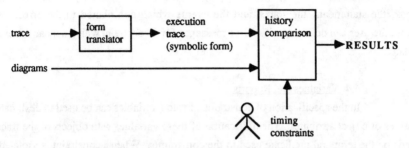

The implementation of the static and dynamic analysis is completed. The implementation of the form translator and history comparison is expected to be completed by June 1988, at which time the implementation of the graphic interface will begin.

This implementation treats all aspects of Ada. However, difficulties were encountered in certain areas. One is the identification of pointers to tasks. To treat this problem, interprocedural data flow analysis techniques would need to be added. Another trouble spot is amount of time and space consumed by the tool when analysing programs with exceptions and arrays related to tasks. One solution would be to have the run-time provide information on a few more types of events.

6 CONCLUSION

Ada was designed to facilitate real-time and concurrent programming, but its additional functionalities lead to new problems in the design and debugging phases of software development. IDEFIX was developed to provide debugging facilities not available in tools made for sequential programs.

One function of this tool is to find the different control paths a program could have followed during an execution on an embedded target machine. This feature does not often exist in such a hard environment without disturbing the real-time aspect. A second function is to allow the user to specify timing constraints of the behaviour of tasks.

One of the characteristics of Ada is to facilitate the portability of programs. The problem is that the different implementations of compilers and run-times provide different performances and behaviours of embedded applications. This tool helps verify the conformity of program performance with its specified behaviour.

® IDAS is a registered trademark of Eletronique Serge Dassault, France.

7 ACKNOWLEDGEMENTS

This work is partially funded by the European Communities under the ESPRIT program (Project DESCARTES No. 937).

We would like to thank Richard Taylor for his suggestions and comments on this project.

8 APPENDIX

Notation:

t = point in time

T = time interval

$<t_1, t_2>$ = time interval from t_1 to t_2

8.1 Time: predefined times, relations, and arithmetic time expressions

Predefined times:

StartProgram (start time of program execution reported in trace)

EndProgram (end time of program execution reported in trace)

Time relations:

All standard arithmetic relations are applicable ($<$ $>$ $<=$ $>=$ $=$ $/=$).

Time expressions:

All standard arithmetic expressions are applicable ($+$ $-$ $*$ $/$, etc.).

8.2 Intervals: predefined intervals, relations, and interval expressions

Predefined intervals:

TOTAL

The interval from the start to the end of the program,

defining $<$StartProgram, EndProgram$>$

Interval relations (Allen 1983):

t belongs to T

t after T ($t > t_{end}$)

t before T ($t < t_{start}$)

T_1 in T_2

T_1 meets T_2

T_1 equals T_2

T_1 before T_2Interval expressions:

T_1 intersect T_2

All comparisons of interval boundaries using the standard arithmetic expressions.

8.3 Duration: relations and duration expressions

Relations:

All standard arithmetic relations are applicable.

Expressions:

dist (t, T)

dist (T_1, T_2)

duration (T)

All standard arithmetic expressions are applicable.

8.4 Examples of constraints

The following constraints can be defined for a program with a *Main* procedure which creates two tasks called *Sender* and *Receiver,* where *Sender* calls the entry *GotMessage* of *Receiver*.

Domain examples:

when (TOTAL)

The constraint applies during the entire history of the program.

when (TaskOccurrence (1), StateOccurrence (n), Task (Sender, 86_49, 7EEB8), s)

The constraint applies only if at least one occurrence of task *Sender* exists and only during the life of its first occurrence. The variable n in StateOccurrence represents the number of occurrences of a state, while the variable s represents the state. By using variable names rather than an explicit number or state name, the constraint applies to any number of any state of this task. Note: a task is identified by three fields, the name Sender, the DIANA node number 86_49 which is its static identifier, and the run-time object pointer 7EEB8 which is its dynamic identifier.

Constraint example:

TaskOccurrence (1), StateOccurrence (1), Task (Sender, 86_49, 7EEB8),

<CallerRendezVous, Task (Receiver, 86_62, 7DE24), GotMessage>,

$<t_{min}, t_{max}>$, StartProgram + 100 < t_{min}

This constraint signifies that the first rendezvous between tasks *Sender* and *Receiver* for the entry *GotMessage* must occur at least 100 ms after the start of the program. The interval $<t_{min}, t_{max}>$ is the interval associated with the first occurrence of the task *Sender* and the first occurrence of its state *CallerRendezVous*.

Complete examples:

when (TOTAL)

FindAll (TaskOccurrence (1), StateOccurrence (1), Task (Sender, 86_49, 7EEB8),

<CallerRendezVous, Task (Receiver, 86_62, 7DE24), GotMessage>,

$<t_{min}, t_{max}>$, StartProgram + 100 < t_{min})

when (TaskOccurrence (1), StateOccurrence (n), Task (Sender, 86_49, 7EEB8),s)

FindAll (TaskOccurrence (1), StateOccurrence (1), Task (Sender, 86_49, 7EEB8),

<CallerRendezVous, Task (Receiver, 86_62, 7DE24), GotMessage>,

$<t_{min}, t_{max}>$, StartProgram + 100 < t_{min})

In the first example, at least one instantiation of task *Sender* must exist and the first rendezvous between tasks *Sender* and *Receiver* for the entry *GotMessage* must occur at least 100 ms after the start of the program. In the second example, the conditions are similar except that if task *Sender* does not exist, the constraint is not violated.

9 REFERENCES

Allen, J.F. (1983). "Maintaining Knowledge about Temporal Intervals." Communication of the ACM, Vol. 26, No. 11, pp. 832-843.

Allen, J.F. (1984). "A Common Sense Theory of Time." In Proceedings of IJCAI 85, L.A. USA, pp. 528-531.

Caillet, J.F., Bonnet, C., Raither, B. (1987). "High Level Interpretation of Execution Traces of Ada Tasks." In Proceedings of ESEC'87 (First European Software Engineering Conference), pp. 329-337. Berlin: Springer-Verlag.

Evans, A., Goos, G., Wulf, W.A., Butler K.J. (1983). DIANA: An Intermediate Language for Ada. Berlin: Lecture Notes in Computer Science, Springer-Verlag.

German, S.M., Helmbold, D.P. , Luckham, D.C. (1982). "Monitoring for Deadlocks in Ada Tasking." In Proceedings Ada-TEC Conference, Arlington Va. USA,

October, pp. 10-24.

German, S.M. (1984). "Monitoring for Deadlock and Blocking in Ada Tasking." IEEE Transactions on Software Engineering, Vol. SE-10, No. 6, pp. 764-777.

Helmbold, D.P. & Luckham, D.C. (1985). "Debugging Ada Tasking Programs." IEEE SOFTWARE, March, pp. 47-57.

Ladkin, P. (1986). "Time Representation: A Taxonomy of Interval Relations." In Proceedings of AIII 86, Fifth National Conference on Artificial Intelligence, pp. 360-366. Los Altos Ca. USA: Morgan Kaufmann.

LeDoux, C.H. (1986). A Knowledge-Based System for Debugging Concurrent Software. Aerospace Report No. ATR-86(8134)-1. El Segundo Ca. USA: The Aerospace Corporation.

Muenier, M. & Dencker, P. (1987). "The Ada-IDAS Project." In Proceedings of the Ada-Europe International Conference, ed. S. Tafvelin pp. 223-236. Cambridge: Cambridge University Press.

Osterweil, L.J. & Fosdick, L.D. (1976). "DAVE: A Validation Error Detection and Documentation System for Fortran Programs." Software Practice and Experience, Vol 6., pp. 473-486.

PrologIA (1985). Prolog II version 2.2 Manuel de Référence. Marseille France: PrologIA.

Schmidt, D., Tress, L., Winterstein, G. (1987). SYSTEAM Ada System Compiler and Tools Description. Karlsruhe Germany: In house publication.

Taylor, R.N. (1983a). "A General-Purpose Algorithm for Analyzing Concurrent Programs." Communications of the ACM, Vol. 26, No. 5, pp. 362-376.

Taylor, R.N. (1983b). "Complexity of Analysing the Synchronisation Structure of Concurrent Programs." In Acta Informatica 19, pp. 57-84. Berlin: Springer-Verlag.

Taylor, R.N. (1984). "Debugging Real-Time Software in a Host-Target Environment." Technique et Science Informatiques, Vol. 3, No. 4, pp. 281-288.

USING MUTATION ANALYSIS FOR TESTING ADA PROGRAMS

W. F. Appelbe
Software Engineering Research Center, Georgia Institute of Technology, Atlanta, GA
30332, U.S.A.

R. A. DeMillo
Department of Computer Science, Purdue University, West Lafayette, IN 47907,
U.S.A.

D. S. Guindi
Software Engineering Research Center, Georgia Institute of Technology, Atlanta, GA
30332, U.S.A.

K. N. King
Department of Mathematics and Computer Science, Georgia State University, University Plaza, Atlanta, GA 30303, U.S.A.

W. M. McCracken
Software Engineering Research Center, Georgia Institute of Technology, Atlanta, GA
30332, U.S.A.

Abstract. Mutation analysis is a method for software testing in which many slightly differing versions of a program are executed on the same test data; the end result is a measure of the data's quality. Over the last ten years, several mutation-based systems have demonstrated the usefulness of mutation analysis for software testing. This paper shows how mutation analysis can be a valuable tool for testing large-scale Ada software systems. We first sketch the general theory of mutation analysis, then show how to apply it to Ada. We then discuss some of the significant new problems that Ada poses for mutation analysis. Finally, we describe a prototype multilanguage mutation system that allows the testing of both Fortran 77 and Ada programs.

1 MUTATION ANALYSIS

Software testing attempts to provide a partial answer to the question "If a program is correct on a finite number of test cases, is it correct in general?" Several techniques have been devised to generate "good" test cases; these include input space partitioning (Howden 1976), symbolic testing (King 1976), functional testing (Howden 1980), as well as mutation analysis. (See DeMillo et al. (1987 c) for a survey of these and other techniques.) Because software testing is insufficient to guarantee program correctness (Howden 1976), these techniques attempt not to establish absolute program correctness but to provide the tester with some level of confidence in the program. Although each of these techniques is effective at detecting errors in the program, mutation analysis goes one step further by supplying the tester with information in the absence of known errors. This unique ability helps the tester predict the reliability of the program and indicates quantitatively when testing can end.

Mutation analysis has been shown analytically and experimentally to be a generalization of other test methodologies (Budd et al. 1978; Girgis & Woodward 1986). Thus, mutation analysis provides the capabilities of other testing techniques as well as features that are unique to mutation.

1.1 *Mutation in theory*

Mutation analysis (DeMillo et al. 1978, 1979) is a powerful technique for software testing that assists the tester in creating test data and then interacts with the tester to improve the quality of the data. We briefly describe the technique here; the reader should consult Budd et al. (1978) and DeMillo et al. (1979) for more details.

Mutation analysis is based on the "competent programmer hypothesis" — the assumption that the program to be tested has been written by a competent programmer. Under this hypothesis, a program that is not correct will differ from a correct program by at most a few small errors. Mutation analysis allows the tester to determine whether a set of test cases is adequate to detect these errors. The first step in mutation analysis is the construction of a collection of *mutants* of the test program. Each mutant is identical to the original program except for a single small change (for example, the replacement of one operator by another or the alteration of the value of a constant). Such a change is called a *mutation*. Next, each mutant is executed, using the same test case each time. Many of the mutants will produce different output than the original program. The test data is said to *kill* these mutants; the data was adequate to find the errors that the mutants represent. Some mutants, however, may produce the same output as the original program. These *live* mutants provide valuable information. A mutant may remain live for one of two reasons: (1) The test data is inadequate. A mutant may remain alive because the test data failed to distinguish it from the original program. For example, the test data may not exercise the portion of the program that was mutated. (2) The mutant is equivalent to the original program. The mutant and the original program always produce the same output, hence no test case can distinguish between the two.

Normally, only a small percentage of live mutants are equivalent to the original program; these are usually easy to locate and remove from further consideration. More test cases can be added in an effort to kill nonequivalent mutants. The quality of a set of test cases is measured by an *adequacy score*; a score of 100% indicates that the test cases kill all nonequivalent mutants.

Although mutation analysis tests only for simple errors, theoretical studies have shown that simple and complex errors are coupled (this is called the *coupling effect*), hence test data that causes simple nonequivalent mutants to die will most likely also cause complex mutants to die (Acree et al. 1979; DeMillo et al. 1979).

As an example of mutation analysis, consider the following Ada function:

```
function Max(M, N: Integer)
   return Integer is
begin
   if M > N then
      return M;
   else
      return N;
   end if;
end Max;
```

One way to mutate this function is to replace the > operator in the **if** statement by some other relational operator (>=, <, <=, =, or /=). This produces a collection of five mutants of Max, which we can attempt to kill by supplying appropriate test data. As a first try, we might choose the values M = 1, N = 2. The original function returns 2; the mutants return the following values:

if M >= N **then:**	2
if M < N **then:**	1
if M <= N **then:**	1
if M = N **then:**	2
if M /= N **then:**	1

Three mutants return different values and are therefore considered dead. The >= and = mutants are still alive. The >= mutant remains alive because it is equivalent to the original function; no test case can kill this mutant. The = mutant can be killed by a second test case, such as M = 2, N = 1.

1.2 *Mutation in practice*

A mutation-based testing system allows a tester to perform mutation analysis on a particular program (or subprogram). The tester supplies the program to be tested (the program is assumed to be valid according to the rules of the source language) and chooses the types of mutations to be performed. The tester also supplies one or more test cases. The testing system executes the original program and each mutant on each test case and compares the outputs produced. If a mutant produces different output on *any* test case, the mutant is marked dead. Once execution is complete, the tester can examine any mutants that are still alive. The tester can then declare a mutant to be equivalent to the original program, or the tester can supply additional test cases in an effort to kill the mutant (and possibly other live mutants as well). (Some mutation systems are able to detect certain kinds of equivalent mutants without the help of the tester.)

Several mutation systems have been built over the past ten years, including PIMS (Budd et al. 1978), EXPER (Acree et al. 1979; Budd 1980; Budd et al. 1980), and FMS.3 (Tanaka 1981), which allow the mutation of Fortran programs, and CMS.1 (Acree et al. 1979; Acree 1980; Hanks 1980), which tests Cobol programs. The most recent mutation-based system is Mothra (DeMillo et al. 1987 b), an integrated software testing environment under development at Georgia Tech and at Purdue University. Mothra has several notable features lacking in previous mutation systems: (1) Mothra provides a high-bandwidth user interface. (Testing requires a great deal of interaction between the tester and the testing system.) (2) Mothra's architecture imposes no *a priori* constraint on the size of software systems that can be tested. Mothra supports the testing of programs ranging in size from 10 lines to 1,000,000 lines or more. (3) Mothra is designed to support multiple source languages. At present, Mothra allows the testing of Fortran 77 programs; this paper describes work underway to extend Mothra to allow the testing of Ada programs. (4) Mothra allows the easy incorporation of new tools. These might include a test case generator (to help the tester create test cases to kill particular mutants) and an automatic equivalence checker (to detect equivalent mutants).

Experience with Mothra and earlier systems has shown mutation analysis to be a powerful tool for program testing. Mutation-based testing systems have a number of attractive features: (1) Mutation analysis subsumes — as special cases — most other test methodologies, including statement coverage and branch coverage. (2) A mutation-based system provides an interactive test environment that allows the tester to locate and remove errors. (3) Mutation analysis allows a greater degree of automation than most other testing methodologies. (4) Mutation analysis provides information that other test methodologies do not. In particular, the mutation score for a particular program indicates the adequacy of the data used to test the program, thereby serving as a quantitative measure of how well the program has been tested.

A potential problem of mutation-based testing systems is the amount of computer resources (both space and time) required for the testing of large programs. The number of mutants generated for a program tends to grow quadratically with the number of names in the program. Storing huge numbers (perhaps millions) of mutants can be difficult on many computer systems; executing that many mutants is an even larger problem. Fortunately, there are several ways to overcome the problem of limited resources: (1) *Mutant sampling*. Mutation systems allow the tester to specify random sampling of a certain percentage of mutants. Often, sampling even a small percentage of the possible mutants is enough to reveal inadequate test data. (2) *Selective application of mutant operators*. Mutation systems also allow the tester to specify that only certain kinds of mutations are to be performed. Thus, the tester can select mutations that are likely to have a high payoff relative to the amount of time they require. (3) *Use of high-performance computers*. The Mothra system is designed to support *resource shifting* — the automatic transfer of computationally intensive tasks (such as mutant execution) to high-speed processors (vector machines, for example).

We feel that mutation analysis is particularly useful for testing Ada programs. Because of Ada's use in mission-critical applications, the testing of Ada programs must be extremely thorough. Mutation analysis is not only a superior testing methodology, but also offers testers the opportunity to match the degree of testing to the criticality of the application and the amount of resources available for testing.

2   ADA MUTATION

A program is mutated by applying a *mutant operator* — a simple transformation — to the program. A number of mutant operators have been defined for Fortran 77 based on error data collected from studies of "competent" programmers. Since many of the Fortran operators are relevant for Ada as well, we first discuss them briefly, then outline a set of Ada mutant operators.

2.1   Fortran mutant operators

The Fortran 77 mutant operators currently supported by the Mothra system can be divided into three classes: *statement analysis, predicate analysis,* and *coincidental correctness.* A simplified list of the operators in each class follows.

Statement analysis. Replace each statement by "trap" (if "trap" is reached during execution, the mutant is killed); replace each statement by CONTINUE; replace each statement in a subprogram by RETURN; replace the target label in each GOTO; replace the label in each DO statement.

Predicate analysis. Take the absolute value or negative absolute value of an expression; replace one arithmetic operator by another; replace one relational operator by another; replace one logical operator by another; insert a unary operator preceding an expression; alter the value of a constant; alter a DATA statement.

Coincidental correctness. Replace a scalar variable, array reference, or constant by another scalar variable, array reference, or constant; replace a reference to an array name by the name of another array.

These operators were derived experimentally to correspond to simple errors that a programmer might make. For example, the coincidental correctness operators represent cases where the programmer uses the wrong variable name or array reference. The predicate analysis operators represent errors that a programmer might make inside an expression — using an incorrect comparison operator or the wrong arithmetic operator. The statement analysis operators check for several types of errors. The "trap" replacement ensures that each statement is reached, the CONTINUE replacement ensures that each statement is necessary, and the RETURN replacement ensures that the code following that statement is necessary. The label replacements, of course, imitate the error of using the wrong label.

2.2 Ada mutant operators

Most of the Fortran mutant operators are still meaningful for Ada (with appropriate changes in nomenclature; e.g., CONTINUE becomes **null**). However, Ada's strong typing requires that mutant operators be applied more strictly. Fortran's simple scope rules and lack of strong typing make it relatively easy to determine when the application of a mutation operator will yield a valid program. Ada's complex static semantic restrictions, designed with the laudable goal of increasing program reliability, make "random" applications of mutation operators much less likely to generate a valid Ada program. For example, determining if the replacement of one operator by another will yield a valid Ada expression is complicated by Ada's overloading rules. Rather than attempting to generate only mutants that will compile successfully, it seems better to define mutant operators that sometimes yield a *stillborn* mutant (one that will not compile). There is a tradeoff involved: by increasing the complexity of the mutant operators — and the software that generates mutants — the number of stillborn mutants can be reduced.

Ada will require a number of new mutant operators in addition to those carried over from Fortran. Unfortunately, the best source of mutant operators — studies of common programmer errors — is not of much help in the case of Ada, because few studies of Ada errors have been conducted (this is not surprising, considering the relative youth of the language and the difficulty of conducting such studies). Most of the errors that recent studies (e.g., Basili et al. 1985; Goodenough 1986) have discovered are errors in Ada syntax and semantics that can be detected during compilation.

Based on the small amount of existing error data and our experience with errors in other programming languages, we have formulated a tentative set of Ada mutant operators (Bowser 1987). A partial list of these operators follows, keyed by sections in the Ada Language Reference Manual (LRM). This set of mutant operators will no doubt require revision as we acquire more experience with error patterns in Ada programs.

Lexical Elements (LRM §2). Ada provides real, integer, string, and character literals. In general, literals of one class appearing in an expression will be replaced by other literals of that class appearing in the same compilation unit. In addition, numeric literals will be replaced by "nearby values" (the Fortran mutant operators alter integer literals by ±1 and real literals by ±10%).

Declarations and Types (LRM §3). Initialization expressions for object declarations will be mutated according to the rules for expression mutation described later. In addition, initialization expressions will be deleted when present.

Expressions occurring within constraints will be mutated. For example, in the declaration

subtype Rainbow **is** COLOR **range** RED .. BLUE;

the literals RED and BLUE would be replaced by other literals occurring in expressions within the compilation unit.

Component declaration lists within records will not mutated by "replacement," since this will always lead to a still-born mutant unless the replaced component is never accessed. For example, in the declaration

```
type aRecord is
record
    list1, list2 : array (1..10) of Integer;
    first1, first2: Integer;
end record;
```

the bounds of list1 and list2 would be mutated, but the names of components would not be replaced by other object names.

Attributes of types and variables are considered to be expressions; mutation operators are defined for each attribute listed in the Ada LRM. Mutants will be generated for each attribute that has the same type as the source program attribute. (For example, X'FIRST would be replaced by X'LAST.) In general, mutation rules for attributes are the same as those for function calls (described later).

Names and Expressions (LRM §4). Any reference to a name in an expression will be mutated to yield names representing objects of the same type. Simple names will be replaced by other simple names; within a compound name, we will mutate each simple name or expression that it contains. For example, suppose that r1, r2, and i are declared as follows:

```
r1, r2: aRecord;
i: Integer;
```

The mutations of

```
r1.list1(i)
```

would be

```
r2.list1(i)
r1.list2(i)
r1.list1(1)
r1.list1(10)
    . . .
```

In general, each occurrence of i could be replaced by any other directly visible object of base type Integer, as well as any other integer literal occurring in the same scope. However, we would not replace r1.list1(i) by either r2.list2(i) or r1.first1, since these require more than a single syntactic change.

Replacing one object by an object of a different type results in a stillborn mutant, except in the presence of overloading. For example, suppose that "+" has been overloaded as follows:

function "+"(l : Integer; r : Float) **return** Integer;

In the assignment

```
i := i + 1;
```

the constant 1 could be replaced by all simple names and constants of base type *universal_real* (as well as those of base type *universal_integer*).

Aggregates in Ada are mutated by mutating the expressions in each component association. For example, the aggregate

aRecord'(r1.list1, r1.list1, 1, 2)

would be mutated to yield

aRecord'(r2.list1, r1.list1, 1, 2)
aRecord'(r1.list2, r1.list1, 1, 2)
aRecord'(r1.list1, r2.list1, 1, 2)
. . .

Permutations of two expressions in an aggregate constitute a *permutation* mutation (provided they are type compatible), so

aRecord'(r1.list1, r1.list1, 2, 1)

is also a mutation of the original aggregate. When named notation is used, choice names must be permuted (again subject to type compatibility) Thus, the aggregate

aRecord'(list1 | list2 => r1.list1, first1 => 1, first2 => 2)

could be mutated to produce

aRecord'(list1 | list2 => r1.list1, first2 => 1, first1 => 2)

An alternative approach to mutating named associations is to mutate them as though it they had been declared positionally, with ranges in array aggregates treated as a single choice. The need to mutate range expressions within aggregates (and also in **case** statement choices) is not clear. Often permuting choices yields the same effect as mutating choice range bounds. Also, range mutations may lead to stillborn mutants even if there is no **others** clause (since choices must be disjoint). For example, if aString is defined as

subtype aString **is** String(1..20);

then the aggregate

aString(1..10 => 'a', 11..20 => 'b')

cannot have the range bounds 10 or 20 mutated arbitrarily. We mutate integer array bounds by ±1, hence the mutants generated would be

```
aString(1..10 => 'b', 11..20 => 'a')
aString(0..10 => 'a', 11..20 => 'b') -- **
aString(2..10 => 'a', 11..20 => 'b')
aString(1.. 9 => 'a', 11..20 => 'b')
aString(1..11 => 'a', 11..20 => 'b') -- **
aString(1..10 => 'a', 12..20 => 'b')
aString(1..10 => 'a', 10..20 => 'b') -- **
aString(1..10 => 'a', 11..19 => 'b')
aString(1..10 => 'a', 11..21 => 'b') -- **
```

The mutants marked "**" would raise CONSTRAINT_ERROR exceptions (and hence probably terminate execution). Such mutants test reachability, but three of the four cases are redundant mutants.

In general, each operator will be replaced by other operators that expect operands of the same type. For example, "+" will be replaced by "-", "*", and "/". The mutation rules for predefined types allow replacement by overloaded operators that are visible. In addition, numeric expressions are mutated by inserting the **abs** operator, and boolean expressions are mutated by inserting the **not** operator.

Type conversions are similar to unary function calls, and hence need not be mutated in the absence of overloading.

Statements (LRM §5). Each statement is replaced by either **null** or **abort**. The Fortran mutation operator that replaces each statement by **return** must be modified in the case of Ada functions so that each statement in a function is replaced by a copy of all other **return** statements appearing in the function.

Each statement within a compound statement is mutated individually. The mutation of simple assignment statements and **if** statements is similar to that for Fortran. The LHS operand of an assignment statement is mutated in the same way as a compound name; the RHS expression of an assignment and the conditional expression of an **if** statement are mutated in the same way as expressions.

Mutating **case** statements is similar to mutating array aggregates. Each statement within a **case** statement alternative is mutated, choices are permuted among alternatives, and the case expression itself is mutated. Consider the following **case** statement:

```
case r2.list1(r2.first1) is
  when 1 .. 10 | 20 => statement_list_1
  when others => statement_list_2
end case;
```

Each of the statements in the two statement lists would first be mutated, then each of the three choices 1..10, 20, and **others** would be mutated to the other case statement alternative, yielding

> **when** 1 .. 10 => *statement_list_2*
> **when** 20 => *statement_list_1*
> **when others** => *statement_list_2*

and

> **when** 1 .. 10 => *statement_list_1*
> **when** 20 => *statement_list_2*
> **when others** => *statement_list_2*

and

> **when** 1 .. 10 => *statement_list_1*
> **when** 20 => *statement_list_1*
> **when others** => *statement_list_1*

The expression r2.list1(r2.first1) would also be mutated.

In **loop** statements with iteration schemes (**for** or **while**), the expressions are mutated following the general rules for expression mutation, and in the case of **for** loops, the use of **reverse** is mutated (deleted if present, added if not present). In **exit** statements, the condition (if present) is mutated and the loop name (if present) is replaced by other loop names. In each **goto** statement, the target label is replaced by all other visible labels.

Subprograms (LRM §6). The mode of each formal parameter will be mutated from **in out** to **in** and **out**, and similarly from **out** to **in** and **in out**, and **in** to **out** and **in out**, although in many cases these will lead to stillborn mutants. Default expressions will be mutated and defaults removed. In a subprogram call, the subprogram name will be mutated in the same way as an operator. It should be noted that mutations of subprogram specifications and declarations must correspond in order to avoid stillborn mutants. Although this violates the rule that a mutant should consist of a single syntactic change, programmers commonly copy subprogram declarations from the corresponding specifications.

Actual parameter lists will be mutated in the same manner as record aggregates (i.e., each expression in the parameter list will be mutated, and parameters will be permuted for named and positional notation).

In a function, the expression in each **return** statement will be mutated.

Packages (LRM §7). In general, the mutation of packages is covered by the earlier rules for mutation of declarations and statements.

Tasks (LRM §9). The major problem in mutating tasks is their potential nondeterminism. In ordinary mutation analysis, a mutant is killed by a test case if the mutant and the original program produce different results when given that test case as input. However, in the presence of nondeterminism, even the original program can produce different results when executed twice with the same input data. The simplest solution is to control the nondeterminism of the scheduler by recording a trace of scheduling decisions, then replaying the same trace when executing mutants. This approach has several problems, however: (1) If the scheduler uses time slicing, then replay is difficult. (2) Some task mutations may make replay impossible (e.g., if a mutation changes one task entry name to another). (3) The death of a mutant may depend upon the choice of scheduling traces.

In general, executing a nondeterministic program on a given test case will generate output in a *feasible output set* of possible legal outputs. A mutant is *equivalent* if it generates the same feasible output set as the original program. A mutant is *weakly equivalent* if its feasible output set is a subset of the feasible output set of the original program. If either definition of equivalence is adopted for killing mutants, it is still necessary to determine the feasible output set of the original program. One approach is static analysis (Appelbe & McDowell 1988), which can determine all possible outcomes by simulating the execution of the original program. The problem is further complicated in Ada by timed entry calls and delays. Our initial implementation will probably use weak equivalence testing, with the tester providing the feasible output set. (Each mutant will be executed once on a test case; only if its output is not in the feasible output set will it be considered dead.) Eventually, a full Ada mutation testing system should incorporate static analysis of input programs, together with user control over task scheduling.

Mutating the tasking statements themselves is straightforward. Entry calls will be mutated in the same manner as procedure calls. Conditional and timed entry calls will be replaced by simple entry calls. **accept** statements will be mutated by replacing the entry name by other visible entries of the same type. **select** statements will be mutated in a manner similar to **case** statements. At present, we do not propose to mutate **delay** statements, since — in the absence of hardware dependencies — the correctness of an Ada program should not depend upon delays. A delay merely notifies the scheduler that a task is not ready to be executed until a specified amount of time has elapsed.

Exceptions (LRM §11). Exception declarations need not be mutated, but both exception handlers and **raise** statements will be mutated. Like other statements, a **raise** statement will be mutated by replacing it by **null** and **abort**. In addition, the name of the exception will be replaced by all other exceptions visible in this scope. However, programmer-defined exceptions will be replaced only by other programmer-defined exceptions, and predefined exceptions will be replaced only by other predefined exceptions. The rules for the mutation of exception handlers are similar to those for **case** statements. In particular, each handler will be deleted and its alternatives permuted.

Generic Units (LRM §12). Generic compilation units cannot be tested stand-alone — they must first be instantiated. Mutating the body of a generic unit (package or subprogram) is the same as mutating the body of a nongeneric unit. In the specification of a generic unit, only expressions appearing in the generic formal part are mutated, since other mutations will be stillborn. Mutating a generic instantiation follows the same rules as mutating a subprogram call.

Representation Clauses (LRM §13). These are not mutated.

Input-Output (LRM §14). Calls to I/O library subprograms are mutated in the same fashion as other subprogram calls. Note, however, that a qualified name, such as

> Text_IO.put('c')

would be mutated by substituting for either Text_IO or put, not both. For example, the mutants

> Text_IO.get('c')

and

> My_Package.put('c')

are valid if My_Package is visible and provides a subprogram named put with appropriate formal parameter(s).

2.3   *Problems and opportunities of Ada mutation*

Ada mutation poses a number of problems that have not been addressed in previous mutation systems. At the same time, we feel that Ada offers significant advantages from a mutation standpoint. In this section, we summarize what we feel are the most important issues of Ada mutation; we have already mentioned some of these issues in our discussion of Ada mutant operators.

Choosing a useful set of Ada mutant operators is difficult, and the number of operators needed appears to be very large. The set of 22 mutant operators supported by the Mothra system seems adequate for Fortran, but Ada will require many more. A large collection of mutant operators not only adds complexity to the testing system, but also requires more effort on the part of the tester, who must decide which operators to apply.

Certain Ada features are difficult to handle within the traditional framework of mutation analysis. For example, generics pose significant problems. A generic subprogram or package is not directly executable—it must first be instantiated. Testing a particular instantiation is straightforward, but provides incomplete information, since data that is good for testing one instantiation is not necessarily good for testing another.

Overloading allows the same symbol to denote different operators, thus complicating the rules for replacement within expressions. Only further experience will enable us to determine whether the rules we have adopted are sufficiently general.

Tasking is also a challenge for mutation, since a program that contains tasking may exhibit nondeterministic behavior. A program and one of its mutants may produce different results, even though the two are equivalent. Testing programs that use tasking requires a weaker notion of input-output equivalence.

Ada's **use** clauses present another problem. In Fortran, the variables visible in a program unit are substituted for one another. Because of Ada's **use** clauses, however, variables (and other entities) declared in packages can be visible in a program unit without actually appearing in the unit. Should these variables be substituted for those appearing in the unit?

While Ada mutation is more complex than Fortran mutation, we feel that strongly-typed languages in general, and Ada in particular, provide one advantage for mutation that Fortran does not. A large number of Fortran mutations are created by substitution: a variable, array reference, or constant is substituted for another variable, array reference, or constant. Most of these substitutions do not require an exact type match, since most Fortran variables — in practice — are arithmetic, and Fortran places few restrictions on the mixing of arithmetic types. If the program (or subprogram) being tested contains many variables, arrays, or constants, this can result in a very large number of mutants. This problem is less likely to occur in Ada, because Ada's strong typing prevents many potential substitutions.

3 DESIGN OF AN ADA MUTATION SYSTEM

We are now building an Ada mutation system as a part of the Mothra software testing environment. Since our system is closely linked to the existing Mothra system, we first describe briefly the architecture of Mothra. Mothra is described in more detail by DeMillo et al. (1987 a,b) and Offutt & King (1987).

3.1 Overview of the Mothra system

Mothra's principal subsystems include the *parser*, the test case formatter (*mapper*), the mutant maker (*mutmake*), the mutant generator (*mutgen*), and the interpreter (*rosetta*). When supplied with a program to test, Mothra first invokes the parser to create a code file and a symbol file. The code file contains instructions in *Mothra Intermediate Code* (*MIC*), a postfix intermediate language. The symbol file contains tables of names and their attributes.

After parsing the program, Mothra invokes *mutmake* to produce a file of *Mutant Descriptor Records* (*MDRs*). Each record describes the change(s) needed to the code file to produce a single mutant. To avoid the cost of storing many copies of the same code, the MDRs are applied to the code file at run time (by *mutgen*) to create mutated versions of the code.

Before executing these mutants, the tester must submit a test case to the Mothra system to produce the original output. Test cases are entered by interacting with *mapper*. When given a test case, Mothra invokes *rosetta* to execute the original code file (*original execution*) and save the output for later comparison. Mothra also saves the test case for use during the execution of mutants (*mutant execution*).

Once a test case and a set of MDRs have been created, Mothra executes the mutant programs. *mutgen* applies each MDR to the code file to produce an (in-memory) mutated version of the code. *rosetta* is then called to execute the mutated program and produce the output. This mutant output is compared to the original output by the output comparator *kilroy*. If the outputs differ, then *kilroy* marks the mutant dead; dead mutants are not executed against subsequent test cases. If the outputs are the same, the mutant is left alive.

MIC instructions are simple operator-operand pairs. Although mutations are defined at the source language level, they are applied to MIC instructions to save the expense of generating intermediate code for every mutant program. Because of this and the decompiling requirement, MIC instructions were designed so that the code produced for a program would have a direct relationship with the original source. This causes MIC to be higher-level than most internal forms. The high-level form of MIC allows easy decompilation and mutation at the expense of some run-time efficiency.

3.2 Modifying Mothra for Ada testing

The development of an Ada mutation testing capability in the Mothra environment involves two major steps: (1) developing a compiler front end to generate MIC, and (2) extending MIC to support Ada programs.

The development of a compiler front end is greatly simplified by the assumption that the input program to be tested is syntactically correct. The translation of Ada into MIC is best accomplished at a high level, e.g., from Diana into MIC, rather than from a low-level abstract machine form. Currently, we are designing a prototype for converting Diana to MIC, using a commercial Ada compiler front end that produces a Diana representation of an Ada program.

The extension of MIC to handle Ada is straightforward. After extension, MIC will resemble an intermediate form such as the ones described by Appelbe & Dismukes (1982) and by Groves & Rogers (1980). At first, Mothra will support only a subset of Ada; the initial prototype will not allow testing of features such as tasking and fixed point numbers. We intend to develop the prototype with a view to testing programs in the Ada software repository, and use the feedback gained in this process to refine the definition of Ada mutant operators, the Diana to MIC translator, and the MIC interpreter.

4 CONCLUSIONS

The numerous mutation-based testing systems developed over the last ten years have demonstrated the effectiveness of mutation analysis as a program testing methodology. We believe that mutation is particularly valuable for testing Ada programs. Ada poses a number of problems for mutation analysis, but we are developing techniques to solve these problems as we add an Ada capability to the Mothra testing environment.

ACKNOWLEDGEMENTS

This work was supported in part under contract F30602-85-C-0255 through Rome Air Development Center and contract 19K-CN982C through Oak Ridge National Laboratory. We also wish to acknowledge the work of John Bowser, who helped to develop the original set of Ada mutant operators, as well as the efforts of the Mothra groups at Georgia Tech and Purdue.

REFERENCES

Acree, A. T. (1980). On Mutation, Ph.D. thesis, School of Information and Computer Science, Georgia Institute of Technology.

Acree, A. T., Budd, T. A., DeMillo, R. A., Lipton, R. J. & Sayward, F. G. (1979). Mutation Analysis, Technical Report GIT-ICS-79/08, School of Information and Computer Science, Georgia Institute of Technology.

Appelbe, B. & Dismukes, G. (1982). An operational definition of intermediate code for implementing a portable Ada compiler. *In* Proceedings of the AdaTEC Conference on Ada, pp. 266-274.

Appelbe, W. F. & McDowell, C. E. (1988). Developing multitasking applications programs. *In* Proceedings of the Hawaii International Conference on System Sciences (HICSS-21), vol. 2, pp. 94-102.

Basili, V. R., Katz, E. E., Panlilio-Yap, N. M., Ramsey, C. L. & Chang, S. (1985). Characterization of an Ada software development. Computer, *18*, no. 9, 53-65.

Bowser, J. (1987). Reference Manual for Ada Mutant Operators, unpublished manuscript.

Budd, T. A. (1980). Mutation Analysis of Program Test Data, Ph.D. thesis, Department of Computer Science, Yale University.

Budd, T. A., DeMillo, R. A., Lipton, R. J. & Sayward, F. G. (1978). The design of a prototype mutation system for program testing. *In* AFIPS National Computer Conference Proceedings, vol. 47, pp. 623-627.

Budd, T. A., Hess, R. & Sayward, F. G. (1980). EXPER Implementor's Guide, Department of Computer Science, Yale University.

DeMillo, R. A., Guindi, D., King, K. N., Krauser, E. W., McCracken, W. M., Offutt, A. J. & Spafford, E. H. (1987 a). Mothra Internal Documentation, Version 1.0, Technical Report GIT-SERC-87/10, Software Engineering Research Center, Georgia Institute of Technology.

DeMillo, R. A., Guindi, D. S., King, K. N. & McCracken, W. M. (1987 b). An overview of the Mothra software testing environment, Technical Report GIT-SERC-87/16, Software Engineering Research Center, Georgia Institute of Technology.

DeMillo, R. A., Lipton, R. J. & Sayward, F. G. (1978). Hints on test data selection: help for the practicing programmer. Computer, *11*, no. 4, 34-41.

DeMillo, R. A., Lipton, R. J. & Sayward, F. G. (1979). Program mutation: a new approach to program testing. *In* Infotech State of the Art Report, Software Testing, vol. 2, pp. 107-126. Maidenhead, U.K.: Infotech International.

DeMillo, R. A., McCracken, W. M., Martin, R. J. & Passafiume, J. F. (1987 c). *Software Testing and Evaluation.* Menlo Park, Calif.: Benjamin/Cummings.

Girgis, M. R. & Woodward, M. R. (1986). An experimental comparison of the error exposing ability of program testing criteria. *In* Workshop on Software Testing Conference Proceedings, pp. 51-60. Washington, D.C.: IEEE Computer Society Press.

Goodenough, J. (1986). Ada Programmer Errors, unpublished manuscript.

Groves, L. J. & Rogers, W. J. (1980). The design of a virtual machine for Ada. SIGPLAN Notices, *15*, no. 11, 223-234.

Hanks, J. M. (1980). Testing Cobol Programs by Mutation: Volume I - Introduction to the CMS.1 System, Volume II - CMS.1 System Documentation, Technical Report GIT-ICS-80/04, School of Information and Computer Science, Georgia Institute of Technology.

Howden, W. E. (1976). Reliability of the path analysis testing strategy. IEEE Transactions on Software Engineering, *SE-2*, no. 3, 208-215.

Howden, W. E. (1980). Functional testing and design abstractions. Journal of Systems and Software, *1*, no. 4, 307-313.

King, J. C. (1976). Symbolic execution and program testing. Communications of the ACM, *19*, no. 7, 385-394.

Offutt, A. J., VI & King, K. N. (1987). A Fortran 77 interpreter for mutation analysis. SIGPLAN Notices, *22*, no. 7, 177-188.

Tanaka, A. (1981). Equivalence Testing for Fortran Mutation System Using Data Flow Analysis, M.S. thesis, School of Information and Computer Science, Georgia Institute of Technology.

Part 2 Industrial Ada Applications

THE USE OF Ada™1 IN A LARGE SHIPBORNE WEAPON CONTROL SYSTEM

Roland Fors, Ulf Olsson, Gunnar Larsson2

ABSTRACT

This paper describes some of the consequences of using Ada in large scale projects, mainly in terms of the training and tool support necessary.

INTRODUCTION

Philips Elektronikindustrier (PEAB) is currently under contract to deliver the electronics suites for several new classes of warships: among others, the Swedish Göteborg-class Coastal Corvette, and the Danish Standard Flex 300 multi-role ship. They are rather small, but carry considerable firepower, and can handle complex missions. As a consequence, the electronics systems must cope with the complexity of weapon systems typical for much larger ships, while still making it possible for a limited crew to control the operation of the system.

The two systems mentioned above are the first to be built out of the new Ship Systems 2000 (SS2000) family of shipborne Weapon Control Systems (also known as 9LV Mk.3) . PEAB has taken the decision to use Ada as the language for SS2000. This presentation intends to describe the practical effects of that decision on design, methodology etc.

Note: it is assumed that the reader has had at least some exposure to the Ada language. If not, see e.g., [1] for a good introduction.

GENERAL PROPERTIES OF SS2000

As is evident from fig. 1 below, SS2000 is a family of distributed systems. The main structural component is the dual Ethernet Local Area Network that ties the nodes of the system together. Furthermore, the nodes themselves can contain several processors (Motorola 68020's, tied together by

---

1 Ada is a trademark of the US Government (Ada Joint Program Office)

2 Philips Elektronikindustrier, S-175 88 Järfälla, Sweden

a VME bus). Thus, the operational software runs in an environment of loosely coupled processors.

In a traditionally designed electronics suite, a number of more or less independent systems would be tied together with point-to-point links. The corresponding role in SS2000 is played by sets of nodes: e.g., the artillery Fire Control System corresponds to the director processors, the gun control processors, and a number of operator consoles. From a design point of view, this means that the network topology is not fixed over time: parts of the system are turned on and off based on operational needs.

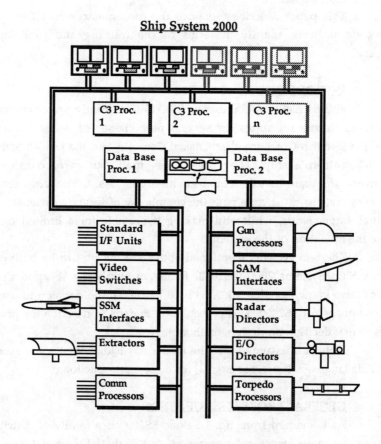

Fig. 1: Structural overview of a typical SS2000 system

When the system is designed towards such requirements, the system structure will as a consequence also have the necessary properties of being adaptable to changing requirements from the current customers, as well as to the requirements for new customers. As we shall see later, this leads to some interesting problems in the Ada context.

Note that it is a further design requirement for the SS2000 family that it should also be possible to build small, low-cost systems. This effectively precludes some design options when dealing with - among others - redundancy issues, as well as posing additional configurability requirements.

WHY Ada WAS SELECTED

It should be noted that Ada was not a firm requirement for any of the two customers, even though it was recommended. Actually, both systems were originally specified to use RTL/2 as the implementation language. The reason was that PEAB had already delivered one large-scale and a few small to medium scale projects using RTL/2. However, the sheer size of the SS2000 project (currently estimated at 1.5 million source lines of code, with an estimated work force of more than 100 SW developers) meant that drastic productivity improvements were necessary. While investigating ways to improve the programming environment and tool support for RTL/2, it became apparent that development environments were becoming available for Ada that not only equalled what was available for other languages, but even constituted a major breakthrough.

In order to put these promises of improved performance to the test, an R1000 development system was bought in May 1986 from Rational of Mountain View, California. A project consisting of the development of a standard operator console for battalion-level artillery staff was selected for development using the Rational Environment. The results were very encouraging: although as usual hard to quantify, programmer productivity was improved enough to motivate the massive investment in hardware, software and training that was required to back the decision. In addition to the improved performance in terms of lines of debugged code written per hour, it was interesting to note that the usual relationship between design, coding and integration/test of 40:20:40 changed - as predicted - to 60:20:20 . I.e., more time was spent thinking about the design, and considerably less time making it work.

In short, then, the main factor behind the Ada decision was the desire to raise programmer productivity considerably, partly through the power of the language, but also because of the quality of the available development environment.The decision was of course also influenced by all the "standard" reasons for choosing Ada: separation of specification and implementation, information hiding, powerful constructs, parallelism etc. .

There are, however, a number of secondary gains that shouldn't be forgotten:

- Personnel: it is remarkably easy to attract qualified SW personnel if you can promise Ada work
- Survivability: Ada can be expected to be around for a significant time. This serves to protect the large investment we are making in terms of writing applications software.
- Reuse: many of Ada's features are expressly in the language to provide for software reuse. This is extremely important for the SS2000 family, in the light of the modifiability requirements that were discussed previously.

Based on the results from this project and other studies, the decision was then taken to buy 7 Rational R1000 processors. In the contract was also included resident technical consulting from Rational for at least a year, and an extensive training program for the transition to Ada. This program will be discussed in more detail below.

IS Ada ENOUGH?

It is often said that Ada is a big language, but is it big enough? This may sound as somewhat heretical [2] but becomes apparent when one tries to organize a large-scale project. Ada's strategy of strictly separating specifications from implementations must then be extrapolated to the next level up in the system design hierarchy. There, the project is broken down into what is known as Subsystems. Where the concept of specs and bodies isolates Ada units from implementation changes, the concept of Subsystems isolate project teams from each other. A key property of the Subsystem is that it can exist in several versions: therefore, all dependent project teams can use a stable version, while the responsible team works with the next version. Thus, even specifications can be evolved, as the project goes through its phases. The development environment supports the Subsystem concept directly.

Ada AND DESIGN METHODOLOGY

One key issue in using the language right is selecting the proper design methods, in terms of the design concepts produced when using these methods, as well as terminology and representation. We have chosen to use the Object-Oriented Design approach (see [1]), for several reasons. Firstly, even though it can be argued that there are other languages (marginally) better suited to the object-oriented approach, there is a straightforward mapping between the concepts used in OOD and the language elements of Ada. This in itself means that the implementation follows naturally from the design structure.

Secondly, we have used Real-Time Structured Analysis techniques and formalisms according to Yourdon and DeMarco [4] to describe the logical model of the system. Much interesting work has been done lately within the Software Engineering community on describing methods for transforming a logical model of a system in terms of Data Flow Diagrams, State Transition Diagrams, and Entity-Relationship Diagrams. Although cookbook methods can be defined to translate virtually any Structured Analysis logical model to an Object-Oriented Design [5], the pragmatic approach seems to be to do the RTSA analysis on a rather high level, keeping in mind that the result is going to be used to find good design objects. I.e., one must try to "see" good objects as early as possible, but acquiring this "20-20 object vision" is a process that takes some time, as we shall discuss further below.

IMPACT ON DESIGN

Ada specifies concurrency: thus, it is quite possible to conceive an entire SS2000 system as one Ada program. Current production compilers normally do not, however, support Ada programs that span more than one CPU. Much research is currently under way to lessen that limitation (see, for instance, [3]). For the present, however, we have no choice but to see the system as a set of cooperating programs.

The next design decision is then: do we allow more than one program per CPU? The answer is yes, and the general structure is shown in Fig. 2 below. The reason is that this opens possibilities for decoupling system design and integration from component design.

A number of reasons can be brought forward in support of such a
model:

- Load balancing: given an inter-program communication facility
  that supports a flat namespace (i.e., it is impossible to deduce from
  the name used in communications on which node the receiver
  resides), it is possible to modify the distribution of programs over
  hardware in a late stage, if load is unevenly distributed over the
  network.

- Testability: the Ada program becomes a very self-contained entity:
  since its behavior is entirely specified by the responses to external
  stimuli, it is fairly straightforward to write test specifications. (Of
  course, testing at this level is preceded by thorough testing on the
  Ada unit level. There, white box methods are used.)

- Easy mapping to the logical model: if the system is built as a set of
  cooperating programs that interact by passing messages, that
  model maps very well onto our basic concepts for analysis and
  design.

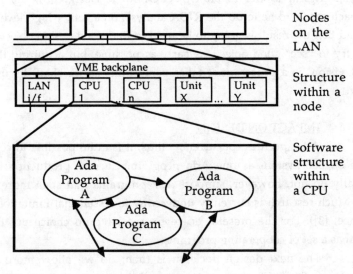

Fig. 2: General software structure

Thus, it is possible to see the runtime structure as a multi-level
hierarchy: a node contains one or more CPU's (or in extreme cases none, if
intelligent I/O units are used) and a CPU contains several Ada programs.

However, due to the flat name space used when programs are addressing each other, what the application programmer sees is better described as an enormous machine with a large number of cooperating programs running.

CONSEQUENCES FOR PESONNEL TRAINING

Experienced real-time software engineers are a very scarce commodity, and such with Ada experience even more so. When trying to transition designers and programmers into the new environment, it becomes very apparent that Ada is not "just any language". From the outset, we realised that we would need to train designers and programmers thoroughly, and the following program was set up:

17 days of classroom instructions, covering

- Ada Language   5 days
- Object-Oriented Design   3 days
- The development environment   9 days

This training package was spread out over 3 to 5 months. However, experience from the pilot projects soon told us that this was not enough: to adopt OOD fully and to make real use of it needs more than classroom training.

The answer to this was to supplement the courses above with a program called "Ada Practice". It is a series of graduated design and development exercises, requiring about half of each student's available time for up to 10 weeks. The first exercises cover general design issues; the later deal with real problems from the SS2000 world. This way, the trainees are gradually brought up to speed, so that by the end of the course, the work they do is directly usable in the project.

The results from this Ada Practice has been very encouraging so far. Interestingly enough, the correlation between previous experience and the ability to change successfully to OOD is not always as one would imagine: normally, an experienced real-time programmer has little trouble grasping the general ideas, but there seems to be a class of people who will unfortunately never leave the assembly frame of mind. As a whole, though, most designers/programmers have come out of this phase with the right mindset for the work ahead of them.

IMPLEMENTATION STRATEGY

The SW effort is divided into the development of SW components (called System Functions) and the development of deliverable systems. The latter process consists of selecting and configuring components, and distributing them over hardware in the best manner in terms of resource utilization. In previous systems, the integration of all the components to form the system did not take place until all components were actually developed. This follows from the strict specify-design-code-test-integrate-verify model that has up to now been taken as the standard way to build systems. The drawback, however, is that the fundamental design problems in terms of interface mismatches, structural imbalances etc. do not become apparent until it is essentially too late: at the beginning of the last development phase before delivery.

To cope with this problem, the Ada paradigm of specifying first and implementing later (with full consistency check between spec and body) has been carried through to the idea of Incremental Integration: once the components in the system have been specified, the integration team actually builds a skeleton system out of those specifications. The interfaces are checked for consistency; statically using the compiler, and dynamically by driving the (message-passing) interfaces with script-based simulators. The component developer then releases versions of his/her component into that framework. This way, the whole system is actually built all the time in the sense that all components are in place, albeit in incarnations with higher and higher functionality. At this stage, however, it is of higher importance to verify dynamic behavior, CPU load, network load, response times etc. than it is to verify functionality.

This emphasis in structure also forces the implementor to address design issues before producing the actual code. Thus, the design is put into focus in the development process. Structural problems can then be detected early. The designer, having developed the specs, can then turn implementation over to other personnel, with full guarantees of at least syntactic consistency. Obviously, semantic consistency (i.e., what actually happens when an operation is exercised) is equally important, but the incremental design and integration approach helps here too, by exposing the developer to the actual system environment early on, so that he/she can verify early that they understand how the basic layers of functionality in the system actually work.

It should be noted that the development environment is entirely built on Ada, both in terms of paradigms, and in terms of tool implementation. Therefore, the developer stays within the language for the whole component life cycle, from design through testing. Cross debugging facilities are supplied, so testing on actual hardware can take place without leaving the basic environment.

REUSABILITY

Some very interesting aspects on Ada have arisen out of the fact that we intend to develop a system family, with several instances of that family being developed essentially in parallel. This highlights the importance of what is normally called reusability, but what should in this case rather be called adaptability.

Our goal is to build components that depend minimally on the configuration, i.e., on what distinguishes one customer system from the other. Ideally, all such information should be read at system startup time from configuration files, i.e., load time binding instead of compile time. The drawback is of course that some of the checking that a compiler might supply at compile time has to be handled by application code at runtime. (For example, the allowed identifiers for track type - FRIGATE, CORVETTE, ... - may be read as strings from a file, instead of as being defined as values of an enumeration type.) Note that this would not be a problem in a non-distributed environment: then, we could build the whole application as one program, compiled within one library. In our context, however, we cannot guarantee that the different programs were compiled in the same library, or, indeed, by the same compiler! In exchange, we gain tolerance against changing requirements.

Sometimes, the differences in requirements for the various customer systems cannot be handled by parametrization only. Instead, new code has to be written. In order to isolate the areas where this may happen, all System Functions have been classified into a layer system, where the lowest layers are expected to be unchanged (at least in terms of their specs) throughout the life of the family, whereas components in the highest layers are tailor-made for the individual customers. A set of rules (tool supported) then control the dependencies so that a more general component is never allowed to depend on a lesser. This way, not only can those components be identified that deserve a lot of attention in terms of making sure that they should be made highly reusable, but we can also single out components that do not stand any chance of ever being reused. Thus, effort can be spared where it would be wasted, and concentrated where it does the most good.

EXPERIENCES

At the time of writing (January 1988), the project situation is such that top level design is essentially complete. Key functions have been prototyped, in some instances several times. Through this effort, the specs for these functions can be considered to be stable and reasonably mature. The factors discussed above have all contributed to this end. The Rational Environment itself has stimulated prototyping by providing rapid turnaround, thereby making sure that the good ideas are actually tried. The Ada Practice sessions also meant that the designs coming out now are of good quality: the important lessons have been learned on less critical stuff.

Equally important, the Configuration Management tools are in full use, which means that the methods for bringing this large project together are also rapidly maturing. Further, the VAX-based documentation environment is being integrated with the Ada development environment. This means that a coherent set of CM tools will be available for both documentation and code.

Finally, let us again stress the importance of pilot projects and training. One does not become a good OOD designer and Ada developer by theoretical studies only! Therefore, it is of prime importance when switching to Ada to ensure the necessary management commitment for investment in training and tools.

CONCLUSION

The changes that Ada has brought with it are more profound than we originally expected. It is interesting to note that several aspects of the development environment have changed simultaneously: for instance the adoption of Ada for implementation and OOD for design. This is obviously not a coincidence, but can rather be seen as a reflection of the fact that the impact of Ada is not tied only to its merits as a language. It will depend just as much to the support it gets from analysis and design methods and the quality of the tools available. Therefore, it is comforting to note that the methods and tools are in fact becoming available, to a large extent because of the inspiration and commercial pressure that the growing usage of Ada creates.

ACKNOWLEDGEMENTS

The authors are indebted to many friends and colleagues who have influenced us significantly. Among these, special thanks goes to Mike Devlin, Grady Booch and Mark Sadler of Rational, California, and Kent Johansson of Devenator, Sweden.

NB: A previous version of this paper has been presented previously at MILCOMP-87 in London and at Ada Expo-87 in Boston; it has also been published in the November 1987 issue of the French software engineering magazine Génie Logiciel.

References

[1] Booch, Grady: Software Engineering with Ada, Benjamin/Cummings 1986 (2nd ed.)
[2] Booch, Grady: Software Components with Ada: Structures, Tools and Subsystems, Benjamin/Cummings 1987
[3] Fisher, David A. and Weatherly, Richard M.: Issues in the Design of a Distributed Operating System for Ada, Computer, May 1986 issue
[4] Structured Analysis for Real-Time Systems (Course material): Yourdon, Inc., 1984
[5] Strandberg, Carlerik: Method for Transition from SART to OOD (unpublished PEAB material)

Ada(1) for CATCAS(2) : a new era in Air Traffic Control .

Jean Francois WETS
Software development director

Marc LEON
Software project manager

Thomson-CSF division SDC (System Defense & Control)
40, rue Grange Dame Rose - B.P. 34
92360 Meudon la foret - FRANCE

Brief history.

The increasing volume of air traffic has led to the development of complex and increasingly automated systems to aid air traffic
controllers.
Early systems presented raw radar displays and left procedural duties and collision avoidance entirely to the operator. These
systems were constructed from the highest level of hardware technology
available and used little or no software.

Modern systems provide synthetic video displays offering
features such as variable range selection, aircraft identification and
map displays (static background information). Depending upon the
assessment of the local authority, a work-station may contain several
input devices and a system may provide collision detection, multiradar
tracking, meteorological displays, flight plan processing and miscel-
laneous features designed to assist a controller with procedural
duties. These systems are substantially software oriented and evolve
as rapidly as developments in technology allow.

Thomson-CSF division SDC (System Defence & Control) has been
supplying ATC systems virtually from their inception. The division
must constantly investigate developments offered by breakthroughs in
technology when proposing new systems.

In 1983 when the Danish Civil Aviation authority specified
the operational functions of a new control centre and associated
simulator, CATCAS 87 and SIMU 87, we estimated that a high performance
32 bit computer was required to fulfil the specification, and that the
development of a completely new software implementation would be
facilited by a highly structured language.

Data General Corporation MV10000 computers were selected and Ada was chosen as the software development language.

CATCAS 87 is an advanced automated air traffic control centre. It is established for a planned operational life of 15 years, and embodies advanced air traffic control functions, including :

* multiradar data acquisition and processing from seven primary and secondary radar stations,

* automated acquisition and processing of flight plan data,

* radar display of aircraft track correlated with flight plans.

The main parameters of the system are :

* 25 radar data visualisation peripherals,

* 150 plots per radar input and per antenna revolution,

* 350 system tracks,

* library of 4000 repetitive flight plans,

* library of 1500 flight plans,

* 300 active flight plans.

Evaluation of a new software language

The final decision to use Ada was taken after six month of evaluation, with benchmarks and timing tests.

Ada was chosen on the basis of the following criteria. Selection of these criteria was based on assessments of languages used in previous implementations.

* Reliability : ATC was introduced to promote safe air transport. The functions of ATC have been designated by ICAO (International Civil Aviation Organization), but the effective-ness of the systems rests with the performance of the implementation. As the volume of air traffic increases, the tolerance of software faults decreases while greater demands are placed on system performance.

* Adaptability : Cost prohibits the total replacement of ATC systems each time extensions are required or specifications are altered. Often, when modifications are requested by a customer it is impossible to assemble the original development team to upgrade the software. Significant time is therefore allocated for comprehension of the original software. This time allocation and the reliability of the modifications vary inordinately with the choice of software development language.

* Maintainability : Languages which are not widely implemented or not directly supported by the manufacturer of the computing system may possibly force a company to divide an area of expertise into software language groups, this is particularly true when the support for a development language is not provided on new generation hardware. Software division reduces flexibility when assembling project teams, and adds overhead for retraining.

* Modularity : While regulations governing the operations in an ATC system and basic system requirements have been specified by ICAO, substantial choices remain when selecting the operations to be implemented. Significant variation is permitted in the system implementation and the size varies greatly from one system to another. What we currently envisage as an ideal situation is a system composed of developed and tested modules with only moderate tailoring provided to suit the customers'requirements. We anticipate that this modularity will greatly enhance system reliability and adaptability.

Software design methodology.

Ada is not just a software language, it is the product of a software philosophy and needs to be combined with efficient methodology and a powerful software development environment.

A study of different methodologies led us to choose the Object Oriented Design (O.O.D.) method, as described by Grady BOOCH in "Software Engineering with Ada" (The Benjamin/Cummings Publishing Company, Inc.).
This method allows the derivation of software structure from the simple formalization of a solution to a problem. It presents major advantages over functionnal methodologies because it is a transcription from the specifications of the real problem. Moreover it is easily applied without the requirement of software expertise.

Representation by objects support the advantages of Ada concepts: modularity and hidden implementation.
Further it may be used with the same efficiency from the top level to the bottom level of the design, in iteration steps.

The Data General Ada Development Environment (ADE) contains the basic tools : text editor, compiler, linker and library manager.
The development of the CATCAS 87 project required additional tools primarily to assist compilation.
Because programs are not independent in their relative order of compilation, due to their dependences (WITH and SEPARATE clauses), compilation or recompilation orders must be determined for successful Ada compilation.

The basic functions of these utilities are to :

* find the correct compilation order for a set of modules previously uncompiled;

* find the minimum number of compilations and their respective orders after modifications to a set of modules.

Certain guidelines have been introduced to simplify these problems.
These guidelines slightly restrict our use of Ada; restrictions which appear reasonable when considering variety of means which the Ada language may satisfy a problem.

The major problem in the design of the software was the general organization of the modules. The definition of types and objects have to be well organized to allow, as much as possible, independance between modules. Otherwise the notion of packages with their visible part and hidden body is very well understood and applied.

The tools and guidelines are described in a manual entitled "Ada Development User's Guide".

Real time implementation.

Multitasking is an efficient means of providing the rapid response times required by air traffic controllers without the use of super computers.
While the Ada multitasking offers all of the features required for the development of an ATC system, several problems were encountered in the use of the tasking with the current Ada compiler implementation :

* The sole tasking primitive (the rendez-vous) creates a substantial overhead and is excessive for the majority of our
  inter-task communications.

* The task scheduling of the Ada implementation suspend all tasks
  during conditions such as the disk access for the page fault
  handling of one task only (At the time of evalution we found no
  implementation which produced a significant improvement in this
  area and catered for our production requirements).

In solving the tasking problems we could neither afford to
wait for significant improvements in performance, nor to remove our-
selves from Ada philosophy and portability.
Our current tasking is written in Data General AOS/VS machine language
and makes use of the efficient task scheduling provided by AOS/VS. The
routines are highly modular, convenient to use and interfaced through
an Ada visible package. It would be possible to write the body completely in Ada, a concept which becomes increasingly viable as the
performance of the implementation improves.
Inter-task   communications   involve similar concepts to
communications between a task and peripheral devices, and both have
been combined into a suite of real time packages developed by SDC.
A description of the basic principles of these real time
packages is given at the end of this paper.

CATCAS 87 development.

To develop the complete CATCAS 87 and SIMU 87 software a
team of 20 persons was involved.
We organized our own Ada training for the SDC staff, including the SDC real time and input-output packages.
Our experience was that a programer with experience of a
structured language (PASCAL or FORTRAN) could program correctly in Ada
after two months of training (theorical and practical).

After one year of development an interview of the staff
showed great satisfaction in the use of Ada. The major requirement was
for an improvement of the compiler speed.

The full project represents about 300.000 Ada code lines,
and the time required to compile the full applications (CATCAS and
SIMU) is 30 hours.

Conclusion.

The impression at the end of this first Ada ATC project is confirmation of the soundness of Ada design.

Despite the risks of using a new language and new environment the CATCAS 87 project was performed on time with the total satisfaction of our Danish customer.

In particular we noted an important time saving during the integration phase of the different software tasks of the application.

Further improvements were noted in error detection and error analysis and in a reduction of the amount of software written in machine language.

The principle disadvantages noted in our use of Ada are :

* the lengthy compilation time due to the number of checks implied by the Ada semantic;

* the increase in disk space used by Ada management files and the associated degradation in response time;

* the code expansion due to the number of dynamic checks performed by the Ada generated code.

These problems can only be overcome by faster processors with greater memories. We estimate that the cost of larger computers is offset by the reduction in software development time, with the result in a better product.

Today SDC is developing many additional ATC systems in Ada; the Belgium Civil Aviation authority and for the Netherlands Royal Air Force as example.

A significant quantity of software from the CATCAS project is scheduled for re-use in these projects.

(1) Ada is a registred trademark of the U.S. government (AJPO).
(2) CATCAS : COPENHAGEN AIR TRAFFIC CONTROL AUTOMATED SYSTEM.

Basic principles of the SDC Ada Real Time System (SDC-ARTS)

The major design guidelines were to keep a solution easily implementable under the operating system AOS/VS and compatible with the Ada real time concepts. Obviously, major advantages of Ada such as (limited) private types and generic units have been used to reinforce the conceptual model.

In the most general cases, a task looks for messages from several other tasks in the system. These messages have to be processed with a different priority. The basic principle is the queuing of messages on a First-In First-Out (FIFO) basis respecting the chronological order of messages received. The SDC Ada Real Time System (SDC-ARTS) associate several FIFOs in a virtual queue. Each FIFO is associated to one type of message by a generic instantiation.

The full definition of a virtual queue will follow the following procedure :

* generic instantiation of the queue giving the number of FIFOs in this queue,

* with these instantiatied procedures there is now the possibility to instantiate as many FIFOs as required with, for each one :

    * type of the queued message,

    * capacity of the FIFO.

The SDC-ARTS method after pertinent instantiations provided in fact a set of queuing/dequeing procedures per FIFO. It is possible to close or open independently each FIFO and to be suspended to wait an incoming message from the set of opened FIFOs. Priority for processing of messages may be controlled selectively by dequeuing messages from chosen FIFOs.

In case of FIFO overflow, the caller has two possibilities :

* suspension until a cell is freed in the FIFO,

* oveflow report (the request is not processed).

This provides efficient flow control between tasks and is achieved by use of generic semaphores (critical time) or server tasks.

Time management.

In all real time systems, three basic needs have to be satisfied :

* reading of the current time and associated operations,

* allocation of a delay to certain events,

* time stamp allocation.

At any time, it is possible to read the current time with a quantum sufficiently low to be compatible with the accuracy needed by radar processing computations. Time stamps are allocated on a universal time basis, supplemented by a discriminant part allowing two different time stamps for two different requests unseparated by a time base quantum.

SDC-ARTS directly offers the possibility of enqueuing delayed events in a FIFO. The message is not really queued at the time of the call but stored and effectively queued later when the attached delay has elapsed. Events may also be enqueued cyclically.

Input/Output management.

Communications with the outside world are ensured with specific I/O front end processors manufactured by SDC. In a task, the receipt of a message from the outside or from another task are two very similar notions. SDC-ARTS manages I/O processing in the same way as intertask messages by using the queuing principle.

In a given queue, it is possible to dedicate a FIFO to receive I/O messages (data or TX acknowledgement). Continuous receiving is achieved for high speed channels (i.e. LAN) and subsequent messages are expressed in concerned FIFOs. For transmission, pools of emitting buffers are provided to reduce the penalty induced by the processing in the case where the CPU is faster than the line, allowing the CPU to prepare messages in advance.

Communication with the outside world are seen by the user as specific Ada packages using the same objects as those used for intertasking. The following packages are currently implemented :

* Asynchronous communications with two major modes :

    * screen manager mode for colour video display units and touch input display management,

* stream manager mode for general purpose point to point
  or multipoint communication,

* synchronous   communications, point to point or multipoint
  communication such as BSC 2780, A500, X25, HDLC, etc.

* Local Area Network (LAN) management : the physical link is
  ETHERNET with IEEE 802.3 procedure and respect of the OSI
  layers.

        In conclusion, the real time implementation used by SDC for
its Ada projects has allowed use of the language as soon as commercialy
available and to take advantages of all the Ada benefits except the
tasking.   However, totally   encapsulated in a doubly generic package,
taking into account the time management and compatibility with the I/O
management,   the SDC model could be easily implemented in full Ada
without code modifications. However, the SDC model is a fully asynchronous one when the Ada model for tasking is synchronous. It could be
certainly more optimal to change the conceptual model used by SDC to be
closer to a synchronous model. This could be done without important
penalties when critical timings are respected and flow control is
properly managed.

CATCAS operational room.
Photo Thomson-CSF Philippe PINAULT

THE APPLICABILITY OF ADA TO HIGH LEVEL VLSI DESIGN TOOLS

C. Daniels
Plessey Information Engineering, Titchfield, PO14 4QA, England

E.B. Pitty
Plessey Research Roke Manor, Romsey, SO51 0ZN, England

C.E. Adams
Advanced System Architectures, Camberley, Surrey, GU15 3PE, England

Abstract. The application of Ada® to the development of two major Computer Aided Design (CAD) software packages is discussed. The discussion covers management and lifecycle issues pertinent to the use of Ada, as well as detail on the use of specific language features. A historical perspective is taken on the two developments which illustrates how our use of Ada has evolved in the light of experience. This supports the primary conclusion which is that Ada has many benefits for the development of CAD software, but these benefits are only realised with both experience and an understanding of the principles behind the language.

1   INTRODUCTION

This paper describes work done at Plessey Research Roke Manor on the development of two Computer Aided Design (CAD) packages for the high-level design of modern integrated circuits. The motivation behind these developments was to provide methods and tools to support the management of complexity in the design of integrated circuits comprised of several tens of thousands of components.

The first package developed was SHADE™ (Burrows 1986) which addresses the problem of high-level hardware design specification. SHADE consists of two major components: an interactive forms-based editor for the entry of design specifications (SBBCAP); and a program which then augments this specification with the details necessary to enable the fabricated integrated circuit to be tested against this specification (CADEPT). The final output of SHADE is a specification of the design in the ELLA™ hardware description language (Morrison et al. 1985). Hardware description languages are formal notations for describing hardware systems at various levels of abstraction (Pitty et al. 1987), and can be loosely thought as being analogous to high-level programming languages. A characteristic of hardware description languages is that they make it possible to simulate (or animate) these abstract design specifications.

Following the development of SHADE, the GATEMAP package was developed (Salmon et al. 1987). The inputs to GATEMAP are the formal ELLA specification of the hardware design generated by SHADE, and a description of a particular semiconductor technology in which this design is to be realised. The purpose of GATEMAP is to efficiently map these ELLA design specifications into implementations in the chosen technology, using the available logic gate primitives. GATEMAP can be likened to a high-level language compiler, aiming to map an input high-level description into an efficient collection of the low-level instructions available on a particular processor.

Both SHADE and GATEMAP have a number of characteristics typical of CAD software, and these result in constraints which are significantly different to those of real-time embedded systems for which Ada was originally devised. Firstly, though CAD software is often interactive it need rarely operate in a real-time environment and hence little or no use of tasking is required. Secondly, with the exception of very specialised applications the target hardware is rarely an embedded processor and so the facilities of Ada to enable this targeting are also unused. Finally, as a consequence of the hardware platform typically being at least a workstation or minicomputer there are generous constraints on the size of both the executable code and its run-time requirements.

Both SHADE and GATEMAP were developed on a Digital Equipment Corporation (DEC™) VAX™ 11/785 using the DEC VAX Ada compiler and Ada Compilation System (ACS) running under the VAX/VMS™ operating system. SHADE contains approximately 730 compilation units (nine executable images) and GATEMAP contains approximately 370 compilation units (one executable image).

The use of Ada within SHADE and GATEMAP is discussed in three main areas. Firstly the role of Ada in the planning and management of the project, secondly details of the use of specific language features within the software, and finally the impact of Ada on the testing and maintenance phases. Further lessons learnt from the GATEMAP development are also discussed, giving pointers as to the way in which Ada may be used in the future.

2   THE DEVELOPMENT OF SHADE AND GATEMAP

2.1   Background To The Development of SHADE

The SHADE software team had a range of experience in the use of high-level languages such as Pascal, FORTRAN and ALGOL. However, none had any specific experience of Ada, and before the project commenced all staff, both technical and managerial, attended a one week course on the language.

2.2   Background To The Development Of GATEMAP

One of the GATEMAP staff had previously worked on SHADE and hence had significant practical experience with Ada. The other staff had a similar background to the SHADE team in that they had considerable familiarity with other high-level languages, but had no specific experience with Ada.

2.3   Project planning, management, methods and tools

The initial project planning stage was not affected by the use of Ada. An initial specification was produced, including a detailed high level diagram of the system which partitioned SHADE into three main areas. This enabled the General Design Documents to be produced. The next phase of the project was to develop Detailed Design documents which were to assist us in breaking down the general design into an implementation.

One difficulty became apparent during these latter stages of the project planning. Although the staff had quickly become familiar with the syntax and semantics of Ada, without an appreciation of the software engineering principles embodied within the language they were not going to fully exploit the possible benefits of using Ada. Indeed, without such an appreciation it was felt that potential misuse of Ada was a serious potential risk.

We addressed this problem by encouraging project staff to read a carefully selected set of references including Myers (1976), Booch (1983) and Barnes (1984). This was effective but in retrospect it may have been better to introduce the appropriate software engineering techniques and design methods first, and only then specifically train staff in the use of Ada.

At the time of the SHADE project, there were no sophisticated software development tools available for use with the project. Primarily the team was restricted to the use of the VAX Ada compiler and Ada Compilation System, standard text-editors, and the VAX/VMS debugger. It was thought that the lack of advanced IPSE-like tools did not impact too severely on software development, however it was felt by the software team that higher productivity and more importantly enhanced quality would have been obtained from the use of such facilities.

2.4   Configuration management and the use of libraries

It soon became apparent to the teams that effective use of program libraries offered many benefits for both software development and software management, and misuse of libraries could cause serious difficulties for the project. There is no doubt that without sub-libraries, or at least inter-library references the control and organisation of the software would have been very difficult.

For SHADE a single main shared library was set up to hold the final software, with individual separate libraries for each team member. Hence this lead to a radial-like library organisation. As each well defined function comprised of one or many units was completed it was copied from one of the separate libraries into the main shared library. Then each team member set up references for these new units from the main library back to their own individual libraries. It was important that all units shared by more than one team member should be entered from the shareable main library, rather than directly from each other's individual libraries. Without strictly enforcing this discipline it would not have been possible to keep consistency between the various libraries.

For GATEMAP, an alternative hierarchical library structure was used in an attempt to simplify the consistency problem whilst maintaining integrity of the development. Here extensive use of sub-libraries was made (Digital Equipment Corporation, 1983). Each sub-library has a single parent library, which could itself be a sub-library. A sub-library automatically had visibility of all the units in its parent library. A single main parent library was set-up with about a dozen sub-libraries, one for each major functional area. New units would be developed in the sub-libraries and when completed would be 'merged' into the parent library from where they would then be visible to all the other sub-libraries.

This library organisation used for the GATEMAP development was felt to be superior to that used for SHADE. It was effective in simplifying the maintenance of consistency between units and the break-down of the software into functional sub-libraries, rather than the libraries of individual team members, eased the management of the project.

As required by the language standard (Ichbiah et al., 1983, section 10.3), the DEC ACS performed checks on the validity of unit compilations. By maintaining details of the date and time of a unit compilation, and a reference to the original source code file, ACS automatically determined which if any units needed to be recompiled at any time. Whilst this was undoubtly a useful feature which helped maintain development integrity it could often lead to the need for an apparent 'avalanche' of recompilations. This was particularly true if (as with ACS) a pessimistic view was taken on the need for a recompilation. For example the addition of a new declaration to a package specification would ideally not require the recompilation of all existing units dependent upon that package.

Until compiler technology becomes more sophisticated, and as a matter of good technique, it is essential to limit the number of interdependencies between units and in particular avoid situations where an avalanche of recompilations could occur. Simple rules like ensuring the minimum of library units were referenced in the context clause associated with a unit specification, were found to be very effective. More fundamentally project staff had to be educated in the consequences of poorly designed software structures, and needed to be encouraged to think very carefully about the grouping of units and the design of packages.

Version control was achieved by creating a separate library for each new issue of software, Figure 1. As soon as an issue was released, a new library was created and all units from the issued library copied to the new library. This method ensured that each baseline was kept completely separate, and could easily be archived. Any maintenance necessary was then carried out in sublibraries using the new library as the parent. Only those units to be modified needed to be transferred to the sub-library and other units were kept visible without duplication. This also saved disk space.

2.5 The use of generics

Primarily the use of generics in SHADE was restricted to the 'obvious' data

Figure 1 Use of Libraries

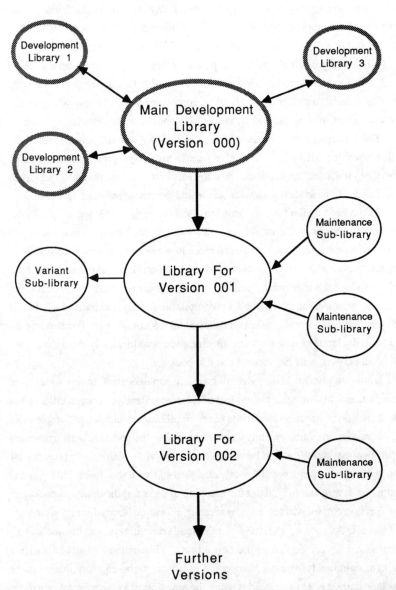

Development
Library 1

Development
Library 3

Main Development
Library
(Version 000)

Development
Library 2

Maintenance
Sub-library

Variant
Sub-library

Library For
Version 001

Maintenance
Sub-library

Library For
Version 002

Maintenance
Sub-library

Further
Versions

structure type applications as covered in most texts on Ada (e.g. Barnes 1984). The only exception to this was the man-machine interface for which generic menu and forms routines were developed. It was slightly disappointing that it was not possible to use generics more generally, though this may be a reflection of the design methods and imagination applied.

The majority of the generic packages for manipulating complex data structures (lists, trees, tables etc.) exported a limited type to represent a data structure object. To allow the composition of these packages, for example lists of trees of tables, it was necessary that each generic package declared a copy and destroy procedure, and required both such procedures as generic formal subprograms. The copy routine would effect a 'real' copy in that a duplicate equivalent data structure would be created. The destroy routine was necessary for dynamic storage management as discussed below in 2.6.

Hence a typical generic package for a complex data structure would take the format :-

```
generic

    type LIST_ITEM_TYPE is limited private;

    with procedure COPY (   FROM        : in list_item_type;
                            TO          : in out LIST_ITEM_TYPE); -

    -- pre-condition 1   : FROM /= null   (designates object x)
    -- post_condition 1 : TO      /= null   (designates object y where y = x)

    with procedure DESTROY (X : in out LIST_ITEM_TYPE);

    -- post_condition 1 : X= null

    package LINKED_LIST is ...
        type LIST_TYPE is limited private;
        procedure COPY      (FROM      : in LIST_TYPE;
                            TO          : in out LIST_TYPE);

        procedure DESTROY  (X : in out LIST_TYPE)
    end LINKED_LIST;
```

To maximise the benefits of reusable generic software it was found essential that potentially reusable routines were discussed thoroughly within the team to make sure all features were incorporated and tested at an early stage. This reduced the necessity for modifications to the generic routine at a later stage, incurring an overhead in terms of recompilations, and encouraged the re-use of these routines. If all staff were not consulted in the development of generic utilities it was often found at a later stage that the specification of these utilities did not completely meet their requirements, and the potential for re-use was hence lost.

The primary disadvantages of generics were found to be the increased re-compilation overheads caused by changes to the bodies of generic units, and the excessive executable code sizes caused by the repeated instantiation of generic units. (At the time of development, code-sharing between instantiations was not supported by the compiler in use.) Both these disadvantages were more inconveniences rather than fundamental problems in our application area.

From our experience during the SHADE development it was felt that generics had been overused and hence to ease the problems encountered with code size and recompilation overheads generics were used less frequently in GATEMAP. Their use was largely confined to the manipulation of common data structures, though this was supplemented with the need to create data structures of varying static sizes to reduce the use of dynamic storage, eg. stacks of different but fixed depths.

As with the SHADE software copy and destroy procedures were formal parameters of each generic package exporting a complex data structure, and copy and destroy procedures were then exported by each package instantiation. For the purposes of testing these procedures were selectively supplemented by procedures to put and get objects of the complex data structure. By supplying these routines at all levels it was possible to create and interrogate complex data structures in isolation.

2.6   Data management - packages and private types

Packages and private types were used extensively in the SHADE design capture system where the manipulation of different types of design objects was largely independent of the composition of such design objects. An object-oriented design style was adopted and found to be very effective with this use of packages. However for the CADEPT component of SHADE it was not found appropriate to use an object-oriented approach and less use was made of private types. Primarily the reasons for this were the complexity of some of the data structures and the ways in which such data structures needed to be accessed. Where a complex network data structure needed to be rapidly traversed and interrogated in a variety of different ways it was found difficult to design this around a package and private type. It was not possible to create a level of abstraction from which to evolve an efficient yet complete set of subprograms for manipulating such complex data structures. If the number of subprograms was kept sensibly small then each would tend to be inordinately complex and hence inefficient. Speed of performance could only be ensured by having a multitude of subprograms whose nature made the underlying data structure effectively transparent anyway.

One minor drawback was found with the use of limited private types. When running programs under the debugging utility, the values of variables of limited private types could not be examined. This however was likely to be an implementation-specific limitation.

In addition to the use of packages with private types, packages were also used to encapsulate type declarations, and sometimes used to group related functions and procedures. As an example of the latter various low level input/output routines were placed in a single package.

The major disadvantage encountered with the use of Ada for VLSI CAD applications was in the area of virtual memory management. The language definition (Ichbiah et al. 1983) states that an implementation may (but need not) perform virtual storage reclamation or 'garbage collection' to free the storage associated with dynamically created objects which have gone out of scope. (This is a consequence of the requirement to support real-time programming). Since many CAD applications involve the manipulation of large dynamic data structures, these objects must be explicitly deallocated (Ichbiah et al., 1983, section 13.10.1) by the program if the compiler does not support garbage collection. To avoid using excessive amounts of virtual memory during program execution this technique was used for the SHADE software.

The problems associated with dynamically allocated storage were addressed in GATEMAP in primarily two ways. Firstly, the use of dynamic storage and access types was reduced and static storage used more often (particularly in conjunction with generics). Secondly, all use of dynamic storage and access types was encapsulated within packages (with the exception of nested access type declarations). This was accomplished by declaring all access types as limited private and providing 'copy' and 'destroy' procedures for all objects of these types. To simplify routines utilising these packages a 'rename' procedure was sometimes provided :-

```
procedure RENAME    (   FROM : in out ITEM_TYPE;
                        TO      : in out ITEM_TYPE);

-- pre-condition 1   : FROM   /= null (designates object X)
-- pre-condition 2   : TO     = null
-- post-condition 1  : TO     /= null (designates object X)
-- post-condition 2  : FROM   = null
```

Hence, with the restriction that access types be limited private and the provision of this procedure and the previously mentioned copy and destroy procedures, not only can the management of dynamic storage be controlled but also the problem of multiple access paths to the same dynamic object is eliminated. In cases where this latter restriction was undesirable a more complex 'keyed' data structure was used (Barnes 1984). For example in a network data structure each item would have associated a unique (limited) key designator. Only possession of the necessary keys allowed changes to the data structure to be made, but non-destructive exploration of the data structure was also permitted with simple (non-limited) designators, of which more than one could refer to a single network object.

As with the SHADE software the copy and destroy procedures used in GATEMAP used the pre-defined generic procedure UNCHECKED_DEALLOCATION to free unwanted dynamic storage. However, the effectiveness of this procedure is implementation dependent. In particular, an implementation may or may not coalesce 'holes' in memory caused by the deallocation of an object. This can cause difficulty if say dynamic length strings are used, where holes for every size of string ever used may be left in memory.

This is a well known problem typically addressed by many operating systems. The simple implementation-independent approach used in GATEMAP was to constrain the size of dynamic objects to a finite set of values, eg. strings of length of powers of two only, and associate a size component with each object, eg. the actual length of the string. This provides reasonable assurance that deallocated storage can then be effectively re-allocated. A further alternative, which provides near complete control of dynamic storage is to maintain a 'free-list' of deallocated objects within the appropriate package body.

2.7   The use of exceptions

The inclusion of exceptions to trap incorrect usage of code and invalid data greatly increases the level of reliability of CAD software.

The SHADE project team identified three possible uses of exceptions in CAD software :

(i) to indicate an incorrect usage of code, (for example to check that initialisation of pointers had occurred before they were accessed);

(ii) to identify if routines have been called with invalid data, (for example trying to access an invalid variant of a record);

(iii) to trap unforseen errors.

The result of these uses of exceptions was (curiously) that the majority (ie. 95% +) of exceptions were never expected to occur and hence were not explicitly handled. So for our application area exceptions degenerated into a mechanism for signalling failures rather than a method for recovering from such failures.

The major use of exception handlers in SHADE was to terminate the programs gracefully after a failure. This was achieved by adding an exception handler to the main procedure of the program, which would handle all exceptions, then re-raise the initiating exception :-

```
procedure MAIN is ...
exception
   when others => SAVE_ALL_DATA;
                      raise; -- traceback starts from here
   end MAIN;
```

Whilst this did in many cases prevent loss of interactively entered data, it did mean that traceback (ie. stack dump) information was lost when such an exception occured.

In GATEMAP exceptions were used in a very similar manner to their use in SHADE, with again the majority of exceptions signalling the failure of internal operations within the software. As with SHADE the majority of exceptions were NOT handled. As GATEMAP is non-interactive no outer-most exception handler was present, and raised exceptions would propagate a full stack dump.

A further alternative considered for GATEMAP was to have exception handlers within each subprogram, which when triggered would write appropriate details into an external error log file and then propagate the raising exception. This would allow the preservation of full traceback information, whilst still permitting exception handlers to operate at any level. If such an option was to be considered then ideally some form of automated tool should be used to construct the necessary code.

2.8 Input/output and operating system interfaces

Predefined Input/Output (I/O) packages are available in Ada for general I/O, but more specialised features will be necessary for most interactive VLSI CAD tools. The language provides comprehensive facilities for interfacing Ada programs to routines in other languages and operating systems, advantageous for many CAD applications.

For the SHADE software additional low level I/O routines were developed to allow more tightly controlled terminal I/O, making use of VAX/VMS utilities. Also a number of routines were implemented to interface to VMS system routines such as assigning symbol values and execution of sub-processes. To allow the SHADE software to be easily transferred to another environment all I/O resources were grouped into a small number of Ada packages, so localising the hardware and operating system dependencies of the software.

2.9 Software testing

The individual team members of both the SHADE and GATEMAP projects carried out initial testing of their own software. Test harnesses were developed to allow testing of certain parts of the software which would necessarily be embedded within the rest of the software with no direct input or output links. This ensured confidence in the individual parts of the code before they were integrated. Packages were found to provide a suitable unit about which to construct such test harnesses. The major difficulty found with such testing was when complex private data types were used, in which case setting-up and interrogating such data structures to perform a test were found to be laborious. This problem was partly addressed by the use of appropriate put and get subprograms as discussed in section 2.5.

Once the software had been tested and integrated by the development team, it was issued for further testing to members of a hardware design team for their day to day use on active VLSI design. From there it was issued for beta-site testing.

2.10 Software maintenance

Sublibraries were used during all maintenance to minimise the number of units to be handled at any one time. Whenever a library unit was to be modified, the unmodified source was first extracted from the main library and compiled into a sub-library of this main library. The unit would then be modified and the software tested within the context of the sub-library. If the tests proved satisfactory then the modified unit and any associated recompiled units were then merged back into the main library.

Many small details in the way SHADE Ada source code was written had a dramatic effect on the ease of maintenance. For example: maintenance was made much simpler if the original authors had always used the full dotted notation, and procedure calls explicitly named parameters instead of relying on positional associations.

Source code could be very confusing if poor naming conventions had been used, for example:

```
procedure MODIFY (  FIRST_INPUT          : in integer;
                    SECOND_INPUT         : in character;
                    RESULT               : out integer;
                    SUCCESSFUL           : out boolean);

- - - - - - - - - - - - - -
SECOND_INPUT     : integer := 1;
FIRST_INPUT      : character := 'P';
RESULT           : integer;
SUCCESSFUL       : boolean;
MODIFY (SECOND_INPUT, FIRST_INPUT, RESULT, SUCCESSFUL);
```

Hence the use of aggregate notation was encouraged at all times, especially where a sub-program had more than one parameter of the same type.

Records with variant parts were used extensively in the data structure of CADEPT. This enabled the data to be handled in a recursive manner which proved beneficial. However the number of possible variants made the task of the maintainer more difficult, since it could be difficult to keep track of which variant was being used at any particular point in the code.

3   CONCLUSIONS

The experiences gained during the development of SHADE and GATEMAP have shown that Ada is well suited for use with CAD software developments. The teams are planning to continue to use Ada in future CAD work.

To gain the full benefits from the use of Ada, it was found necessary to have a thorough knowledge of software engineering techniques and the principles behind the language. To write practical software it was also found necessary to have an appreciation of lower-level activities behind the language. In particular the management of dynamic storage needs to be considered at the outset of a project.

Ada has an impact with large projects as the construction of the language permits systematic software development, the formal specification of interfaces between units, and a means to spread development of large programs between members of the software team. The need for a well-planned and strictly controlled library environment is essential to secure development.

4   ACKNOWLEDGEMENTS

The GATEMAP work described was funded by the UK Ministry of Defence (PE), under contract number NNS32A1A91418.

The authors would like to thank all staff within the Silicon Design Technology Division at Plessey Research Roke Manor who directly or indirectly contributed to the work described.

5   REFERENCES

Barnes, J.G.P., (1984). Programming in Ada. USA: Addison-Wesley Publishing Company.2nd ed.

Booch, G., (1983). Software Engineering With Ada. Menlo Park, California: Benjamin/Cummings Publishing Company.

Burrows, D.F (1986). SHADE: Plessey's Structured Hardware Design Environment. Silicon Design,3, no.5.

Digital Equipment Corporation (1985). Developing Ada Programs On VAX/VMS. Maynard, Massachusetts: Digital Equipment Corporation.

Ichbiah, J.D. et al. (1983). Reference Manual For The Ada Programming Language. ANSI/MIL-STD-1815A-1983.

Morrison, J.D. et al. (1985). A Hardware Design and Description Language. Proc. of Computer Hardware Description Languages and their Applications.

Myers, G.J., (1975). Reliable Software Through Composite Design. New York, New York: Van Nostrand Reinhold Company.

Pitty, E.B., Daniels, C. and Adams, C.E. (1987). Languages for Hardware Specification and Design. Ada User, 8, Supplement.

Salmon, J.V. Pitty E.B., Abrahams M.S, (1987). Syntactic translation and logic synthesis in GATEMAP. IEE colloquium on VLSI Systems Design: Specification and Synthesis. Savoy Place, London, October 1987.

TRANSIT

an Ada-Package for Multitasking, with an Application to

Airport-Simulation

Harry Feldmann

Universität Hamburg,
Betriebswirtschaftliche Datenverarbeitung,
Von-Melle-Park 5, 2000 Hamburg 13

Abstract

This paper presents an Ada package TRANSIT for statistical supervising of parallel processes of the kind 'transit of individuals through parallel stations', well known from SIMULA and GPSS .
Ada(1983) with TRANSIT(1983) combines the advantages of SIMULA
(1967) with SIMULATION(1967) and of FORTRAN(1957) with GPSS(1977):
free multitasking in a universal programming language, automatical
protocolling and release from all statistical efforts. In addition
Ada offers the modern rendezvous concept and TRANSIT offers
print-plot procedures for graphical presentation of the model
and the statistical results. We apply TRANSIT to the 'transit of
airplanes through the holdings, taxiings and the runway of an airport (Flughafen Hamburg)', showing the TRANSIT-protocol (Fig. 4) ,
the graphical presentation of the model with statistical TRANSIT -
results (Fig. 5) , and from these the HISTOGRAM-bar-chart of
the runway occupation in the months January and August (Fig. 6) .

1. The Package-Hierarchy

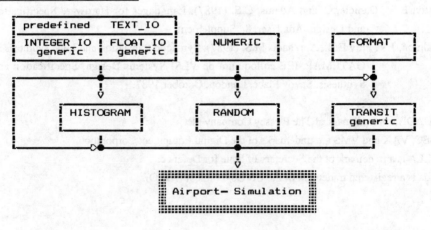

Fig. 1: Package Hierarchy

The package hierarchy for airport-simulation , see Figure 1 above, includes the Ada-predefined

- generic package TEXT_IO for IO-procedures put,get

and the authors

- package NUMERIC   for numerical functions ent,sum,min,med,max,
                      sqrt,ln,exp,sin,cos,tan,arctan,
- package RANDOM   for random - values rand,draw,roul,pois_come,
                      nexp_wait,norm_rand,
- package HISTOGRAM for histogram types,functions sum,min,med,max,
                      freq,chisq_test and dot_plot, bar_plot,
- package FORMAT   for format fmt (default 6) for the TRANSIT-
                      protocol and the TRANSIT-plot,
- generic package TRANSIT for transit of individs(1..population)
                      through stations(1..transition) , with
                      on(individ,station), automatical protocol
                      and plot(station).

2. The Generic Package TRANSIT

Similar to GPSS the package TRANSIT will relief the programmer from all statistical effort which usually will be a multiple of the simulation effort. TRANSIT also offers a protocol of all the moves.

In contrast to GPSS the package TRANSIT will not take care of the multitasking simulation which remains a domain of Ada . This separation of powers is realized mainly by the two procedures

                    ON(individual,station)

which informs TRANSIT that the Ada-program wants to put a certain individual on a certain station, and

                    PLOT(station)

which enables the Ada-program to plot out all statistical TRANSIT-results concerning this station. If an individual or a station is associated with a parallel process, the programmer has to do a double entry book-keeping: an individual or a station in the package TRANSIT belongs to a task in the Ada-program.

The author doesn't have the ambition to invent the wheel twice and to start a restricted rendezvous-technique in TRANSIT . Thus the TRANSIT-user is not restricted in his free Ada-multitasking . Restriction is a lack of GPSS and even of GPSS-FORTRAN.

2.1   The Specification of the Package TRANSIT

The following programtext 1 describes the specification of the
generic library package TRANSIT for transit of individuals through
parallel stations.

```
WITH TEXT_IO,NUMERIC,FORMAT;USE TEXT_IO,NUMERIC,FORMAT;
GENERIC
 POPULATION:POPULATION_RANGE; -- number of individs
 TRANSITION:TRANSITION_RANGE; -- number of stations

PACKAGE TRANSIT IS ...

 TYPE IND IS RECORD
  PROTOCOL    :BOOLEAN                    :=TRUE        ;
  NAME        :STRING(1..12)              :="      Individ";
  VALUE1      :INTEGER:=0;VALUE2:FLOAT:=0.0             ;
  STATION     :AC_STA                                   ;
  TIME_ON     :FLOAT                                    ;...
 END          RECORD                                    ;

 TYPE STA IS RECORD
  PROTOCOL    :BOOLEAN                    :=TRUE        ;
  NAME        :STRING(1..12)              :="      Station";
  VALUE1      :INTEGER:=0;VALUE2:FLOAT:=0.0             ;
  CAPACITY    :NATURAL                    :=POPULATION  ;
  FIRST,LAST  :AC_IND                                   ;
  TIME_LAST_EX:FLOAT                                    ;...
 END          RECORD                                    ;

 INDIVID: AR_AC_IND(1..POPULATION  );PRAGMA SHARED(INDIVID);
 STATION: AR_AC_STA(0..TRANSITION+1);PRAGMA SHARED(STATION);
 SOURCE :    AC_STA RENAMES STATION(0           )       ;
 SINK   :    AC_STA RENAMES STATION(TRANSITION+1)       ;
 FUNCTION EMPTY (S:AC_STA) RETURN BOOLEAN               ;
 FUNCTION FULL  (S:AC_STA) RETURN BOOLEAN               ;

 PROCEDURE ON   (I:AC_IND;S:AC_STA)          ;
 PROCEDURE PLOT (S:AC_STA);PLOT(S1,S2:AC_STA);...

 LONG_PROTOCOL:BOOLEAN:=FALSE; PRAGMA SHARED(LONG_PROTOCOL);
 LONG_DIAGRAMS:BOOLEAN:=FALSE; PRAGMA SHARED(LONG_DIAGRAMS);
 PROCEDURE       PROTOCOL_RESTART                   ;

 FUNCTION  TIME RETURN              NONEG_FLOAT ;
 PROCEDURE TIME_LAPSE (TIME_DIFF:NONEG_FLOAT);
 PROCEDURE TIME_DELAY (TIME_DIFF:NONEG_FLOAT);
 PROCEDURE TIME_ABORT                    ;...

END TRANSIT;
```

Progr. 1: TRANSIT, Specification

The package TRANSIT has two generic parameters, POPULATION, the
number of all individuals, and TRANSITION, the number of all stations. An instantiation of TRANSIT automatically defines all

INDIVIDs in the population and all STATIONs in the transition , plus STATION(0) named SOURCE and STATION(TRANSITION+1) named SINK. In the beginning all INDIVIDs are put automatically on the station SOURCE.

As mentioned above, TRANSIT is used for statistical supervising and does not take active part in multitasking. Thus the types IND and STA are not tasks but records. In order to keep these pages easily comprehensible we don't show all the components of IND and STA and have omitted some aspects of PRIVATE specification.

2.2 All that TRANSIT needs is ON(Individual,Station)

A move of an individual I to a station S has to be announced to the package TRANSIT by calling a procedure ON(I,S). With regard to this, TRANSIT goes through all the moving formalities, updates the statistics and issues a protocol line.

An event-controlled reduction of the protocol can be achieved by assigning LONG_PROTOCOL:=FALSE; .

2.3 Any Print/Plot Port in a Storm

The statistical results of all movements through a station S since the last PROTOCOL_RESTART can be obtained from TRANSIT by calling a print-plot procedure PLOT(S).

The plots can be arranged to produce a print-plot flow chart of the entire station-model. The programtext 5 and the resulting figure 5 may be taken as an example. A less detailed PLOT can be achieved by assigning LONG_DIAGRAMS:=FALSE;

Graphical tools are not yet available in the Ada-Standard (83a). Thus and in order to ensure TRANSIT a broad area of application, its PLOT-procedure was not implemented for a special plotter, but was written with TEXT_IO in print-plot-version for any printer .

Nevertheless the reader nowadays expects a minimum of graphical presentation-comfort and would be rightly disgusted with rough typewriter-print-plots, as there were some in GPSS .

The author would recommend to solve this very problem by using a matrix printer with a redefinable character set and to redefine for instance the following characters:

typographical 'Normal' Characters ! # ' * + , - ; < > 0 V ^ \
typographical ' Plot ' Characters ! ⠿ ⌐ ● + ⌐ — ⌐ ◁ ▷ O ∇ △ ∟

2.4   TRANSIT-TIME is not Ada-Realtime

The following programtext 2 shows the task TIME_SLICE and the procedures TIME_LAPSE and TIME_DELAY for time-slicing in TRANSIT .

Time-slicing is simply realized by Ada-rendezvous - technique : if TIME_LAPSE or TIME_DELAY want to make a rendezvous with TIME_SLICE, they are put into the rendezvous-waiting-queue and are elaborated subsequently.

```
TRANSIT_TIME:NONEG_FLOAT:=0.0;

TASK TIME_SLICE IS ENTRY PLEASE;END TIME_SLICE;
TASK BODY TIME_SLICE IS
  BEGIN LOOP ACCEPT PLEASE;END LOOP;END TIME_SLICE;

PROCEDURE TIME_LAPSE(TIME_DIFF:NONEG_FLOAT) IS BEGIN
   TIME_SLICE.PLEASE;TRANSIT_TIME:=TRANSIT_TIME+TIME_DIFF;
   END TIME_LAPSE;

PROCEDURE TIME_DELAY(TIME_DIFF:NONEG_FLOAT) IS
   TIME_LIMIT:NONEG_FLOAT:=TIME+TIME_DIFF;BEGIN LOOP
   TIME_SLICE.PLEASE;EXIT WHEN TIME>=TIME_LIMIT;
   END LOOP;END TIME_DELAY;

PROCEDURE TIME_ABORT IS
   BEGIN ABORT TIME_SLICE;END TIME_ABORT;
```

Progr. 2: TRANSIT Body, Timeslicing

TRANSIT_TIME is not Ada-realtime CALENDAR.TIME and our TIME_DELAY is not Ada DELAY, but if desired, it could be achieved by a very few alterings in TRANSIT.

Non-realtime is better suited for simulation - purposes than realtime. Simulating the Airport-Movements of one day in non-real-time will perhaps take 5 minutes, in realtime again one day. It is not possible to reduce the Ada-realtime CALENDAR.TIME arbitrari-ly by applying a diminishing factor to the Ada-duration , because DURATION needs not to be implemented below 20 milliseconds (83a) .

3.   Airport-Simulation

A starting airplane passes through the stations start-taxiing, start-holding and runway, and a landing airplane through the sta-tions land-holding , runway and land-taxiing. Multiple or further stations like parking or service could be added . Further models for passenger-clearance, for baggage or air freight could be linked to this airport-movement model.

3.1 Airport Initial Values, Flight-Table, Turbulence

A first survey of the airport-model and its initial values is given below in figure 2. A comparison with figure 5 shows that the entire model with all initial and resulting values can be print - plotted with TRANSIT.PLOT procedures.

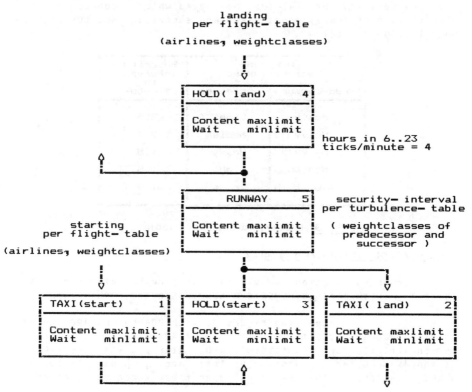

Fig. 2: Airport, Initial Values

Initial values for the model are the limits for the content maxima of the stations and the limits for the waitingtime minima of the individuals passing through the stations.

In calm times the contents will decrease and in the rush hour the waitingtimes for the individuals will increase . This depends on the flight-table, which gives the model-input: the time (hour, minute), the airline (reduced here to commercial, non commercial), the move (start, land) and the weightclass (light <= 7 tons , 7 < medium <= 136 tons, heavy > 136 tons) of every flight . Flight - table entries for noncommercial flights are gained from annual report statistics (long-term model) or ad hoc (short-range model).

The moving of an airplane over the runway will cause air-turbulence of a certain degree which will be proportional to the weightclass of the airplane. This turbulence may be dangerous for the following airplane on the runway, especially for an airplane of medium or even light weightclass.

Thus a security interval must be obeyed which depends on the weightclasses of runway predecessor and successor, see turbulence-table in figure 3 below.

Airplane Weightclasses		Security – Interval in Minutes
Predecessor	Successor	
Heavy	Light	2.5
Heavy	Medium	2.0
Heavy	Heavy	1.5
Medium	Light	1.5
O t h e r s		1.0

Fig. 3: Runway, Turbulence - Table

3.2 The AIRPORT Multitasking-Program

The Airport-Simulation model has a package hierarchy , see figure 1 , with TEXT_IO,NUMERIC,RANDOM,HISTOGRAM,FORMAT,TRANSIT .

TRANSIT is initiated, see figure 2, with POPULATION=190 individuals (in January, 260 in August) and TRANSITION=5 stations : station(1)=TAXI(start) , station(2)=HOLD(start) , station(3)=RUN , station(4)=HOLD(land) , station(5)=TAXI(land) , plus station(0)= SOURCE, station(6)=SINK. Renaming specifies successor-stations .

The Ada program AIRPORT has a main-task, its begin-end part, and four depending tasks: TAXIING with parameter move=start , TAXIING with parameter move=land,HOLDING_RUNNING with parameter move=start and HOLDING_RUNNING with parameter move=land.

```
TASK BODY TAXIING IS move:MOV;BEGIN
  ACCEPT PARAMETER(M:MOV);DO move:=M;END PARAMETER;LOOP
  IF NOT(EMPTY(TAXI(move))OR ELSE FULL(TAXI_SUC(move)) OR
    ELSE TIME-TAXI(move).FIRST.TIME_ON<TAXI(move).VALUE2)
  THEN ON(TAXI(move).FIRST,TAXI_SUC(move));END IF;
  TIME_DELAY(TIME_INCREMENT);EXIT WHEN TIME>CLOSING_TIME;
  END LOOP;END TAXIING;
```

Progr. 3: AIRPORT, task body TAXIING

Programtext 3 above shows the task TAXIING . The task TAXIING
time-incrementally asks whether the individual FIRST in the station TAXI(move) has waited for a longer time than the given limit
for the waiting-time minimum TAXI(move).VALUE2, and whether the
successor station TAXI_SUC(move) is empty. Then it puts the individual FIRST on the successor station TAXI_SUC(move) . TAXIING is
activated and parametrisized by the main-task AIRPORT at the time
OPENING_TIME= 6.00 . It loops until time is greater than
CLOSING_TIME=23.50 and then terminates by EXIT.

```
BEGIN -- main task AIRPORT
   ...
   TIME_LAPSE(OPENING_TIME);
   FOR HOUR   IN HOR LOOP PROTOCOL_RESTART;
    FOR MINUTE IN MNT LOOP
     FOR LINE   IN LIN LOOP
      FOR MOVE   IN MOV LOOP
       IF FLIGHT(HOUR,MINUTE,LINE,MOVE) THEN
        IF EMPTY(SOURCE) OR ELSE FULL(INPUT(MOVE)) THEN
         PUT(MOV_STR(MOVE));RAISE CONSTRAINT_ERROR;ELSE
         SOURCE.FIRST.NAME  :=LIN_STR(LINE);
         SOURCE.FIRST.VALUE1:=ROUL(WEIGHT_PROBS(LINE));
         ON(SOURCE.FIRST,INPUT(MOVE));
         PUT(" "&       INPUT(MOVE).LAST.NAME(1..4)
            &" "&WGT_STR(INPUT(MOVE).LAST.VALUE1  )
            &" "&MOV_STR(       MOVE));END IF;END IF;
       END LOOP; -- MOVE
      END LOOP; -- LINE
      FOR TICK IN TIC LOOP TIME_LAPSE(TIME_INCREMENT);
      END LOOP; -- TICK
     END LOOP; -- MINUTE
    ...
   END LOOP; -- HOUR
   ...
END AIRPORT;
```

Progr. 4: AIRPORT, task MAIN

The main task AIRPORT which can be seen above in the programtext 4 causes a TIME_LAPSE(OPENING_TIME), OPENING_TIME=6 o'clock ,
and then loops from 6.0 o'clock to 23.59 o'clock. Every minute it
causes a TIME_LAPSE(TIME_INCREMENT) , TIME_INCREMENT=1.0/60.0/
FLOAT(TICKS_PER_MINUTE)=0.004, TICKS_PER_MINUTE=4 .

The loop cascade HOUR,MINUTE,LINE,MOVE provides actual parameters for the FLIGHT table, which decides whether an airplane from
the SOURCE shall move (start or land) ON the INPUT (TAXI(start)
or HOLD(land)). The airplane is marked with the airline-name
LINE_STR(LINE) and with a statistically suiting weightclass
ROUL(WEIGHT_PROBS(LINE)). An appendix to the automatically output
ON-protocol-line is given by PUT(...) . The PUT-result can be seen
below in figure 4 at the right border.

3.3   Airport, TRANSIT-Protocol

The PROTOCOL_RESTART in programtext 4 delivers a new protocol-heading for every HOUR-loop. Figure 4 below gives a protocol for the hour from 8.00 0'clock up to nearly 9 o'clock.

```
Time ON(Ind,Stat)  Station.Content    Long_Protocol=&
                   ┌──1────5──────────────────────────▷  260
 8.00    13      1 │●●●●OOOOOOOOOOOOOOOOOOOOOOOOOO           1&  Comm  heavy   start
 8.00    14      4 │●●●●OOOOOOOOOOOOOOOOOOOOOOOOOO           1&  Comm  medium  land
 8.00    15      1 │●●●●●OOOOOOOOOOOOOOOOOOOOOOOOO           2&  NonC  light   start
 8.00    16      4 │●●●●●OOOOOOOOOOOOOOOOOOOOOOOOO           2&  NonC  light   land
 8.02    14      5 │●●●●OOOOOOOOOOOOOOOOOOOOOOOOOO           1&
 8.02    13      3 │●●●●OOOOOOOOOOOOOOOOOOOOOOOOOO           1&
 8.02    15      3 │●●●●OOOOOOOOOOOOOOOOOOOOOOOOOO           2&
 8.04    14      2 │●●●●OOOOOOOOOOOOOOOOOOOOOOOOOO           1&
 8.04    13      5 │●●●●OOOOOOOOOOOOOOOOOOOOOOOOOO           1&
 8.05    13      6 │●●●●●●●●●●●●●OOOOOOOOOOOOOOOOO          13&
 8.06    16      5 │●●●●OOOOOOOOOOOOOOOOOOOOOOOOOO           1&
 8.06    14      6 │●●●●●●●●●●●●●●OOOOOOOOOOOOOOOO          14&
 8.10    16      2 │●●●●OOOOOOOOOOOOOOOOOOOOOOOOOO           1&
 8.10    15      5 │●●●●OOOOOOOOOOOOOOOOOOOOOOOOOO           1&
 8.11    15      6 │●●●●●●●●●●●●●●●OOOOOOOOOOOOOOO          15&
 8.12    16      6 │●●●●●●●●●●●●●●●●OOOOOOOOOOOOOO          16&
 8.17    17      1 │●●●●OOOOOOOOOOOOOOOOOOOOOOOOOO           1&  Comm  medium  start
 8.19    17      3 │●●●●OOOOOOOOOOOOOOOOOOOOOOOOOO           1&
 8.19    17      5 │●●●●OOOOOOOOOOOOOOOOOOOOOOOOOO           1&
 8.21    17      6 │●●●●●●●●●●●●●●●●●OOOOOOOOOOOOO          17&
 8.25    18      4 │●●●●OOOOOOOOOOOOOOOOOOOOOOOOOO           1&  Comm  medium  land
 8.27    18      5 │●●●●OOOOOOOOOOOOOOOOOOOOOOOOOO           1&
 8.29    18      2 │●●●●OOOOOOOOOOOOOOOOOOOOOOOOOO           1&
 8.31    18      6 │●●●●●●●●●●●●●●●●●●OOOOOOOOOOOO          18&
 8.33    19      1 │●●●●OOOOOOOOOOOOOOOOOOOOOOOOOO           1&  Comm  medium  start
 8.33    20      1 │●●●●●OOOOOOOOOOOOOOOOOOOOOOOOO           2&  NonC  light   start
 8.35    19      3 │●●●●OOOOOOOOOOOOOOOOOOOOOOOOOO           1&
 8.36    19      5 │●●●●OOOOOOOOOOOOOOOOOOOOOOOOOO           1&
 8.36    20      3 │●●●●OOOOOOOOOOOOOOOOOOOOOOOOOO           1&
 8.37    19      6 │●●●●●●●●●●●●●●●●●●●OOOOOOOOOOO          19&
 8.38    20      5 │●●●●OOOOOOOOOOOOOOOOOOOOOOOOOO           1&
 8.40    20      6 │●●●●●●●●●●●●●●●●●●●●OOOOOOOOOO          20&
 8.50    21      1 │●●●●OOOOOOOOOOOOOOOOOOOOOOOOOO           1&  Comm  medium  start
 8.50    22      4 │●●●●OOOOOOOOOOOOOOOOOOOOOOOOOO           1&  Comm  medium  land
 8.50    23      4 │●●●●●OOOOOOOOOOOOOOOOOOOOOOOOO           2&  NonC  light   land
 8.52    22      5 │●●●●OOOOOOOOOOOOOOOOOOOOOOOOOO           1&
 8.52    21      3 │●●●●OOOOOOOOOOOOOOOOOOOOOOOOOO           1&
 8.54    22      2 │●●●●OOOOOOOOOOOOOOOOOOOOOOOOOO           1&
 8.54    21      5 │●●●●OOOOOOOOOOOOOOOOOOOOOOOOOO           1&
 8.55    21      6 │●●●●●●●●●●●●●●●●●●●●●OOOOOOOOO          21&
 8.56    23      5 │●●●●OOOOOOOOOOOOOOOOOOOOOOOOOO           1&
 8.56    22      6 │●●●●●●●●●●●●●●●●●●●●●●OOOOOOOO          22&
 8.58    23      2 │●●●●OOOOOOOOOOOOOOOOOOOOOOOOOO           1&
 8.60    23      6 │●●●●●●●●●●●●●●●●●●●●●●●OOOOOOO          23&
 8.67    24      1 │●●●●OOOOOOOOOOOOOOOOOOOOOOOOOO           1&  Comm  heavy   start
 8.67    25      1 │●●●●●OOOOOOOOOOOOOOOOOOOOOOOOO           2&  NonC  light   start
 8.69    24      3 │●●●●OOOOOOOOOOOOOOOOOOOOOOOOOO           1&
 8.69    24      5 │●●●●OOOOOOOOOOOOOOOOOOOOOOOOOO           1&
 8.69    25      3 │●●●●OOOOOOOOOOOOOOOOOOOOOOOOOO           1&
 8.71    24      6 │●●●●●●●●●●●●●●●●●●●●●●●●OOOOOO          24&
 8.71    25      5 │●●●●OOOOOOOOOOOOOOOOOOOOOOOOOO           1&
 8.75    26      4 │●●●●OOOOOOOOOOOOOOOOOOOOOOOOOO           1&  Comm  medium  land
 8.75    25      6 │●●●●●●●●●●●●●●●●●●●●●●●●●OOOOO          25&
 8.77    26      5 │●●●●OOOOOOOOOOOOOOOOOOOOOOOOOO           1&
 8.79    26      2 │●●●●OOOOOOOOOOOOOOOOOOOOOOOOOO           1&
 8.81    26      6 │●●●●●●●●●●●●●●●●●●●●●●●●●●OOOO          26&
 8.83    27      1 │●●●●OOOOOOOOOOOOOOOOOOOOOOOOOO           1&  Comm  medium  start
 8.85    27      3 │●●●●OOOOOOOOOOOOOOOOOOOOOOOOOO           1&
 8.86    27      5 │●●●●OOOOOOOOOOOOOOOOOOOOOOOOOO           1&
 8.87    27      6 │●●●●●●●●●●●●●●●●●●●●●●●●●●●OOO          27&
                   ▽
```

Fig. 4: Airport, TRANSIT-Protocol

Time is protocolled in hours with decimal-minutes. The station-
contents are graphically presented in an exponential scale , their
numerical values can be seen to the right.

For instance the protocol shows that at 8.33 o'clock the individual (airplane) with the (flight) number 20 is put on station 1
(land-holding) , which then has content=2 . The airline of this
airplane 20 is "NonC"ommercial, its weightclass "heavy" and its
move is a "start". The further ON-moves of individual 20 are protocolled at the times 8.36 , 8.38 and finally at 8.40 o'clock when
the individual 20 is put on station 6 (SINK) and thus leaves the
airport model.

A complete protocol with LONG_PROTOCOL=TRUE is needed for
test purpose . An event - controlled protocol reduction with
LONG_PROTOCOL=FALSE would only give a short survey. Protocols are
essential for chronological registration of content peaks . A
TRANSIT-PLOT-diagram , see figure 5, only registrates the minimum,
the medium and the maximum of the station-content within a certain
time interval.

3.4 Airport-Model with TRANSIT-Results

The best way to watch and control the course of events in a
model simulation would be a cinema-like animation of the transit
of individuals through the stations and a synchronous presentation
of statistical results in condensed tabular form.

TRANSIT comes close to this ideal. Figure 5 below shows a 'photo
snap' of the model near 9 o'clock with all the stations and the
statistical results in tabular form. The contents of all stations
are momentary 0,that is to say there are no individuals to be seen
at this time. If their would be some individuals at another time ,
they would be listed up at the end of the station diagrams with
name, number, values et cetera. Such a TRANSIT-snap-shot can be
made repeatedly and at any time of the simulation. The statistical
results refer to the time interval from the last PROTOCOL_RESTART
(Time min) up to now (Time max).

All stations are presented uniformly. Whether a station serves
as a source, a queue, an active or passive aggregate or as a sink
or whether a station is associated with a task, is of no signifi-
cance for TRANSIT. Furthermore Figure 5 does not constitute a
'program flow chart' or a so-called 'structured programming
diagram' - Ada programs do not walk on such crutches.

An often required statistical result is the idle time of a station in the time interval. In the case of the runway station the
complement of the idle time would deliver the wanted business-time
or occupation of the runway, see section 3.5 .

Oddly GPSS does not deal with idle times.

Figure 5 below shows that the runway had been idle in 70.00 % of the time between 8.00 and 9.00 o'clock (on a day in the month of January). 15 airplanes have passed the runway , 9 started through the start-taxiing and start-holding , 6 landed from the land - holding and left through land-taxiing.

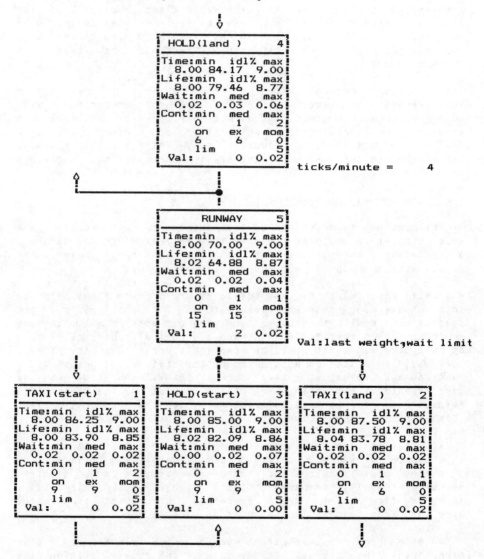

Fig. 5: Airport, Model with TRANSIT-Results

A question often asked in discussions is: ' How does TRANSIT
know the configuration of the simulation-model for plotting down
the model-diagram like that of figure 5 ? ' . The answer is very
simple: ' TRANSIT does not know the configuration of the simulation-model at all . TRANSIT only deals with single stations and
a TRANSIT.PLOT only plots a single station-diagram . But the user
of TRANSIT knows the configuration of the simulation-model and he
can plot the station-diagram freely in Ada , using TRANSIT.PLOT
procedures !'

```
        O;              I                       ;NEW_LINE;
        O;              V                       ;NEW_LINE;
    PLOT(Op,   HOLD(land));PUT("ticks/minute =");
                         PUT(TICKS_PER_MINUTE,FMT);NEW_LINE;
        A;              I                       ;NEW_LINE;
        I;              I                       ;NEW_LINE;
        NE;             WI                      ;NEW_LINE;
        O;              I                       ;NEW_LINE;
    PLOT(Op,            RUN);PUT("Val:last weight,wait limit");
                                                 NEW_LINE;
        O;              I                       ;NEW_LINE;
        I;              IE;         WS          ;NEW_LINE;
        I;              I;          I           ;NEW_LINE;
        V;              I;          V           ;NEW_LINE;
    PLOT(TAXI(start), HOLD(start),  TAXI(land)  );NEW_LINE;
        I;              A;          I           ;NEW_LINE;
        I;              I;          I           ;NEW_LINE;
        NE;             WN;         V           ;NEW_LINE;
```

Progr. 5: AIRPORT, Plot of Figure 5

Programtext 5 above is part of the Ada program AIRPORT and
plots the model-diagram of figure 5.

The overloaded TRANSIT-procedure PLOT is able to plot an arbitrarily long series of station-diagrams in a row.A 'zero-station',
that is to say blanks over one station width , can be plotted by
inserting the plot parameter Op.

Diagram branches in station-width can be plotted by using the
TRANSIT-procedures A (arrow up), V (arrow down), I (north,south),
WI (west,north,south) , IE (north,south,east) , NE (north,east) ,
WS (west,south), WN (west,north). A 'zero-branch', that is to say
blanks over one station width, can be plotted by calling the
procedure O .

The numbers in the station-diagram of figure 5 all have a width
which is equal to the format FMT (default 6) of the package
FORMAT. If FMT would be enlarged, then the numbers and thus the
station-diagrams and branches would become broader .

3.5   Runway Occupation in the Months January and August

Figure 6 below shows the runway occupation in percentages on average days in the month of January and in the month of August over the hours 6 to 22 o'clock. In the calmest month January the runway peak-hour is 8-9 o'clock, in the most lively month August the runway peak-hour is 18-19 o'clock.

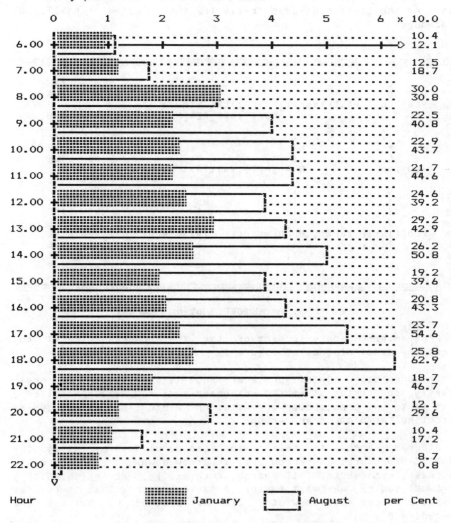

Fig. 6: Runway, Occupation in %

The runway-occupation-values are complements of runway-idle-times which themselves are TRANSIT-results of airport-simulations, see sections 3.1-3 . The runway-occupation print-plot of figure 6 results from calling the procedure BAR_PLOT of the package HISTOGRAM, see section 1 .

Summary

The generic Ada-package TRANSIT for statistical supervising of Ada-multitasking and the auxiliary packages FORMAT,NUMERIC,RANDOM, HISTOGRAM constitute a medium "large" software system for industrial applications like airport simulation (Flughafen Hamburg) . The system is developed and planned for productive use like flight-table proof correction and possibly airport-extension.

The hardware and software runtime environments were a big IBM-compatible SIEMENS-FUJITSU computer with Telesoft Ada , a medium DATA GENERAL computer with Rolm Ada and a smaller DIGITAL EQUIPMENT computer with DEC Ada . In the near future there will be an installation on an IBM PC/AT personal computer with Meridian Ada (supplier GSE Munich). Experience has shown that system - migration from one full-Ada-environment to another would take less than an hour. No machine-dependent questions appear. Other than in FORTRAN with GPSS, in Ada with RANDOM the random-procedures can be automatically fitted to the available number length INTEGER'LAST .

Discussions on Ada- and simulation-congresses have shown that the quality of the resulting system mainly lies in the statistical service, in the print-plot comfort and in the nonexistence of re-strictions for free multitasking in Ada rendezvous-technique.

References

(80) Feldmann, H.: "SIMULATRANSIT , structured Simulation with Print Plot Statistics and Output", brings the example: "Simulation of a steeple chase " , SIMULA NEWSLETTER, 4 pp. , August 1980.
(83a) US Department of Defence: " Reference Manual for the Ada Programming Language", ANSI/MIL-STD 1815 A , Lecture Notes in Computer Science 155 , Springer:Berlin, Heidelberg, New York, Tokyo, ca. 250 pp., 1983.
(83b) Feldmann, H.: "Einführung in Ada" , Lecture Script , brings TRANSIT and examples'Jobs in parallel Shops', 'Epidemic Infection', Universität Hamburg, ca. 280 S., 1983.
(86) Feldmann, H.: "Erfahrungen in der Anwendung von Ada am Bei-spiel "Simulation des Flughafens Hamburg " , 2. Deutscher Ada-Anwendercongress : München , 5 S., April 1986. mentioned in Ada Letters VI, 6 (Nov,Dec) 1986 p.27 by Ralph Duncan
(87) Feldmann, H.: "TRANSIT, ein Ada-Paket zur Überwachung paral-leler Prozesse, mit Anwendung auf Kunden-Ab-fertigung , Epidemie-Bekämpfung , Flughafen-modell", 3. Workshop "Simulationsmethoden für paralle-le Prozesse": München, 2 S., April 1987.

Part 3 Introducing Ada

PRACTICAL METHODS FOR INTRODUCING SOFTWARE ENGINEERING AND ADA INTO AN ACTUAL PROJECT

Lisa Brownsword
Rational, Box 165, Sturegatan 22, S-172 25 Sundbyberg, Sweden

INTRODUCTION

Introducing new software technologies such as object-oriented development and Ada is a challenging process. This paper discusses an effective way in which to make such a transition. First, the paper summarizes the project and presents an initial strategy for dealing with some of the issues involved in the transfer of technology. Then it describes an important modification to this strategy and the results produced in the project.

PROJECT SITUATION

The methods discussed here evolved for the 9LV Mk3 project under development by Philips Elektronikindustrier AB (PEAB) in Sweden. This is a ship-borne command, communication, and control system, including navigational and weapons functions. The 9LV Mk3 project could be characterized in early 1987 by the following:

- Limited Ada experience. Team members had some reading knowledge of the language but limited actual usage.

- Limited high-level language experience. Past projects primarily had been in languages such as assembly or RTL/2, with some Pascal. Structured programming concepts were fairly well known.

- Limited experience with tool sets or software development environments. Many team members were unfamiliar with integrated tools. Most development tools had been fairly primitive.

- Team-size expansion over the next one to two years would increase from 30 to 150–200. There would be a surge of new personnel with continuing training requirements.

- The project management structure consisted of a matrix organization. Thus, one part of the organization was responsible for the total end product but did not have direct authority for all subproject areas.

- The development team was geographically distributed. The five sites ranged from 5 to 500 kilometers apart, spanning two countries.

- The application was a very large, very complex system with an aggressive delivery schedule. The current estimated size exceeds 1000K lines of code.

EARLY STRATEGY

The overall strategy aims to assist in the transition of the 9LV Mk3 project to Ada, software engineering, object-oriented development, and a sophisticated development environment, the Rational® Environment™. It initially consisted of two components: consulting and formal classroom instruction. Each is discussed below.

Consulting

The first part of this strategy is consulting. It provides a way for an organization to acquire new technologies at a faster pace and with less project risk. This is vital on actual projects with aggressive delivery schedules.

Two levels of consulting are provided: specialized and general purpose. Specialized consultants provide expertise in design, development, or the integration of large Ada systems. They have done this themselves, can share their experiences, and provide advice on possible approaches relevant to a particular project. General-purpose consultants have an overall knowledge of Ada, project development, and the project development environment. They help the project to apply the recommendations of the specialists. The specialists provide consulting several times a year as needed; the general-purpose consultants provide ongoing support. This will continue for at least a year until the project has stabilized in its transition to the new technologies.

Formal Classroom Instruction

Formal instruction in Yourdon's Real Time Structured Analysis, project documentation methods, and the project development environment are provided for each developer, in addition to instruction in Ada and object-oriented design. Approximately one-third of the total time is allocated to Ada, and two-thirds is devoted to training in the other project-specific methods and environment.

The formal instruction is spread over a three- to five-month period. This allows the team members time to assimilate and use the course material. It also provides team members time to continue with other project activities, which is an essential consideration on a project. In addition, the scheduling of courses is geared to the rate of new members added to the project and the overall project schedule.

Initially, the project used a typical training approach to the introduction of Ada, object-oriented design, and software engineering. This included a one-week, hands-on Ada course plus a three-day, object-oriented design course. The Ada course consisted of the standard focus on Ada syntax and constructs plus an introduction to the terms and concepts surrounding object-oriented development. Approximately 40% of the class time was devoted to hands-on programming exercises. The design course was composed of lecture, case studies, and in-class design exercises. Both courses were well regarded by the participants.

Early Training Results

The above training approach was used for several months with some of the more experienced developers. It was discovered that few were able to develop designs and the subsequent code in an object-oriented manner. The designs and code still reflected their previous language experience.

One of the stated goals of the 9LV Mk3 project was to avoid repeating the difficulties of previous projects and to find design, development, and integration methods that are more suited to large, complex systems. PEAB had made the decision to use an object-oriented design and development approach with this project. Thus the inability of their best developers to adequately employ these new technologies to their respective project areas was very discouraging.

Analyzing the situation revealed that the developers seemed to have little difficulty in understanding which Ada constructs to use and how to use them in a semantically valid way. They could create legal Ada programs that would run correctly. Learning the syntax and form of the language is relatively easy, but discovering how to really use the language is more challenging. For example, knowing how to syntactically and semantically create a legal Ada package is easy relative to knowing what to put in the package and where to use the package. Thus, using object-oriented design and development approaches is not a matter of following a set of prescribed steps. It is, potentially, a totally new way of solving a design problem.

The 9LV Mk3 project revealed that classroom instruction provides an efficient method for introducing concepts, features, and mechanisms, but it does not easily show students how to put into practice software engineering principles. Students need time to become familiar with—and actually use—new ways of approaching problems and their solutions. This assimilation process generally requires significantly more time than a one- or two-week course can offer. Class time is needed just to acquire the basic ideas and methods. Then additional "processing" time is needed by most people to begin to make the new methods a part of their general problem-solving approach.

A further limitation of classroom instruction is that it provides little opportunity to determine the level of expertise a participant has attained relative to the actual use of the material on a real project. PEAB experienced this with the first few Ada classes it held. The students who performed well in class did not necessarily perform well on projects after class.

The goal then is to employ all the "good" software engineering principles and disciplines that promise to lead to more maintainable and reliable code. This means observing good examples, making mistakes, and having someone to point out those mistakes and suggest alternatives—in other words, actually using the language to reflect those principles. The work at PEAB and Rational's own internal training proved that this generally does not come in a one-week or even a two- or three-week course. Thus, a method of teaching problem solving, or a new way of thinking, needed to be added to the existing curriculum.

Finally, in a large project that crosses organizational boundaries, a consistent development methodology and style is needed. Again, the formal instruction can introduce these, but something else is needed to ensure that team members actually know how to use them effectively.

NEW STRATEGY

A method was developed to answer the above objections and form a natural bridge between formal classroom instruction and actual project development such as the 9LV Mk3 project. The original technology transition strategy of consulting and formal classroom instruction was augmented to include a practical workshop, called "Ada Practice," in applying Ada, object-oriented design, and software engineering. Key portions of the design course were incorporated into Ada Practice. Both the implementation and the results of this workshop will be described in the remainder of this paper.

It should be noted that, in the development of a possible strategy, it became apparent that a potentially more significant amount of time would be needed for training. Management commitment was required to implement the plan effectively, and this was achieved readily from the project managers at PEAB.

Ada Practice

Ada Practice is a series of development exercises providing individual and group feedback that uses progressively more aspects of Ada, object-oriented design, and software engineering on the project development environment. Ada Practice consists of two primary components: lecture and feedback sessions plus the actual exercises.

Logistics. Ada Practice currently is organized as follows:
- Total elapsed time is scheduled for six weeks.
- A maximum of twelve participants is allowed.
- One instructor devoting approximately 100% of his/her time is generally required. This assumes that the exercises and scheduling are already completed.
- Informal lecture and feedback sessions are held once or twice a week for two hours per session.
- Each participant submits exercise solutions for review by an instructor.
- Participants spend 50–80% of their time on the exercises. Other time is spent on their various project tasks.
- An instructor is available for questions regarding Ada, design, the exercise, or the Rational Environment as participants encounter problems in working out their solutions.

Lecture and Feedback Sessions. The group lecture sessions are used for the following purposes:
- Discussion of the previous exercise. In the process of reviewing the exercise solutions, the instructor collects a series of relevant topics and examples of positive and negative portions of the solutions that illustrate the topic. These become the focus of the discussion. Questions as to which of several solutions on a topic are the most preferred (and why) may be posed to stimulate discussion. Students benefit from the solutions of other participants.
- Return of the previous exercise with individual feedback. Students receive feedback on areas that may not have been covered in the general discussion.
- Discussion of conceptual material as background for the next exercise. Any preliminary information that would be useful in understanding the next

exercise or how to approach its solution is discussed. This includes video tapes of a design seminar by Grady Booch, director of software engineering programs at Rational; white-board informal lectures; and reprints from various Ada articles.

- Introduction of the next exercise. The new exercise is distributed and the instructions are reviewed.

A total of 50–70% of the group sessions is spent on reviewing and discussing the previous exercise. The remainder of the time is spent in providing the background for the following exercise and introducing it. Additional sessions are scheduled for viewing the longer segments of the video seminar. These sessions range from one to two hours.

The Exercises. The focus of the exercises is not on the syntax or form of Ada but on the use of design and coding styles that encourage easier integration and maintenance in a more object-oriented manner. All aspects of Ada are used, including generics and tasking.

Exercises are devised to give students an opportunity to use the project development methods. In the 9LV Mk3 project, for instance, an incremental development and test approach is used. This means that design, implementation, and test are applied iteratively, with each iteration providing increased functionality.

Currently, there are eight basic exercises. Most are structured around a single application that can be implemented by six to ten Ada packages with an overall size of 500–1000 lines of code. This will be referred to as "the small Ada system" in the following exercise descriptions.

- Exercise 1: Review of algorithmic uses of Ada. This includes an introduction to the use of the project incremental development and test approach.

- Exercise 2: Implementation of an abstraction. Students are introduced to the concepts of abstraction, constructors, selectors, and iterators in Ada. They then apply these concepts to a bottom-level abstraction or package of the small Ada system that they will design and build over succeeding exercises. Students are given the visible part of the package defining the abstraction and must determine an appropriate implementation for the private types, implement the package body, and test the package.

- Exercise 3: Design and implementation of an abstraction and using layers of abstraction. Students are given the definition of another abstraction in the small Ada system. This new abstraction can be implemented on top of the previous abstraction to introduce students to the practical aspects of layering abstractions. Students must define the complete package specification for the new abstraction plus implement and test the set of packages.

- Exercise 4: Design of a complete system. Students are given the complete set of requirements for the small Ada system (the need for tasks and generics has been removed). Students use diagrams as well as Ada package specifications to represent their designs.

- Exercise 5: Implementation of design. Students are given the opportunity to redesign Exercise 4 and implement their design. They also must document any changes made to the design as a result of their implementation.
- Exercise 6: Design and code review. Students are given a solution to Exercises 4 and 5 and must critique the design and the code.
- Exercise 7: System requirement change (design extension). A further requirement to the small Ada system is introduced. Students must modify their design to accommodate it. Tasks generally will be needed and a review of tasking is provided.
- Exercise 8: Implementation of design extension. Students must now implement their proposed design change.

This series of exercises is explicitly structured to provide students with time to learn the application of object-oriented styles in progressively larger contexts. Thus, Exercise 1 focuses primarily on algorithmic style issues. The next exercise focuses on how an abstraction as a package is implemented, and Exercise 3 requires that the student start understanding how to design a single abstraction as a package. From there, the design activity is applied to a larger set of packages. This is the first time that many of the students actually grasp how an Ada system behaves. Having students implement their designs allows them to discover firsthand what was lacking in the original design, with the intent that they then can apply these discoveries in the future. The design and code review also increases the overall quality of future design and code as students verbalize the concepts and techniques used in the previous exercises. The final two exercises allow students to discover how robust their design is for future changes and what they could have done to improve the maintainability of their design and code. It also provides them with experience in designing and implementing tasks.

The small Ada system used as the basis for the above exercises was chosen to meet the following criteria: familiarity of the instructor with the application to reduce initial exercise breakdown and definition time, general ease of understandability by students, and suitability for participants from a wide range of project areas, such as weapons systems or communications. The amount of time required for each exercise depends on the particular application. For the current Ada Practice, the time allowed for each exercise is shown in Figure 1.

Figure 1.   Student Solution Time per Exercise

Exercise	Duration (days)
1: Review of algorithmic uses of Ada	2.5
2: Implementation of an abstraction	2
3: Design and implementation of an abstraction	2
4: Design of a complete system	3
5: Implementation of design	4
6: Design and code review	1
7: System requirement change	2
8: Implementation of design extension	4
	20.5

Scheduling. Ada Practice provides the continuity and actual usage experiences
between various formal courses. A typical partial scenario might contain
the following components, with a timing sequence as depicted in Figure 2.

Figure 2.   Scheduling of Ada Practice and Formal Classroom Instruction

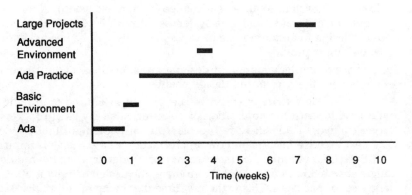

- Introduction to Ada in a hands-on formal course.
- Basic course in the project development environment.
- Beginning of Ada Practice with several exercises of increasing size and
  complexity.
- Advanced course in the project development environment.
- Additional exercises in Ada Practice.
- Large-project development course on the project development environment.
- Beginning of subproject design and implementation work.

The actual length of Ada Practice can be extended as required by the
skill levels and project schedules of the participants.

Experiences and Results

For the 9LV Mk3 project, a total of 150 or more developers need
to be trained. Using Ada Practice in its current form allows the project to train
12 team members every 6 weeks and requires a minimum of 1 full-time
instructor. Attempting to use this approach for all project members in a timely
manner would require a very large (and well-trained) training staff, the overall
expense of which may not be justifiable.

As a result, the general strategy is to thoroughly train the key
designers and project leaders as outlined in this paper. The project leaders then
work with their own groups. This can be implemented through the packaging
of the exercises, lectures, and approaches to solutions for use by noninstructors.

In addition to the general exercise phase of Ada Practice, an
optional designers' phase has been developed, allowing designers learning Ada
to work with more experienced Ada designers. This optional phase provides
for direct work on the subproject areas leading to actual project end products.

The participants work individually and in small groups, with periodic review by the project design group and consultants.

The initial three offerings of Ada Practice focused on training the key designers and project leaders, a total of 30 people. The first and second groups have completed both the general exercise phase and the optional designers' phase. They currently are involved in further design work for their subproject areas. In addition, they have started to pass on their experiences and knowledge to those in their own areas. In this bootstrapping mode, the project development styles and methods are being put into practical use.

Participants in Ada Practice have had various backgrounds. Some are very experienced designers and implementors; some have graduated from the university only recently. Some have used assembly-language programming with little formal requirements analysis and design methods; others are quite experienced with formal methods and high-level languages.

So far, the experience has been that previous background has had little to do with participants' success or failure in Ada Practice. It has been only an indicator of how much time, relative to other participants, they have had to devote to the exercises. Further, it has been found that participants either do quite well in Ada Practice or do quite poorly, with few in the middle. The prime indicator of success has been the attitude or motivation toward Ada, software engineering, and object-oriented development. Those who are open to learning a new way of designing and developing software do well; those who would rather retain their old methods do poorly. Ten-year veteran assembly "hackers" have done extremely well and newly graduated university students have done extremely poorly (as well as the reverse).

The role of the subproject manager cannot be overlooked. Managers who do not perceive the value of the workshop are not as supportive of their team members. This has made it much more difficult for students to prioritize conflicting tasks to gain enough time for the exercises.

So how can success with a program such as the Ada Practice be measured? The key criterion should be whether participants are able to design and implement their own subprojects in a more object-oriented manner. So far, it has been found that those who do well in Ada Practice are able to apply what they have learned.

Another criterion of program success could be the perceived value that participants feel they have received. Those who do well in Ada Practice almost universally feel that they have learned a great deal, that they are much better equipped to start work on their subprojects, and that this practical approach is the only way to understand how to apply the new technologies being introduced on the project. They are more excited about what they are doing. They generally are so "sold" on the practical approach to learning Ada that they want all their subproject members to go through the same process. For example, one of the key members of one subproject area has been through the practice. As a result of her experiences, the other subproject members are trying to go through the exercises in their own spare time. They have recognized that the formal Ada course is not sufficient for actual applications of object-oriented approaches to Ada.

SUMMARY

Many of the challenges faced by the 9LV Mk3 project are not unique to this particular company or project; they are very typical of most organizations throughout the world. Further, transition problems are not unique to Ada or modern software engineering; they have been with the industry for the last 15 years. More complex applications with more complex software are being built. Without more cost-effective ways of producing that software, companies become less competitive. Like the hardware side of the industry, the software side is learning the importance of adequate tools. However, new tools and methods require time to be assimilated.

New technologies require adequate training and consulting resources. Introducing new technologies requires adequate time for personnel to understand and make effective use of the technologies. Formal courses play an important role in introducing the various technologies, but they are not sufficient. An efficient method for the transfer of technologies is a practical workshop that allows project personnel to learn to actually use these technologies and avoid making those first mistakes on actual project design and code. Consulting rounds out this process. Finally, it should not be underestimated that introducing new technologies takes great dedication and commitment on the part of the management.

Part 4 System Design with Ada

Design and Development of Distributed Software using Hierarchical Object Oriented Design and Ada™

Maurice HEITZ, Bertrand LABREUILLE,CISI-INGENIERIE
13 rue Villet, 31400 Toulouse, France tel (33) 61.34.95.82

ABSTRACT : This paper reports on an Ada pilot project (janv86 to Sept87) which was conducted for the EUROPEAN SPACE AGENCY (ESA) by CISI-INGENIERIE as main contractor and CARLO GAVAZZI SPACE as subcontractor. The main objectives of this study were to provide information on issues of using the Ada technology for the design and implementation of large distributed systems in the context of the COLUMBUS space station program by developing a prototype of an on-board Data Management System (DMS). Results and lessons learnt by applying a virtual node approach together with Hierarchical Object Oriented Design (HOOD) may contribute to a better understanding and management of the use of Ada technology and provide alternative approaches to current practice in the field of large distributed system development. Experimental data gathered over a development of 30 man*month which yielded a 15000 Ada source line system, are given.

0.ABREVIATIONS

ADMS	Ada DMS Prototype	AOCS	Attitude and Orbit Control Sub-system
CCIP	Calling Communication Interface Package	CIP	Communication Interface Procedure
DMS	Data Management System	HCS	Housekeeping Control Sub-system
HOOD	Hierarchical Object Oriented Design	NC	Inter Node Communication
MDS	Monitoring Display Sub-system	NI	Network Interface
OBCS	OBject Control Structure	OSI	Open System Interconnection
PADS	PAckage Distribution System	PLS	PayLoad Sub-system
PN	Physical Node	REC	Remote Entry Call
RCIP	Receiving Communication Interface Package	RPC	Remote Procedure Call
SIP	Service Interface Procedure	VN	Virtual Node

1. OVERVIEW

1.1. Background of the study

The clear trend towards more complex on-board data functional requirements and higher performances which is characteristic of the European space mission scenario has been dramatically enhanced by the new space station program COLUMBUS, the most demanding and challenging project for the next few years. Major efforts will be required in many areas of technology and expertise. The software technology required for the implementation of such on-board functions as the Data Management System and other automated sub-systems, represents a technological step forward with respect to previous missions. Moreover, the adoption of state-of-the-art advanced software technology must be traded-off with the tight time schedule in the definition of a technology transition strategy. The choice of Ada as the mandatory programming language for all COLUMBUS software is one of the essential elements in this transition. It is worth recalling the main justifications for this decision :
- **The Ada language is explicitly oriented to embedded systems** and therefore supports, at a high level, the concurrent aspects which are typical of this type of system (tasking, rendezvous, exception handling).
- **The aspects of modularity, maintainability and modifiability are deeply integrated in the concepts** of the language. They are required, in general, in space

---

[1]Ada is a registered trade mark of the U.S. governement (Ada Joint Program Office)

software to allow for changes, to partition software development, etc., particularly in retrievable, reusable and long life cycle manned systems in order to provide reconfiguration, adaptation and growth capabilities.
- The above point is enhanced by the **strong typing and the high level built-in checking**, providing a high quality code and supporting the early identification of programming errors and detailed design inconsistencies.
- **The language definition is machine-independent,** providing the software developer with a unique level of abstraction. It supports the reusability of design concepts and techniques,and makes efficient portability of actual Ada packages and systems possible.
- **Ada is standardized. This affects portability, maintenance and long lived systems support.** What is possibly even more important is the fact that this aspect relates directly to the multinational cooperative nature of European space projects.
- **The availability of Ada compilers and tools is ensured for a   very wide spectrum of host and target machines.** Moreover, the quality of compiler implementation (e.g. performances of the codes generated) is continually improving.

However, the applicability of Ada to Columbus software is subject to at least two major constraints :
- **distributed nature of the execution environment** : the Columbus DMS will be based on a distributed target architecture consisting of a hierarchical local area network of computers, each of which has well defined functions (PLS, AOCS, Thermal control, etc.).
- **distributed concurrent software development** : individual application software systems will be integrated and localized on dedicated processors and they will be developed by different teams. The long operational life and the maintenance/upgrade replacement requirements will imply different development and integration schedules and different levels of stability and standardization for payloads, sub-systems and DMS functions.

Although the Ada language directly supports multi-tasking, the reference manual does not impose any constraints on the target implementing a parallel execution. At present, manufacturers have generally chosen to associate the notion of an Ada task relatively closely with the notion of the process that is generally available on the executive system (run-time) considered. The development of distributed Ada run-time kernels enabling the generation of executable code on distributed target systems such as the one planned for Columbus DMS has yet not be announced. Moreover, the setting-up of an effective methodology capable of supporting partitioning, interfacing, developing and integrating very large and distributed Ada applications is far from being straightforward.

1.2. Study approach

In 1986 CISI-INGENIERIE was awarded a contract from ESA in order to investigate the implications and techniques related to the utilization of the Ada programming language for the implementation of complex distributed on-board software systems. The project was split into :
1) **Studying of the implications of using Ada in distributed** execution and development **environments** in the framework of space station requirements.
2) **Demonstration of the use of Ada technology** based on the approach defined previously , by means of a case study to be specified, produced and tested as a prototype of the functions derived from the Columbus space station scenarios.The objectives were to define a specific and practical minimum set-up for the use of Ada on on-board distributed systems, providing well defined methods and guidelines by going through the process of designing and coding.
Both CISI-Ingéniérie and Carlo Gavazzi Space were involved in the two phases. For phase 2, ESA acted as the customer, Cisi-Ingéniérie and Carlo Gavazzi Space as the software developers.

2. ADA FOR PROGRAMMING DISTRIBUTED TARGET SYSTEMS

2.1. Classical Approach

Ada compilers presently available are exclusively intended for single-processor type host/target machines. But, real time applications increasingly rely on distributed hardware architectures including several physical processing nodes connected through one or several networks. In this context, the development of a distributed application in Ada seems only possible using a multiprogram approach : an Ada program is written for each machine of the target configuration and the interactions between remote programs are implemented using communication primitives provided by each local operating system (e.g. SEND and RECEIVE primitives of a networking communication medium).This approach, which is certainly easy to implement, means that the advantages of concepts intrinsic to Ada are lost. It would not be possible to expect to validate the application uniformly with respect to the semantics of the Ada language. The control flows would be implemented differently depending on whether they are local to a program (rendezvous, call procedure) or remote between two separate programs (network primitive calls). **So that the possibility of validating the software interfaces in a consistent way is ruled out.** Furthermore, the abstraction and information hiding possibilities become highly compromised as it would be necessary to know the target system configuration, the application's partitioning scheme on this configuration and the inter-processor communication facilities, right from the design phase. Several studies have explored alternatives to the multi-program approach; the major idea consists in distinguishing between two phases in the development of a distributed Ada application :
- **Functional design** corresponding to the development of a unique Ada program.
- **Distribution of the application** by allocating Ada program units to the physical nodes of the target system.

Such 'post-partitioning' and 'pre-partitioning in virtual nodes' approaches (still being explored [WEL87]) consist then in defining an Ada program satisfying the functional specifications of the distributed system to be developed and to validate this first model on a conventional single-processor machine with a standard Ada compiler. The distribution aspect is only envisaged in a second step as a specific implementation constraint imposed on an Ada program.

2.2. "Post-partitioning" approach

This strategy is based on the **hypothesis that all Ada entities (data or control) can be distributed.** Therefore, this enables an initial program to be designed without any restrictions. This approach is attractive, but it is also the most complex to implement as mechanisms guaranteeing the coherency between different copies of variables shared by the various modules distributed throughout the distributed system have to be foreseen. Hence a specific distributed operating system capable of providing such mechanisms must be available.

2.3. "Pre-partitioning in virtual nodes" approach

In the perspective of using standard Ada compilers, the **approach of choosing a specific Ada construction as the only possible partitioning unit,** is the most attractive and was the one experimented in our study. This amounts to fixing the distribution granularity of an Ada program. This strategy relies on the notion of **virtual node**, offered in languages specifically designed for programming distributed systems (e.g. "task module" construction in C O N I C language [SLO84]).**The application is seen as a network of communicating virtual nodes.** The essential properties of a virtual node are as follows :
- It has activities (control flows), which consists of local actions, communication and coordination actions with the other nodes of the system.
- Its internal state is invisible to the other nodes.
- It communicates with the other nodes through well defined interfaces and according to message like transmission protocols (communication by shared variables is excluded).

- It can be executed autonomously on a physical node of the target system or be incorporated in a group of virtual nodes to form a new executable program.

Furthermore, it must be possible to define a virtual nodes configuration by explicitly indicating the connections between these nodes, thus enabling **the separation of the components programming phase from that of the definition of the final system's configuration.** The interfaces of the virtual nodes are then described through their communication ports with the outside world, and a system configuration can then be defined using the external interfaces and a specification of the ports connections

2.3.1. The Ada representation of the virtual node

Two Ada constructions may represent the notion of virtual node : **the task** and **the package**. On one hand the Ada **task** has its own control flow,executes in parallel with other tasks, communicates and synchronizes through rendez-vous,but since it is not a library unit, cannot be an autonomous executable entity. On the other hand the **package**, with opposite characteristics, is a library unit and the most suitable Ada tool for encapsulation and modularization but it does not have its own control flow (the initialization part excepted). Faced with this dilemma, two attitudes can be observed at present :
- The first one illustrated in the DIADEM project [DIADEM 86]considers that the package or the task are not suitable for implementing the virtual node concept. The virtual node is seen as a collection of Ada units structured according to well established composition rules. The notion of Ada library unit is thus assimilated with that of virtual node.
- The second attitude taken from [INN 85] and [WEL 87] is based on the package as the only Ada support for the virtual node, while accepting the limitations imposed by this choice.

2.3.2. Transformation of the Ada program into a distributed configuration

When an application has been designed according to the "virtual node" approach described above, its distribution on the target system is made easier : all that has to be done is to define the allocation of virtual nodes on the target configuration's physical nodes. The following transformation rules are then deduced :
- Communications between virtual nodes allocated to the same physical node remain unchanged.
- Communications between remote virtual nodes are transformed, according to a mechanism ensuring that the Ada semantics are maintained.

3. DEVELOPMENT METHODOLOGY USING HOOD

The properties of a virtual node are very similar to those of an object in the Object-Oriented Design sense:
- well defined interfaces : they are only procedural interfaces because the sharing of global variables is not permitted. Moreover, the parameters can only be transmitted by value and not by reference.
- independence : each object may have its own control flows.
- cooperation : each object interacts with others to perform certain system-wide functions.

Thus a design method used for defining the virtual nodes should provide concepts supporting identification of communicating objects directly mappable into Ada packages. HOOD([HOOD87],see also appendix 1) as an improved version of Object-Oriented Design (OOD), was a unique candidate, since :
- HOOD objects are defined by their external properties only, whereas the internal structure is hidden from the user, thus giving a view of "how it appears to other objects".
- HOOD objects can be mapped directly into Ada packages
- the **use relationship** between objects can directly map the communication schemes between objects.

These concepts were found to be completely suitable for the use of HOOD in the design phase of the virtual nodes, thus prohibiting unstructured identification of Ada packages by 'derivation' from requirement analysis.

4. DESCRIPTION OF THE ADA CASE STUDY

4.1. Baseline for the case study

The case study considered in the pilot project is a simplified model of an On-board Data Management System [CISI87]. The Ada Data Management System (ADMS) is composed of four logical nodes, each one being in charge of specific functions and implemented in a simulated distributed environment. The nodes shown in Fig. 4.1 (ADMS Prototype General Block Diagram) have been identified as :
- **Housekeeping and Control Sub-system** (HCS) : responsible for the general control of the mission and for Earth_Station communication management.
- **Monitoring and Display Sub-system** (MDS) : responsible for crew interface management.
- **Attitude and Orbit Control Sub-system** (AOCS) : responsible for the control of navigation and stabilization of the space station.
- **Payload Sub-system** (PLS) : responsible for the execution of the various operations foreseen for the scientific experiments or industrial processes.

ADMS also includes simulation of the external environment of the above mentioned nodes, i.e. Attitude and Orbit Data Simulator and a Scientific Experiment Data Simulator.

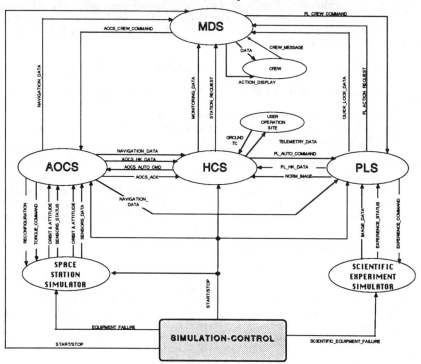

Fig. 4.1 - ADMS Prototype General Block Diagram

4.2. Representativeness of the Ada DMS prototype

The aim of the project was not to model the Columbus DMS accurately in Ada, but rather to support a study of the evaluation of the suitability and reliability of Ada technology for the most significant aspects of an on-board DMS, including distribution to different targets.Thus, it is important to point out if and how the ADMS manages typical DMS situations, such as distributed services and operations, management of multiple concurrent activities, data flow control, multi-user environment and crisis management.The main architectural differences between the ADMS and the Columbus DMS can be summarized as follows :

a) The number of processing nodes in the ADMS prototype is less than in the Columbus DMS; furthermore, some ADMS nodes embody different parts of DMS nodes, even if in a simplified manner.For example, HCS contains some Mission Management and Control (MMC), Telecommand Unit (TCU) and Telemetry Formatter functions, MDS is a simplified version of the Multipurpose Workstation (MPWS) but PLS is conforming with the Payload Manager (PLM), even if it manages only one simulated experiment.

b) The ADMS architecture seems flatter as the one expected for COLUMBUS DMS where several layers are foreseen, however a mapping of ADMS architecture to these layers can be defined as:

- **Application layer** (containing DMS Management software and user application software) and **Services layer** (including general services as telemetry and telecommand link support, data acquisition and distribution, data processing and monitoring, command processing) into ADMS first levels of decomposition.

- **Distributed Operating System layer** (including a Distributed Service Manager, to manage the distribution of the services through the network and a Local Operating System consisting of an Executive Kernel and of I/O Device Drivers) into PADS node communication layer.(see §4.3.3). And **Network Communication Software layer** into PADS network interface layer.

4.3. Description of ADMS prototype development

Following the approach defined in phase 1 of the project, the development of ADMS was phased into:
- **Functional specification and requirement analysis**
- **Non distributed design and implementation**
- **Distributed implementation**

4.3.1. Functional specification

Data Flow analysis method allowed identification of the system's functional activities, and the messages exchanged between these activities.The only support provided by Ada was the possibility of giving preliminary definitions of the message structures in the form of Ada types definitions.

4.3.2. Non-distributed design and implementation

a) **Pre-partitioning into HOOD objects/virtual nodes** : The functional activities previously identified have been grouped into six objects :AOCS, AODS (Attitude and Orbit Data Simulator), MDS, HCS, PLS, SEDS (Scientific Experiment Data Simulator). All these objects include at least one permanent activity that is executed in parallel with the rest of the system. This approach enables thus to take into account the environmental parallelism induced by the simultaneity of interactions. Each Hood object (see figure 4.2 below) has been represented and described according to Hood notation including :
- an external description : (interface provided, interface required)
- an internal description : (object control structure/behavior, operation control structure per operation provided using an Ada like notation (ADA-PDL))

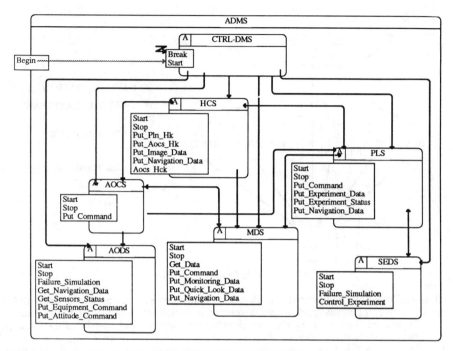

Figure 4.2 : HOOD TOP-LEVEL Object

HOOD objects implementation rules towards Ada enable the direct derivation of the package specifications and derivation of implementation outlines through body stubs and skeletons.

b) Definition of the system configuration and prototyping : Figure 4.3 below describes the application's Ada architecture. The boxes represent Ada units (packages) and the arrows represent the inter-unit 'use' links in the Ada sense (with relationships) :
- **CTRL_DMS** : a package controlling and managing the DMS simulation environment according to a number of events triggered by an operator (e.g. default at the level of an attitude data sensor).
- **DMS-body-configurator** : a package containing the instantiations of the six virtual nodes as well as the definitions of the procedures required for these instantiations. The composition of the system is entirely defined at this level.
- **HCS, AOCS, PLS, MDS, AODS and SEDS**: packages corresponding to the six objects/virtual nodes.
- **Type_Dictionary** : a package containing all the types defining the messages exchanged between the objects.

This configuration has been prototyped at the static and dynamic levels :
- static level : compilation of packages allowing the validation of the syntactic coherency of the interfaces.
- dynamic level: **Design prototyping is performed by implementing** body skeletons according to Object Control Structures thus making partial execution of the application as a whole possible and enabling checking of the coherency of the communication and synchronization schemes selected. In particular, it was ensured that for a given operating mode the object/virtual nodes transmit or receive messages in compliance with the behaviors identified at requirement analysis level.

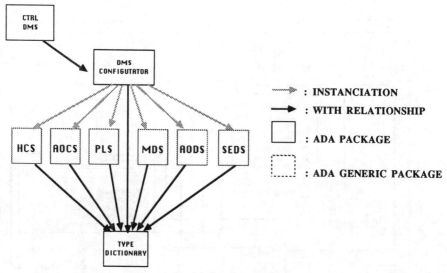

Fig. 4.3 - Ada Prototype Architecture

c) Distributed development of objects/virtual nodes : Using the above interface specifications, the virtual nodes were developed in parallel in Toulouse and in Milano. The HOOD method was used by the two development teams, and considerably facilitated communication during the design phase by providing a standard methodological framework. HOOD decomposition and structuration rules were used to identify objects and derive Ada units at each stage of the breakdown. By applying this method, each virtual node/object was treated in turn as an object to be broken down into children objects on which the same process was reiterated. This decomposition process resulted in the identification of 60 objects distributed over three levels of decomposition.

The AODS and SEDS were designed and realized beforehand so as to permit the development and testing of the **AOCS, MDS, PLS and HCS** nodes,which could then be tested autonomously in a specific configuration containing :
- A test driver responsible for selectively causing the activation of the operations provided by the node under test.
- An emulation of the other nodes provided by the remaining part of the design prototype of first level decomposition and ensuring an interconnection complying with the interfaces previously established.
- Data dialogues and display units enabling control of the behaviour of the node under test.

d) Functional integration and validation of the application : Following unit validation of each of the virtual nodes, application integration was performed at Toulouse site by :
- progressive enrichment of the architectural design prototype, with replacement of the implementation skeletons of each object by the corresponding final implementations..
- execution and validation of the application at each enrichment step.

This integration was carried out rapidly (see § 4.4.1) and did not imply any modifications at the level of the interfaces validated during the design phase.

4.3.3. Distributed implementation of the application

a) Transformation of the single Ada program into its distributed version : The strategy for the static allocation of the six top-level virtual nodes of first decomposition level to the target system's physical processors was defined as :
- AOCS and AODS on physical node 1
- MDS on physical node 2
- HCS on physical node 3
- PLS and SEDS on physical node 4.

This distribution scheme lead to the definition of a software configuration for each of the physical nodes, obtained from the previous single Ada program and by applying a transformation mechanism relying on a PADS (PAckage Distribution System) implemented in Ada as result of a feasibility study in phase1 of the project. This mechanism consists in replacing calls to the remote packages by local surrogate packages providing the same Ada interfaces. These surrogate entities then manage the interactions between remote virtual nodes through the communication medium (Bus or Local Network). The software configuration corresponding to physical node 1 is given in Fig. 4.5 (See [CISI87] for a more complete description of the PADS mechanism).

b) Final integration and operational validation : When the application was transformed according to the PADS mechanism, the distributed execution was simulated using a network model by means of a FIFO mechanism managing the messages received and transmitted by each of the physical nodes. The principle of the approach was thus validated and all of the functional tests were run through again in a way similar to that of the previous integration stage for the non-distributed program.

Fig. 4.5 - Configuration of Physical Node 1

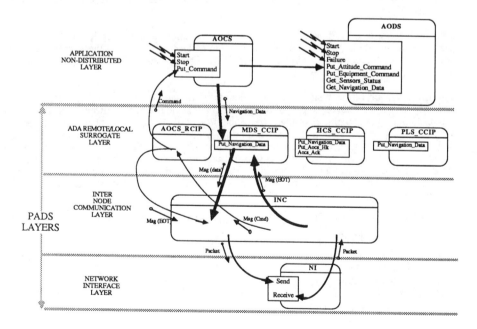

4.4. Essential results derived from the case study

4.4.1. Distribution of manpower over the various project phases

Development of the ADMS prototype was performed in accordance with the ESA Software Engineering Standards.The project life cycle was therefore split into the following classical phases, up to the transfer of the prototype to ESA : 1) User Requirements, 2) Software requirements, 3)Architectural Design, 4) Detailed Design and Implementation.The output of each of the above phases complied with ESA standards.

The first two phases, **User and Software Requirements**, required 143.5 man days.

During **Architectural Design phase**, a 'design prototype' of the system (implementing the children behaviors of the six top-level objects/virtual nodes). was produced and validated in addition to the Architectural Design Document. The AOCS and MDS prototypes were developed in Toulouse and the HCS and PLS prototypes were developed in Milano. Prototype integration was performed in Toulouse and demonstrated at the time of the Architectural Design Review. Early validation of the Architectural Design was thus allowed by execution of the prototype, and so checking the inter-object interfaces and behaviors with respect to data and/or commands. The use of the Hierarchical Object Oriented Design (HOOD) methodology ensured a natural transition from the requirements to design and implementation, trough use of a graphical and textual formalism, allowing smooth transitions from informal to formal descriptions.. Mapping of finite state automata descriptions into object behaviours expressed in Object Control Structures using Ada like notations, was found specially helpful for expressing a coherent high-level HOOD object model, whereas parent-child transformation rules ensured consistency throughout the decomposition and refinement process down to objects directly implementable in Ada units. The AODS and SEDS were developed during the ADMS Architectural Design phase, in parallel in Milano and Toulouse. Architectural Design phase required 159 man days.

Detailed design of individual objects, implementation and object level testing were performed in parallelat the two sites (Toulouse and Milano), in line with the approach already adopted for Architectural Design phase.The Detailed Design required 128 man days, including unit testing test phase.

Final integration of the system (centralized and distributed versions) took place in Toulouse and only required 5 man days, part of which was spent standardizing the library procedures for Input/Output management. Given the size of the project, this integration phase was performed very rapidly. This is mainly due to the methodology used (virtual node approach and HOOD); and to the fact that inter-object interfaces were specified and validate early at each level in the design decomposition .Also final integration took place only three months after the Architectural Design Review; this schedule was helped by the use of the HOOD methodology allowing parallel and independent developments distributed between different teams in different development sites.

The total effort required for the project was actually 27 man months and the total manpower for the various project phases was distributed as follows :

- User/Software Requirements :   24 %
- Architectural Design :   27 %
- Detailed Design, coding and Final Integration,including Simulators : 42 %
- Prototype Distribution :   7 %

4.4.2. Assessment of Productivity

Approximately 15000 source lines (comment lines are excluded) were produced in this project, this includes the code for the centralized ADMS version, the distribution software package and the code specifically developed for the various single nodes and partial integration test configurations;
- AOCS :   1,607 ASL
- MDS , including implementation of the User Crew :   2,353 ASL
- HCS, including implementation of the User Operation Site :   3,385 ASL
- AODS: 1,279 ASL
- SEDS: 267 ASL
- Other high-level prototype units (Type_Dictionary, DMS-Configurator):   687 ASL
- Ada re-usable packages (such as library routines) :   2,146 ASL

On the basis of the above data, the overall productivity assessed for the development of the ADMS prototype was 500 non commented Ada source lines/man month (1000 ASL are figures given in the litterature), taking into account the complete development from the URD/SRD phases up to final integration in Toulouse. The productivity achieved in the project was really good, considering the nature of the study and the specificity and innovative nature of the topics to be investigated during the ADMS case study.

4.4.3. Assessment of the Ada virtual node approach

4.4.3.1. The virtual node concept and its Ada implementation

The notion of the virtual node supported by the Ada package was found to be particularly powerful by allowing:
- easy partitioning of an application by grouping together highly coupled activities, while providing a very comprehensible interface, the definition of which can be limited to provided and required services.
- definition ,with great flexibility, of an application as a composition of virtual nodes interconnected according to a scheme defined only at the interface level.

However, the choice of the package as the only virtual node support does not allow definition of dynamic configuration of virtual nodes, i.e. configurations where inter-node connections can be modified during execution. Furthermore, such choice implies the following restrictions:
- communications between objects/virtual nodes are restricted to three kinds of control transfer: procedure call, entry call (rendezvous) , exception propagation.
- for a distributed entry call, the following features are difficult to handle in a distributed context, and therefore can only be used according to the implementation of the distribution mechanism : conditional and timed entry calls, family of entries, testing task attributes (terminated, completed and entry count)
- access and task type parameters must not appear in remote transfers of control as these types require that the caller accesses the caller's address space.
- declarations of global data in the specification part of packages implementing virtual nodes are strictly forbidden.

4.4.3.2. Principle of transformation into a distributed configuration

The PADS mechanism for distributing an application's packages has permitted validation of the proposed approach. **The distribution of an Ada application designed according to the virtual node principle has thus been proven**. The PADS mechanism does not affect the original application design and it only adds a specific software layer for the realization of "syntactically" transparent communications between virtual nodes. However, the

mechanism was only implemented in our study for demonstration purposes. Implementation of PADS for industrial developments would mean that the following points must be taken into account :
- **automatic transformations** : although transformation was applied manually for ADMS this distribution transformation mechanism could easily be automated, as it would only require that the services provided/used by a node, and those to be remotely called, to be known. (An analysis of the specifications of the virtual nodes, where the services to be remotly called could be explicitly indicated, would be sufficient).
- **Network support** : because PADS is limited to the distribution of procedure calls, the advantage of using an RPC (Remote Procedure Call) type protocol should be considered for inter-processor communications. Moreover, the [INTEC 87] study recommended that this type of primitive be present at the level of the NOS (Network Operating System) communication kernel.
- **Performances aspect** : the PADS mechanism and its support were entirely written in Ada in this study. This results in overheads during the distribution of a procedure call (requiring approximately ten procedure and/or task calls for each distributed transaction).

4.4.4. Assessment of the methodological results for Ada distributed programming

The HOOD method was found to be very useful as a support for an Ada application development process according to the "virtual node" approach :
- the "virtual node" concept is very close to that of the object as defined by HOOD
- HOOD provides a structuration model that enables a virtual node hierarchy to be established in such a way that the entities at the lowest level are reduced to server nodes.
- HOOD provides a virtual node implementation model based on a successive breakdown of objects with associated validation rules.

5. CONCLUSIONS

This study has illustrated the various problems posed by the development of distributed Ada applications. It has been shown that the pre-partitioning into virtual nodes approach would be a satisfactory solution providing the following advantages :
- use of standard Ada compilers,
- good usage of the language features (packages, tasks, type checking and Ada communication mechanisms).

Moreover, the importance of a methodological support, such as that provided by HOOD, has been underlined, in particular because of the very close links between the notions of HOOD object, of virtual node and of mechanisms provided in HOOD to support distributed design and development (see Appendix here after).

Furthermore, the virtual node approach combined with HOOD would enable the definition of a development framework very well adapted to the Columbus DMS context :
- by defining application and service software as Ada virtual nodes it would be possible to design the whole system as a single Ada program, structured according to the architecture model planned for the DMS.
- the applications could be developed in parallel on geographically distributed sites and be validated individually using this initial model and the corresponding interface specifications
- the final integration process could be essentially concentrated on the operational validation of the system in distributed configuration (the functional validation in centralized configuration being obtained at the end of the first phase).

Finally, the efficient implementation of this method requires support tools for :
- checking the rules imposed by the virtual node approach.
- scanning virtual node specifications (Ada packages) in order to generate a surrogate software layer which would provide "syntactically" transparent communication between virtual nodes located on distinct physical processors.

6. ACKNOWLEDGEMENTS

This work was funded by the European Space Agency under the contract number 6512/85/NL.We acknowledge Mr A. CIARLO, project manager, and Mr P. GOMEZ-MOLINARO technical monitor, as well as the contributions of members of the team not listed as authors.

7. REFERENCES

[CISI87]   ESTEC contract 6512/85/NL, **Final Report,** november 87.

[CORN 83]   D.Cornhill "**A survivable Distributed System for embedded application programs written in Ada**" ACM Ada Letters Vol. 3, No. 3, Nov-Dec 83

[DIADEM86]   **A compiler independent approach to distribute a single Ada program,** CEC-MAP project, 770 intermediate report, March 86

[HOOD87]   M.Heitz **une méthode de conception hiérarchisée orientée objets pour le developpement des logiciels techniques en temps réel.** Journées ADA-AFCET 1987. .

[INN85]   Y.J.Inn, M.Rosenberg, **An Ada Distributed System**, Annual Conference on Ada Technology, 85

[INTECS87]   Intecs Toscana S.r.l., "**Study of Communication Options in a Distributed Data Handling System**" ESTEC/Contract No. 6653/86/NL/PB, Final Report April 87.

[SEIDE86]   Seidewitz and Stark, **Generalised Object Oriented Development,** NASA Software Engineering Laboratory Report. SEL-86-002

[SLO84]   M.Sloman, J.Magee, "**Building flexible distributed computing systems in CONIC**", Distributed Computing Systems Program, ed. D.A. Duce, Peter Pevegrinus Ltd, 84

[WEL87]   Wellings, **Programming and Debugging Distributed Real Time Applications in Ada,** International Workshop on Real Time Ada Issues, May 87.

APPENDIX 1 : A HOOD ABSTRACTED DESCRIPTION

Hood is a design and development method for large technical and real-time software and was derived from industrial experience gained through applying the approaches of OOD and Abstract Machines (AM). HOOD integrates engineering principles relying on the concepts of objects, hierarchies (as worked out in methods such as SADT and AM)and on expression of control. It provides severals mechanisms to overcome the limitations of OOD in the field of large and complex systems:

1) The formalisation of the Object Concept in Hood is intended to capture both its static and dynamic properties:

   - **Static properties :** An object has a visible part (the interface), and a hidden part (the body) which cannot be accessed directly by external objects. An object is known to the external world by a name.

     * The **interface** defines the operations and resources **provided** by the object and the associated parameters and types, as well as the operations **required** from other objects.

     * The **body** is the implementation of the provided operations and resources, as described in the interface, using internal operations and data, or using internal objects.These internals implement the object internal state.

   - **Dynamic properties:** The execution of an operation, as seen from the user of an object, can be done in two ways :

     * **sequentially**: the control is transferred from one object to another and the operation is executed immediately along an **operation control structure** (OPCS). After completion, the control is returned. This defines a **passive** object with respect to control flow.

     * **concurrently**: the control is transferred following a control protocol depending on the internal state of the object, and according to incoming control flow dependencies. This defines an **active** object. The control protocol is fully described in the **object control structure** (OBCS). The external world may

"trigger" a flow of control in an operation ; in this case a "zigzag arrow" sign is used. Asynchronous interrupts are thus taken into account.
In both cases, if the operation cannot be performed successfully, an **exception** can be raised and propagated to the user.
- **The object relationships are structured** according to **use** and **include** relationships.
  * Objects may be decomposed in other objects, so that a system can be represented as a **parent** object including **child** objects.
  * Objects may use operations of other objects, so that a system can be represented as **senior** objects using **junior** objects in a hierarchy[Seide86].

2) **Particular support is given to the top-down decomposition process** by viewing a system under design as a parent-child hierarchy where each object is a parent incorporating several children using one another. The design process closely follows this model: an object is first identified at a given level of decomposition through OOD like techniques, and is then described throughout two successive design steps:
  * **at child level** (i.e. when a given object is identified as a child component), only the object interface and its general behaviour is described.
  * **at parent level** (i.e; when this object is in turn broken down into other child components), the object definition is refined and its internals are described.
Parent-child decomposition rules in HOOD allow to achieve top-down design in a consistent and verified way. A system is first defined as an abstract high-level object model with an associated abstract behaviour, and is then broken down into several lower level object models and behaviors up to they can be directly implemented into target languages units and environment services.

3) The **clear separation** in the design process of a phase where an **external description** (both structural and behavioral) of an object is produced, from the phase where its implementation is described provides a key abstraction mechanism,which is used for managing the complexity and for producing phase-based verifiable products. Hence **design validation can be enforced** :
  * at the end of a **basic design step** where parent-child signature checks can be performed, and executable models of children produced in order to perform **requirements traceability** checks (against requirement analysis models).
  * at the end of a level decomposition, where **a complete design can be prototyped** by implementing all children together on behalf of their associated object control structure descriptions, and testing the resulting model against their parent executable models. Such design prototyping at appropriate points in the process brings up means to validate both a behavioral parent-child decomposition on the basis of the same executable model support, and to validate it against requirements analysis models on the basis of same test data.

4) Hood allows geographical **distribution of the design and development** since:
  - **the scope of a given design step is limited** to its nearest levels of decomposition according to the parent-child relationships. Each design steps produces specifications of objects which define as much new problems and can be validated by prototyping against requirement models.
  - **production of such validated specifications** of both the objects and their test environment (i.e.the brother prototypes) **allows to subcontract** their design and development to other teams.
  - Finally **level validation prototypes may be reused as test and pre-integration** environment for all objects of a same level, i.e. all brothers of a given object, thus minimizing the effort of developers whereas improving management procedures by providing better visibility.

Combining CSP and Meta-IV into an Ada Related PDL for Developing Concurrent Programs

H. Morell Heerfordt
DDC International A/S, Lundtoftevej 1C, DK-2800 Lyngby, Denmark

Abstract. Since CSP makes no assumptions on the objects that can be communicated among CSP processes, these objects can be datastructures, which in Meta-IV are modelled as mathematical entities. Based on this observation this paper suggests a simple way of combining CSP with the applicative parts of Meta-IV. The combination is suitable for writing designs for programs which embodies concurrency and also operate on complicated datastructures. A large class of non-trivial designs expressed in this notation are easily transformed into functional prototypes written in Ada. Used as a Program Design Language (PDL) the suggested notation is thus particularly interesting for Ada system designers.

1 INTRODUCTION

The ability to write down designs of large software systems is mandatory to the successful implementation of such systems. A written down design is useful as a starting point for discussions and should form the basis for prototyping critical parts. Meta-IV (Bjørner & Jones (1978)) and CSP (Hoare (1985)) have both proved to be valuable for capturing different design aspects of a system (Oest & Bjørner (1980), Clemmensen & Oest (1984), George & Grosvenor (1986)). While Meta-IV easily describes complicated data structures and operations on these, models of the concurrent behaviour of a system can be expressed using CSP. This paper suggests a way of combining the applicative parts of Meta-IV with CSP. The notation so formed allows writing down designs of large systems which involve both operations on complicated data structures and exhibit concurrency.

The main idea behind the combination is that CSP makes no assumptions on the objects being communicated among processes in a CSP model. These objects can thus be datastructures, which in Meta-IV are modelled as mathematical entities. The work and the ideas described in this paper have been influenced by Folkjær & Bjørner (1980) and Palm & Pedersen (1986). But while a total integration of CSP and Meta-IV both syntactically and semantically is attempted in Folkjær & Bjørner (1980), no such integration is made for the combination suggested here. There is no reason, however, to believe that such an integration is not possible, except for the fact that providing a semantic foundation for a notation of this kind will always be difficult and be a big task. If the concept 'Program Design Language' or 'PDL' signifies that a semantic foundation is guaranteed, the CSP/Meta-IV combination described in this paper should rather be denoted a notation for program design.

Functional prototypes of models written in CSP/Meta-IV is the second issue of this paper. A small but powerful subset of the constructs used in CSP process models is chosen. Rules are given for transforming each of these into

Ada tasking constructs. The technique described in Heerfordt & Villadsen (1987) for turning Meta-IV models into prototypes written in Ada is used together with the CSP construct transformations. In this way a large class of non-trivial designs written in the CSP/Meta-IV combination can be transformed directly into Ada prototypes. A prototype constructed in this way will exhibit a behaviour similar to that of its model. Naturally, the speed with which the prototype executes cannot be gauranteed.

Following this introduction chapter 2 describes how CSP and Meta-IV are combined. Chapter 3 explains how prototypes are derived. A specification of a simple airline reservation system is introduced in the opening paragraphs of Chapter 2. This reservation system is used throughout the paper for the purpose of illustrating ideas, and concepts being described. The reader is assumed to have fundamental knowledge of Ada tasking, CSP, and Meta-IV.

2 COMBINING CSP AND Meta-IV

Consider a simplified airline reservation system, which is specified to have the following characteristics:

- The system includes a centralised database, which contains departure and booking information. This database is handled by a database server.
- A remote controller serves two terminals used for entering reservations. The controller is connected to the database server through a single wire.
- The database is updated with respect to information about new departures or changes to already scheduled ones from a terminal connected directly to the database server.

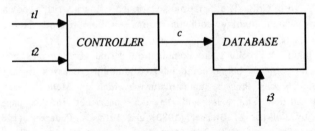

$$\alpha t1 \text{ } CONTROLLER = \alpha t2 \text{ } CONTROLLER = \alpha c \text{ } CONTROLLER = \{reservation\}$$
$$CONTROLLER = t1?x \rightarrow c!x \rightarrow CONTROLLER \text{ } [\![t2?x \rightarrow c!x \rightarrow CONTROLLER$$
$$\alpha c \text{ } DATABASE = \{reservation\}$$
$$\alpha t3 \text{ } DATABASE = \{departure\}$$
$$DATABASE = c?x \rightarrow DATABASE \text{ } [\![t3?y \rightarrow DATABASE$$
$$RESERVATION\_SYSTEM = CONTROLLER \text{ } \| \text{ } DATABASE$$

Figure 1. CSP model of a simplified airline reservation system.

A model of this system is easily described using CSP (fig. 1). We restrict our use of CSP to the parts dealing with communication. This implies that processes communicate through channels. By convention channnels are used for communication in only one direction and between only two processes. The airline reservation system consists of two processes running in parallel. One process (*DATABASE*) takes care of the database, the other (*CONTROLLER*) serves the remote terminals. These terminals are connected to the controller through the channels *t1* and *t2* . The fact that reservations (and only reservations) can be made from these terminals is reflected in what is called the alphabet associated with the channels. The alphabet associated with a channel is the set of messages that a process using that channel may output or input from it. It is required that the alphabet associated with the output end of a channel is the same as the alphabet associated with the input end of that channel. The alphabets associated with *t1* and *t2* ($\alpha t1_{CONTROLLER}$ and $\alpha t2_{CONTROLLER}$) contain only one legal message: *reservation* . The exchange of information which this implies will be explained shortly. The controller is connected to the database server through a single channel *c*. Only the message *reservation* can be communicated on this channel ($\alpha c_{CONTROLLER}$ = $\alpha c_{DATABASE}$ = {*reservation*}). The terminal used for scheduling departures is connected through channel *t3*. Only messages of the kind *departure* can be entered via this terminal since $\alpha t3_{DATABASE}$ = {*departure* }.

The process *CONTROLLER* is initially ready to accept a request for a reservation entered either through *t1* or *t2*. But when a request has been accepted from one or the other terminal, no further requests will be served until the one made first has been output on channel *c* and accepted at the database server end. The database server process: *DATABASE* will accept a request for a reservation input via channel *c*, or an update of the departure information input via channel *t3*.

The model reflects the fact that only one terminal at a time is allowed to get access to the database. Whether this is a satisfactory solution is irrelevant in this context. Note that the model in fig. 1 does not take the actual updates of the database with respect to departure and reservation information into account. This issue is dealt with next.

The specification of the reservation system is now extented with the following requirements:

- A person is only allowed to book one seat on a particular flight. He can, however, make reservations on as many different flights as he pleases.
- New departures can be added freely, but when one kind of aircraft is substituted for another on a particular departure, there must be at least as many seats available on the new aircraft as the number of reservations made for that departure beforehand.
- Overbooking is allowed. Reservations can be made for 20 more seats than are actually available on a particular departure.

This part of the specification is not easily modelled in CSP. Meta-IV however offers a suitable way of expressing such requirements. First an abstaction of the database is established. This is done by means of socalled Meta-IV domain equations (fig. 2).

$$
\begin{aligned}
TICKET\_BASE &= FLIGHT\_NO \xrightarrow{m} FLIGHT\_REC \\
FLIGHT\_REC &:: NO\_OF\_SEATS \ NAME\text{-}\underline{set} \\
FLIGHT\_NO &= \underline{TOKEN} \\
NO\_OF\_SEATS &= \underline{N_1} \\
NAME &= \underline{TOKEN} \\
\underline{inv}\text{-}TICKET\_BASE \ (tb) &\overset{\Delta}{=} (\forall \ r \ \in \ \underline{rng} \ tb) \\
&\qquad (\ \underline{let} \ \underline{mk}\text{-}FLIGHT\_REC \ (nos, nas) = r \ \underline{in} \\
&\qquad\qquad \underline{card} \ nas \leq nos + 20 \ ) \\
\underline{type}: TICKET\_BASE &\rightarrow \underline{BOOL} \\
\\
RESERVATION &:: FLIGHT\_NO \ NAME \\
DEPARTURE &:: FLIGHT\_NO \ NO\_OF\_SEATS
\end{aligned}
$$

Figure 2. Meta-IV definition of the reservation system database

The database is modelled as a mapping from flight numbers to Meta-IV trees having two components. The first component is a positive integer, specifying the maximum number of seats available on the aircraft associated with the departure. The second component is a set of names, one name for each passenger who has booked a seat on the plane. How passenger names and flight numbers will eventually be represented is of no interest at the current stage of the design. Both are specified as *TOKEN*. This means that a person can be identified uniquely, and thus different persons may be distinguised from each other. Similarly for flight numbers. The requirement that a person can only book one seat on a particular flight is enforced by modelling the passenger list associated with a departure as a set of names. Since each element of a set appears only once in that set, any attempt by a passenger to reserve two seats on the same flight will be in vain.

For a database of the kind *TICKET_BASE* to be legal, the function inv-*TICKET_BASE* must hold true. This function reflects the specification of allowed overbooking. It states that for any departure in the database, the number of persons on the passenger list ($\underline{card}(nas)$) must not exceed the number of seats available on the plane by more than 20.

Finally, it is stated what information is needed in order to make a reservation or add or modify a departure. In both cases the model is a Meta-IV tree having two components, where the first component identifies the departure by means of the flight number. *RESERVATION* has the passenger's name as the second component, while the maximum number of seats available is the second component of *DEPARTURE*.

Having defined the database to be an object of the type *TICKET_BASE* it is now possible to state the operations we allow on this database, and the prerequisites that must hold for such operations to be legal. Again Meta-IV offers suitable means for doing this.

make_reservation (*r, tb*) $\triangle$ let   mk-*RESERVATION* (*fno, na*) = *r*,
                                                          mk-*FLIGHT_REC* (*nos, nas*) = *tb* (*fno*) in
                                                          (*tb* + [*fno* → mk-*FLIGHT_REC*(*nos, nas* ∪ {*na* })]])
type: *RESERVATION TICKET_BASE → TICKET_BASE*

pre-*make_reservation* (*r, tb*) $\triangle$ let   mk-*RESERVATION* (*fno, na*) = *r* in
                                                          (if *fno* ∈ dom *tb* then
                                                                    let mk-*FLIGHT_REC* (*nos, nas*) = *tb* (*fno*) in
                                                                    (card *nas* < *nos* + 20)
                                                          else false)

add_departure (*d, tb*) $\triangle$ let   mk-*DEPARTURE* (*fno, nos*) = *d* in
                                                     (if *fno* ∈ dom *tb* then
                                                               let mk-*FLIGHT_REC* (*nos1, nas*) = *tb* (*fno*) in
                                                               (*tb* + [*fno* → mk-*FLIGHT_REC* (*nos, nas*)])
                                                     else
                                                               (*tb* + [*fno* → mk-*FLIGHT_REC* (*nos,* {})]))
type: *DEPARTURE TICKET_BASE → TICKET_BASE*

pre-*add_departure* (*d, tb*) $\triangle$ let   mk-*DEPARTURE* (*fno, nos*) = *d* in
                                                          (if *fno* ∉ dom *tb* then
                                                                    true
                                                          else
                                                                    let mk-*FLIGHT_REC* (*nos1, nas*) = *tb* (*fno*) in
                                                          (*nos* ≥ card*nas*))

Figure 3. Meta-IV definition of *TICKET_BASE* operations.

Two operations are defined in fig. 3: *make_reservation* and *add_departure*. The latter is used not only for adding new departures but also for modifying already scheduled ones. The definition of each operation consists of three parts:
- a definition of the impact of the operation on the ticket base,
- an indication of the type of the operation, stating the types of the parameters to the operation and the type of the result. This type indication is made with reference to the *TICKET_BASE* definition of fig. 2,
- a predicate function, stating the conditions which must be fulfilled, for the operation to be legal.

The details of *make_reservation* and *add_departure* will not be explained here, they are fairly obvious from the Meta-IV definition. Note, however, that the requirement related to the change of aircraft for an already scheduled departure is reflected in the predicate function pre-*add_departure*.

2.1   Parameterisation of CSP process descriptions

So far, we have seen how concurrent aspects of a system are modelled using CSP, while characteristic data structures of the same system and operations on these structures are modelled using Meta-IV. The question is: How do the two descriptions fit together? In order to answer the question, we need the notion of a parameterised process. C.A.R. Hoare defines in his book on CSP (Hoare (1985)) a process named *UNPACK*. Its definition is repeated in fig. 4.

$$\alpha left = \{s \mid s \in \alpha right \ast \wedge \#s = 80\}$$
$$UNPACK = P_{<>}$$

$$P_{<>} = left?s \rightarrow P_s \quad \text{where}$$
$$P_{<x>} = right!x \rightarrow P_{<>} \quad \text{and}$$
$$P_{<x>\wedge s} = right!x \rightarrow P_s$$

Figure 4. Hoare's CSP model of *UNPACK*.

UNPACK inputs a sequence of 80 characters from its left channel and outputs the characters again one by one on the right channel. Note how the process description given by Hoare depends on the interpretation of the suffixes:

      $<>$ (the empty sequence),

      $<x>$ (the sequence containing only one element: x),

      $<x>\wedge s$ (the sequence having x as its first element and s as its tail).

In essence these suffixes constitute what is known as a parameterisation of the process description. With a slight change in syntax this parameterisation can be made more explicit. This is done in fig. 5. The definition utilises Hoare's own notation: s_0 and s', meaning the first element of the sequence s and s with its first element removed (the tail) respectively.

$$\alpha left = \{s \mid s \in \alpha right \ast \wedge \#s = 80\}$$
$$UNPACK = P (<>)$$
$$P (s) = \text{if } s = <> \text{ then}$$
$$left?t \rightarrow P (t)$$
$$\text{else}$$
$$right!s_0 \rightarrow P (s')$$

Figure 5. Parameterised CSP model of *UNPACK*.

The if-then-else construct is only one of many constructs which can be used when describing parameterised processes. The readers are referred to Jørgensen, J. et al. (1988) for a fuller treatment of this issue. All that should be noted here is that the simple construct of fig. 5 is powerful enough for describing a large class of non-trivial parameterised processes.

2.2   Adding   Meta-IV

The parameterisation shown in fig. 5 depends on a datastructure known as a sequence. It also depends on certain operations on sequences, such as counting the number of elements in a sequence, or removing the first element.   One of the virtues of Meta-IV is its ability to express exactly such datastructures and operations. Not only sequences but much more complex datastructures (like *TICKET_BASE* defined in fig. 2) are easily   described using Meta-IV. A natural way of embedding Meta-IV into CSP would therefore be to use Meta-IV for expressing the parts of a process description that deal with the parameterisation. Furthermore the alphabets (the messages communicated on channels) are adequately described using Meta-IV domain equations. This scheme is adopted in the definition of *UNPACK* shown in fig. 6.

$$CARD = CHAR^*$$

$$CHAR = \underline{TOKEN}$$

$$\alpha left = CARD$$

$$\alpha right = CHAR \qquad UNPACK = P(\langle\rangle)$$

$$\beta P = CARD \qquad P(s) = \underline{if}\ s = \langle\rangle\ \underline{then}$$

$$left?t \rightarrow P(t)$$

$$\underline{inv}\text{-}\alpha left\ (s)\ \triangle\ \underline{len}\ s = 80 \qquad \underline{else}$$

$$\underline{type}:\ \alpha left \rightarrow \underline{BOOL} \qquad right!\ \underline{hd}s \rightarrow P(\underline{tl}s)$$

Figure 6. *UNPACK* defined using CSP/Meta-IV.

The CSP notation for the first element s_0 of a sequence s corresponds to $\underline{hd}s$ in Meta-IV. Similarly, s' in CSP is equivalent to $\underline{tl}s$ in Meta-IV. One piece of new notation unfamiliar to both CSP and Meta-IV has been introduced: $\beta PROCESS$ (pronounced "type of PROCESS' parameter"). $\beta PROCESS$ denotes the type of the parameter to the process named *PROCESS*.

The benefit of introducing Meta-IV in the definition of *UNPACK* is not obvious. The expressive power of the CSP/Meta-IV combination becomes apparent, however, when the datastructures under consideration are more complicated. Fitting together the two models associated with the airline reservation system nicely illustrates how the combination works. With reference to fig. 2 and fig. 3, the CSP model in fig. 1 is replaced by the parameterised model in fig. 7.

The messages that can be communicated on channels $t1$, $t2$, and c are Meta-IV trees of the type *RESERVATION* defined in fig. 2. The Meta-IV tree type is very similar to the Ada record type. Similarly, trees of the type *DEPARTURE* are communicated on $t3$. The process *CONTROLLER* is not parameterised. *DATABASE*, however, behaves like *DB*, parameterised with respect to an empty ticket base. Finally, the process *RESERVATION_SYSTEM* behaves like *CONTROLLER* running in parallel with *DATABASE*.

The combination of CSP with Meta-IV implies in summary that the overall system behaviour is modelled using CSP processes. The alphabets of the

$$\alpha t1_{CONTROLLER} \ = \ \alpha t2_{CONTROLLER} \quad = RESERVATION$$
$$\alpha c_{CONTROLLER} \ = \ \alpha c_{DB} \qquad\qquad =RESERVATION$$
$$\alpha t3_{\ DB} \ = \ DEPARTURE$$
$$\beta DB \quad = \ TICKET\_BASE$$

$$CONTROLLER \ = \ t1?x \to c!x \to CONTROLLER \quad \| \ t2?x \to c!x \to CONTROLLER$$
$$DATABASE \quad = \ DB \ (\, [] \,)$$
$$DB \ (tb\,) \ = \ c?x \to \ \underline{if} \ \underline{pre}\text{-}make\_reservation \ (x, tb\ ) \ \underline{then}$$
$$DB \ (make\_reservation \ (x, tb\,))$$
$$\underline{else} \ DB \ (tb\,) \ \|$$
$$t3?y \ \to \ \underline{if} \ \underline{pre}\text{-}add\_departure \ (y, tb\ ) \ \underline{then}$$
$$DB \ (add\_departure \ (y, tb\,))$$
$$\underline{else} \ DB \ (tb\,)$$
$$RESERVATION\_SYSTEM \ = CONTROLLER \ \| \, DATABASE$$

Figure 7. CSP/Meta-IV model of the airline reservation system. Figures 2, and 3 are also part of the model.

processes are defined using Meta-IV domain equations. The CSP processes are, where necessary, parameterised with data structures relevant for describing the internal behaviour of the process under consideration. These data structures and operations on them needed in the process description are also described using Meta-IV.

```
generic
  type ELEMENT_TYPE is private;
  ...
package SET_PACKAGE is

  type SET is private;

  function IS_MEMBER ( E : ELEMENT_TYPE; S : SET) return BOOLEAN;
  function IS_EQUAL (S1, S2 : SET) return BOOLEAN;
  function IS_SUBSET (S1, S2 :  SET) return BOOLEAN;
  function IS_TRUE_SUBSET (S1, S2 : SET) return BOOLEAN;
  function CARD (S : SET) return NATURAL;

  -- Constructing sets
  function EMPTY_SET return SET;
  function SINGLETON_SET ( E : ELEMENT_TYPE ) return SET;
  function "+"  (S1,  S2 : SET)  return SET; -- set union
  function "*"  (S1,  S2 : SET)  return SET; -- set intersection
  function "-"  (S1,  S2 : SET)  return SET; -- set difference

  -- Traversing sets
  procedure INIT_SCAN (S : in out SET);
  procedure NEXT_ELEMENT (S : in out SET; E : out ELEMENT_TYPE);
  function MORE_ELEMENTS (S : SET) return BOOLEAN;

private
  ...
end SET_PACKAGE;
```

Figure 8. Generic Ada package implementing the Meta-IV set data type.

3 PROTOTYPING MODELS WRITTEN IN CSP/Meta-IV

Designs written in the CSP/Meta-IV combination proposed in the last chapter can easily be turned into prototypes written in Ada. This is fortunate for the system designer, who intends to use Ada for implementing the system. First of all, it is easier to use one and the same language for prototyping and for implementation. Secondly, parts of the prototype may be reused.

3.1 Prototyping Meta-IV models in Ada

A Prototype of *TICKET_BASE* (fig. 2) and the operations defined in fig. 3 is easily obtained using the generic packages described in Heerfordt & Villadsen (1987). These packages implement the more common Meta-IV data types. An outline of the package implementing the set data type is shown in fig. 8. Instantiating this package with an Ada type makes it possible to build sets of objects of that type and to manipulate such sets in the usual manner.

Maps from one type of objects to another can be built and manipulated by proper instantiation of the generic package outlined in fig. 9. Note that before the package can be instantiated, SET_PACKAGE must be instantiated twice: once for the domain type and once for the type of the map range. This is necessary due to the functions DOM, RNG, RESTRICT, and COMPLEMENT_RESTRICT defined within MAP_PACKAGE. These functions need for their definitions the two sets mentioned above.

```
generic
  type DOMAIN_TYPE is private;
  type RANGE_TYPE is private;
  type DOMAIN_SET_TYPE is private;
  type RANGE_SET_TYPE is private;
  ...
package MAP_PACKAGE is

  type MAP is private;

  function DOM ( M : MAP) return DOMAIN_SET_TYPE;
  function RNG ( M : MAP) return RANGE_SET_TYPE;
  function IS_EQUAL ( M1, M2 : MAP)  return BOOLEAN;
  function APPLY ( D : DOMAIN_TYPE; M : MAP) return RANGE_TYPE;

  -- Constructing maps
  function EMPTY_MAP return MAP;
  function SINGLETON_MAP(D : DOMAIN_TYPE; R : RANGE_TYPE) return MAP;
  function MERGE (M1, M2 : MAP) return MAP;
  function "+" (M1, M2 : MAP) return MAP;  -- overwrite merge
  function RESTRICT ( M : MAP; D : DOMAIN_SET_TYPE) return MAP;
  function COMPLEMENT_RESTRICT ( M : MAP; D : DOMAIN_SET_TYPE) return MAP;

private
  ...
end MAP_PACKAGE;
```

Figure 9. Generic Ada package implementing the Meta-IV map data type.

Implementing *TICKET_BASE* defined in fig. 2 is now straight forward (fig. 10) using these packages. Note that the order in which the types are introduced is changed from that of fig. 2 in order to satisfy Ada's visibility rules. The package does not need a body.

```
with SET_PACKAGE;
with MAP_PACKAGE;

package TICKET_BASE_DEFINITION is

    subtype NAME is CHARACTER;     --dummy implementation of TOKEN
    subtype FLIGHT_NO is NATURAL;  --dummy implementation of TOKEN
    subtype NO_OF_SEATS is POSITIVE;

    package NAME_SET is new SET_PACKAGE (NAME,...);
                         -- see Heerfordt & Villadsen (1987) for explanation of "..."
    type FLIGHT_RECORD is
      record
        SEATS : NO_OF_SEATS;
        NAMES : NAME_SET.SET;
      end record;

    package FLIGHT_NO_SET is new SET_PACKAGE (FLIGHT_NO,...);   --Needed by MAP_PACKAGE
    package FLIGHT_RECORD_SET is new SET_PACKAGE (FLIGHT_RECORD,...); -- same as above

    package TICKET_BASE is new MAP_PACKAGE (FLIGHT_NO,   FLIGHT_RECORD,
        FLIGHT_NO_SET.SET,   FLIGHT_RECORD_SET.SET,...);

    type RESERVATION is
      record
        FLIGHT : FLIGHT_NO;
        PERSON : NAME;
      end record;

    type DEPARTURE is
      record
        FLIGHT : FLIGHT_NO;
        SEATS : NO_OF_SEATS;
      end record;

end TICKET_BASE_DEFINITION;
```

Figure 10. Ada prototype of *TICKET_BASE* defined in fig. 2.

The package TICKET_BASE_DEFINITION makes available all the datastructures and operations needed for implementing the operations defined in fig. 3 directly. As an example, the implementation of pre-*MAKE_RESERVATION* is given in fig. 11. Note the close similarity of the Meta-IV definition and the Ada prototype.

```
-- 'WITH TICKET_BASE_DEFINITION' and 'USE TICKET_BASE_DEFINITION' assumed
function PRE_MAKE_RESERVATION (R : RESERVATION; TB : TICKET_BASE.MAP)
                                                    return BOOLEAN is
   FR : FLIGHT_RECORD;
begin
   if FLIGHT_NO_SET.IS_MEMBER (R.FLIGHT, TICKET_BASE.DOM(TB)) then
     FR : = TICKET_BASE.APPLY (R.FLIGHT, TB);
     return NAME_SET. CARD(FR.NAMES) < FR.SEATS + 20;
   else
     return FALSE;
   end if;
end PRE_MAKE_RESERVATION;
```

Figure 11. Ada prototype of pre-*make_departure* defined in fig. 3.

3.2   Prototyping CSP models in Ada

As mentioned earlier, Ada implementations are attempted only for a few selected CSP constructs. These constructs and an outline of the rules used for implementing them in Ada are listed below.

- A process is implemented as an Ada task.
- Each input channel of a process is implemented as an entry of the corresponding task. The entry has one input parameter of a type determined by the alphabet associated with the input channel.
- Parallel composition of processes, such as *CONTROLLER∥DATABASE* is implemented by declaring the associated tasks within the same Ada package.

The three rules given above is enough for deriving a specification of an Ada package (fig. 12) implementing the reservation system defined in fig. 7. The rules needed for deriving the associated body are outline below.

```
with TICKET_BASE_DEFINITION; use TICKET_BASE_DEFINITION;
package RESERVATION_SYSTEM is

   task DB is
     entry C (R :  in RESERVATION);
     entry T3 (D : in DEPARTURE);
   end DB;

   task CONTROLLER is
     entry T1 (R : in RESERVATION);
     entry T2 (R : in RESERVATION);
   end CONTROLLER;

end RESERVATION_SYSTEM;
```

Figure 12. Specification of package implementing
              the   airline reservation system.

- A sequence of input and output commands $(c1... \to c2... \to ... cn... \to ...)$ is implemented as a sequence of Ada entry calls and accept statements.
- An output command $(... \to c!... \to ...)$ is implemented as an entry call, placed properly in the sequence of other entry calls and accept statements.

```
package body RESERVATION_SYSTEM is

  function MAKE_RESERVATION (R : RESERVATION; TB : TICKET_BASE.MAP)
                                    return TICKET_BASE.MAP is separate;
  function PRE_MAKE_RESERVATION (R : RESERVATION; TB : TICKET_BASE.MAP)
                                    return BOOLEAN is separate;
  function ADD_DEPARTURE (D : DEPARTURE; TB : TICKET_BASE.MAP)
                                    return TICKET_BASE.MAP is separate;
  function PRE_ADD_DEPARTURE (D : DEPARTURE; TB : TICKET_BASE.MAP)
                                    return BOOLEAN is separate;
  task body DB is
    TB : TICKET_BASE.MAP := TICKET_BASE.EMPTY_MAP;
  begin
    loop
      select
        accept C (R : in RESERVATION) do
          if PRE_MAKE_RESERVATION (R, TB) then
            TB := MAKE_RESERVATION (R, TB);
          end if;
        end C;
      or
        accept T3 (D : in DEPARTURE) do
          if PRE_ADD_DEPARTURE (D, TB) then
            TB := ADD_DEPARTURE (D,TB);
          end if;
        end T3;
      end select;
    end loop;
  end DB;

  task body CONTROLLER is
  begin
    loop
      select
        accept T1 (R : RESERVATION) do
          DB.C (R);
        end T1;
      or
        accept T2 (R : RESERVATION) do
          DB.C (R);
        end T2;
      end select;
    end loop;
  end CONTROLLER;

end RESERVATION_SYSTEM;
```

Figure 13. Body of package implementing the airline reservation system.

- An input command (... → $c?$... → ...) is implemented as an accept statement also placed properly in the sequence of other entry calls and accept statements.
- A recursive process definitions, such as $P = (... → P)$ is implemented by an Ada loop around the sequence of accept statements and entry calls guarding the recursion. Most recursive process definitions of interest can be implemented in this way.

- The general choice $(c1?... \to P1) \; \square \; (c2?... \to P2) \; \square ... \square \; (cn?... \to Pn)$ is implemented as an Ada selective wait statement. This implementation can only be used when the guards participating in the choice are all input commands (implemented as accepts statements). If a mixture of input and output commands appears like in $(d1!v \to P) \; \square \; (d2?x \to P)$ the simple implementation by means of a selective wait cannot be used. A full discussion of this issue together with suggestions for implementations can be found in Welch (1985) and will not be repeated here.
- A possible parameter associated with a process description is implemented as a variable local to the task implementing the process under consideration. The parameter is thus conceived as a task state.
- The if-then-else construct used in parameterisation is simply implemented by an Ada if statement.

Using these rules the body of the package RESERVATION SYSTEM (fig.13) can be derived from the model in fig. 7. The model specifies that the initial value of the parameter of the process *DB* is an empty *TICKET_BASE* map. This is reflected in the initialisation of the state variable TB in task DB. Finally a very simple environment for trying out the system can be set up (fig. 14).

```
with TICKET_BASE_DEFINITION;   use TICKET_BASE_DEFINITION;
with RESERVATION_SYSTEM;   use RESERVATION_SYSTEM;

procedure PROTOTYPE is
begin
    ...
end PROTOTYPE;
```

Figure 14. Simple environment for trying out the reservation system.

Within procedure PROTOTYPE it is possible to call the entries CONTROLLER.T1, CONTROLLER.T2, and DB.T3. This enables trying out the functionality of the reservation system. In terms of the model in fig. 7 it does not make sense to call DB.C from outside the task CONTROLLER. Unfortunately, it is possible to call the entry from within PROTOTYPE. Such unmeant entry calls may in the general case lead to deadlocks and must be avoided.

4 CONCLUSION AND FUTURE WORK

A notation for writing designs of concurrent programs has been proposed. The notation combines CSP and Meta-IV in a way that allows concurrency as well as operations on complicated datastructures to be modelled. The notation is of particular value for designs which will eventually be implemented in Ada. The reason is that a large class of designs written in the CSP/Meta-IV combination can be turned into functional prototypes written in

Ada by means of simple transformations. This opens for reuse of parts of the prototype in the final implementation. A number of areas for future work can be identified:

- A large part of the prototype derivation process may be automated. The extent to which this is possible has not been investigated yet.
- For models written entirely in Meta-IV, Heerfordt & Villadsen (1987) describes possible ways of deriving final implementations from a prototype. The idea is that an efficient implementation of the Meta-IV set data type can be obtained under circumstances where an ordering can be devised for the set of data under consideration. A similar technique might be applicable to the CSP/Meta-IV combination. This has not yet been investigated
- Syntactic integration with semantic underpinning of the CSP/Meta-IV combination is an obvious but difficult future task.

5 ACKNOWLEDGEMENTS

The author wishes to thank the employees of Dansk Datamatik Center and DDC-International A/S for many valuable comments. Special thanks go to Klaus Havelund, Steen Ulrik Palm, and Claus Bendix Nielsen, all Dansk Datamatik Center, and Peter Villadsen, DDC-International for clarifying discussions.

6 REFERENCES

Bjørner, D. & Jones, C.B. (eds.)(1978): The Vienna Development Method: The Meta-Language. Springer Verlag, Lecture Notes in Computer Science, Vol. 61.

Clemmensen, G.B. & Oest, O. (1984): Formal Specification and Development of an Ada Compiler - A VDM Case Study. In Proceedings 7th International Conference on Software Engineering, March 26-29, Orlando, Florida.

Folkjær, P. & Bjørner, D. (1980): A Formal Model of a Generalized CSP-like Language. In IFIP 8th World Computer Conference Proceedings, Amsterdam: North-Holland Publ. Co.

George, C.W. & Grosvenor, D.A. (1986): Development of the alternating bit protocol. STC Technology LTD, Harlow, RAISE/STC/CWG/9/v3

Heerfordt, H.M. & Villadsen, P.(1987): A Set of Ada Packages Supporting the use of VDM for Ada Program Development. In Proceedings of 6th Ada UK Conference, York, 7th to 9th January.

Hoare, C.A.R. (1985): Communicating Sequential Processes. Prentice-Hall International.

Jørgensen, J. et al. (1988): Preliminary Definition of the RAISE Specification Language. Dansk Datamatik Center, København, RAISE/DDC/JJ/14/v6.

Oest, O.N. & Bjørner, D. (eds.)(1980): Towards a Formal Description of Ada. Springer Verlag, Lecture Notes in Computer Science, Vol. 98.

Palm, S.U. & Pedersen, T.N. (1986): Applicative RAISE Language Constructs related to Concurrency. Copenhagen: Dansk Datamatik Center, RAISE/DDC/SUP/10.

Welch, P.H.(1985): Structured Tasking in Ada? In ACM Ada Letters, vol. V, nr.1, J July - August.

Welch, P.H.(1986): A Structured Technique for Concurrent Systems Design in Ada.In proceedings of the Ada-Europe International Conference, Edinburg 6-8 May.

Part 5 Tailoring the Ada Environment

AdLog : an Ada components set to add logic to Ada

Gilles PITETTE
CR2A
19, avenue Dubonnet
92411 COURBEVOIE CEDEX
FRANCE
phone : 33 1 47 68 97 97

Abstract: Many applications, that would otherwise be liable to be coded in Ada, exhibit features that outstretch the capabilities of imperative languages. To overcome this problem, AdLog offers a deductive kernel which can be used in any Ada application. AdLog's principles and results are presented here, as well as information on its coding in Ada and on future developments. A few portability experiments are also discussed.

1 SYSTEMS THAT NEED A MIXED STYLE

Although initially targeted toward embedded systems, Ada was designed and is now promoted as a universal language, as evidenced by the wide variety of application for which the use of Ada is being contemplated, or even required.

In spite of the great progress made in software engineering, only the problems which can be solved using algorithms are presently suitable for direct and natural processing by the techniques offered by imperative languages, of which Ada is the most recent example. But due to the increasing complexity of the tasks performed by software, more and more systems locally feature characteristics for which these conventional languages lack satisfactory mechanisms.

For instance, some of their functions process possibly incomplete data, or follow strategies that may be altered during program execution. Such characteristics can be found in functions performing situation recognitions, diagnoses or choices of strategy. More generally, the description and evolving nature of a large number of processes are better expressed using a declarative style than a purely imperative style. Such situations arise in fields as diverse as *embedded systems*, *robotics* or *software engineering,* Ada's prime targets.

Thus, large systems, intended to be coded using imperative languages because most of their functionalities are conventional, can include modules (often quite isolated) requiring better-fitted description techniques. As an example in the field of software engineering tools for Ada, [Ledoux & Parker 85, Buhr et al.85, Hendler & Wong 87, Dobbins et al. 87] describe Ada systems using non-imperative techniques locally .

Among these techniques, *deductive descriptions* are very well suited to code such modules, thanks to their expressive power and dynamic features.

Implementing by means of imperative languages, such as Ada, processes expressed deductively is quite delicate. Indeed, since they cannot be described by pure algorithms, a problem representation and a problem-solving strategy must be developed and then simulated in Ada.

Indeed, for efficiency reasons, the specifics of the problem and the strategy used to solve it will often be hard coded in the program, without the support of an adequate language. In other words, implementations of the problem-solving mechanism and of the description of the problems processed will be tightly intertwined, making it impossible to sort out what is output by which. Accordingly, the implemented knowledge base will not be modified easily, although an open-ended structure, both static and dynamic, is one of the most important requirements in this type of functions.

Coding in Ada modules that deal with problems not expressible naturally into algorithms thus requires developments that are each time specific, costly, and often cumbersome. As a consequence, those developments are seldom reusable in other applications, even in different versions of the same application.

2 AN INFERENCE ENGINE IN THE ADA WORLD

The purpose of AdLog is to provide a portable standard deductive kernel that can be used by any Ada application perform computations expressed deductively. Such computations will be described in isolated components called *deductive bubbles*.

In order to avoid the problems mentioned above, AdLog applies a principle widely accepted in the world of artificial intelligence : separating the knowledge base (containing the facts and rules that guide deductive processes) from the inference mechanism. This promotes both the modifiability of the declarative expression of an application deductive parts, and the reusability of the problem-solving mechanism in other applications. This approach requires :

- the definition of an external language needed to describe the deductive processes,
- the availabilty of an engine linked to this language and capable of performing the deductions.

Accordingly, using a knowledge base in an Ada application consist in declarating data (knowledge) that can be dynamically exploited and enriched through an inference engine. AdLog is thus made up of two series of components entirely coded in Ada :

- a *compiler* which transforms the declaration of the knowledge expressed using the defined formalism into an Ada form which can be inserted in the application ;

- a *run-time executive* containing, on the one hand, the inference engine, and the primitives used to manipulate and query the obtained data base.

3 ADLOG'S MAIN CHOICES

Many works were conducted to find ways in which to mix deductive and imperative styles within the same system. These works used two different approaches :

- developing software interfaces between a deductive language and a conventional imperative language. Most often, these interfaces offer a two-way communication, but in non-standard fashion and based on very low level implementation characteristics of both languages (data representation, call stack management, and so forth) ;

- developing a deductive language either on top of, or with, an imperative language. This approach is widely used above Lisp. It was recently explored with Modula-2 [Muller 86] and Ada [Attali & Franchi 87, Ice et al. 87]. It provides for a more natural interface between the two languages since the terms submitted to deductive evaluation become objects of the imperative language used.

The contexts and the objectives of these systems are varied and the best way to explain what makes the specificity of AdLog consists in describing the principles which guided its development. These principles flow directly from its initial functional positioning :

to provide Ada applications with the services of a standard deductive language.

A deductive standard : Prolog, and nothing but Prolog

The first issue raised by the AdLog approach is choosing the language in which to express the deductive bubbles.

The world of artificial intelligence seems to suffer from a cruel lack of application portability caused by the sheer number of languages or dialects offered by the available development tools. The few artificial intelligence tools existing in the Ada environment reflect this diversity, even though they often do make reference to Prolog.

For example, [Attali & Franchi 87] proposes an Ada package kit built around a tree rewriting component. It can be used to build different inference engines by changing the components implementing the various strategies used by the resolution (resolution tree traversal, clause choice, and so on). Accordingly, *interpreters* can be built with this tool for several different deductive languages. Also, if communication mechanisms from Prolog to Ada are included, they imply the static typing of the Prolog terms handled.

Likewise, [Ice et al. 87] proposes an expert system shell featuring a Prolog-based language but with several changes and extensions, both in terms of syntax and semantics.

Beyond the portability problem, the diversity of deductive languages raises other issues :

- each language requires a minimum development environment that fits it (tools for coding, debugging, analysis, etc.) ;
- the knowledge bases used by mixed applications must be validated (certified ?) just like the more conventional parts. Validation techniques adapted to each deductive language or dialect must therefore be developed. This aspect becomes particularly important when the applications using this technology are very sensitive.

AdLog did not opt for defining yet another deductive dialect. On the contrary, AdLog rests on a language which, thanks to its wide dissemination throughout the academic and industrial world, appears today as the only possible standard in the field of deductive programming : Prolog. Furthermore, this choice makes it possible to reuse all the works conducted around Prolog, whatever the domain.

Finally, since this approach considers Prolog a standard, introducing extensions or variants which would make the language processed by AdLog yet another dialect of Prolog is thus prohibited.

Until work on standardization presently under way at AFNOR, BSI and ISO is completed, the so-called Edinburgh Prolog [Clocksin & Mellish 84] is used by AdLog as the reference for syntax and semantics.

An AdLog application : Ada components only

The inference engine provided by AdLog is encapsulated in 100% Ada-written components. It is used by Ada applications as a run-time, along the same lines as the primitives supplied by the standard input/output packages (TEXT_IO, etc). The Prolog clauses, contained in the deductive bubbles, are merely the external declarative form of data guiding the deductions which are carried out. Thus, the operations supplied by the run-time package process them somewhat in the same way as the primitives PUT and GET process data from external files.

The clauses are transformed beforehand by the *compiler* into an Ada form, and then inserted in the using application. *Each deductive bubble thus gives rise to a new Ada package.*
Accordingly, all the components in an AdLog application are Ada components, both with respect to

its imperative part and its deductive part. Viewed in this way, AdLog can be defined simply as a means to *describe Ada components in Prolog*.

Thus, *an Adlog application is fully supported by Ada*. It can be carried and executed on any computer where Ada is installed.

This maximum portability sets AdLog apart from systems that only provide an interface between the implementation of two languages. In these systems, migrating an application from one computer to another requires, on the latter, the availability of Ada and of the same Prolog dialect featuring exactly the same interface mechanisms as on the first computer.

Several deductive bubbles

An AdLog application can use several separate deduction fields, each one described by a different bubble. Each bubble can be thought of as a clause base, sealed and separate from the others. But all the bubbles share the same executive (term management operations, dictionary, inference engine). The Prolog source of a bubble is stored in a separate source file, involving a separate Ada package.

The application, through the executive package, can initiate successive evaluations in different bubbles. To this effect, initiating operations select the bubbles on the basis of the same mechanism as that used by the I/O predefined Ada packages for the files (default bubble).

The production diagram of an AdLog application is shown below :

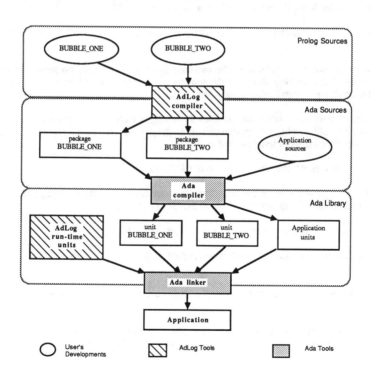

Purely deductive Prolog bubbles

As the scope of Prolog got progressively larger, it became clear that no sizable software could ever be purely deductive, and thus ever be developed in *pure* Prolog, solely on the basis of the mechanisms of deduction. For this reason, and to render Prolog a genuinely usable *programming language, evaluable* predicates have been *pre*defined. These predicates are used to introduce extra-logical side effects (I/O,etc.) inside the logical clauses. Moreover, they represent the least standardized part among all the existing Prolog implementations.

In a software entirely developed in Prolog, the declaration of facts and of logical rules is thus interspersed with programming heavily reliant on Prolog procedural semantics and the use of evaluable predicates.

For the Prolog application developer, the communication capabilities between Prolog and conventional languages represent first and foremost a means to write new evaluable predicates.

The idea underlying the AdLog product is entirely the opposite. AdLog is mainly intended for Ada application developers.

AdLog merely considers Prolog as a means to express deductive computations to be used where an application includes isolated functions difficult to express imperatively in Ada, but not as a programming language per se. An AdLog application is an Ada application that merely utilizes deductive computation services. Accordingly, it needs to be designed and structured like any Ada application, while clearly defining the needs for purely deductive computations. Each language must be used to develop the functions for which it was designed. Here, Prolog is used simply to help Ada in specific functions. It should not be used, for instance, to code I/O.

This approach, at the opposite of that commonly used, determines two characteristics specific to AdLog :

- the privileged communication between the two languages puts *Prolog at the service of Ada and not Ada at the service of Prolog*. Accordingly, the present version of AdLog does not provide any communication facilities from Prolog toward Ada ;

- the number of predefined predicates offered by AdLog is kept down to the minimum reasonably required to carry out symbolic computations (manipulation of terms), arithmetic operations, and pragmatic deductive development (cut, not, call, ...).

No restrictions on the use of Prolog

Certain features specific to Prolog explain the wide variety in the form of Prolog programs (clause bases), and particularly in the ways they can be exploited (queried) :

- *non-determinism* : resolving a goal may generate several solutions ;

- *inversibility* : an argument can be used as an input or an output, depending on the way the predicate is called ;

- *lack of hierarchy* : a clause base has no top and any predicate, whatever its level, can be queried directly,

- *dynamicity* : any clause can be modified at any time, and the same goal may give rise to different resolutions depending on the date it was submitted during the lifetime of the base.

A Prolog program, or part of a program, using none of the properties mentioned above could certainly be better coded using imperative techniques, Ada in this case. Conversely, the need to use deductive techniques, and AdLog, arises precisely when developing the components of an Ada application which naturally require these properties.

Contrary to certain Prolog optimization techniques which tend to make Prolog more and more a programming language [Mellish 85], AdLog pushes aside all the restrictions on the structure of deductive bubbles. A deductive bubble is not a program, taken as a hierarchical structure with only one entry point, but indeed a clause base which can be queried at any level. It provides Ada programs with most of the traditional interactive capabilities between a clause base and its user. But here, the user simply is an Ada program using the procedural interface offered by AdLog to exploit the base.

Efficiency

In order to be preferred over specific developments, even with all their drawbacks, using a standard deductive kernel in Ada applications should generate acceptable levels of performance in the deductions. Accordingly, optimizing efficiency while staying within the bounds of the defined approach became one of AdLog's major objectives. The technical solutions it has adopted were thus guided by this objective, but without challenging the others.

AdLog is not a production environment

The purpose of AdLog is first and foremost to offer standard deductive facilities fit to describe deductive bubbles and the Ada component required to exploit them in an application. Therefore, the tasks specific to the development of deductive sources do not fall within its scope.

For these tasks, the choice of Prolog as a standard deductive language enables developers to use existing specialized development environments [Poplog, BIM_Prolog, Quintus, VM/PROLOG]. These environments provide the tools required to develop Prolog sources under the best conditions (editing, debugging, cross-references, source management, and so on).

The *compiler* included in AdLog stands merely as the static tool required to *introduce* Prolog bubbles in the Ada sources of the application.

4 USING A DEDUCTIVE BUBBLE : AN EXAMPLE

The sole purpose of the example below is to show briefly how a deductive bubble is used in an Ada program. In this respect, it is not entirely typical of AdLog applications. In particular, the Ada part is quite short and only enquires the Prolog bubble in a very simple way.

This bubble manages a knowledge base describing elementary air routes and the relationships defining what a route between two points is. It can be used to search out all the possible itiniraries between two cities, as well as for other questions.

The Prolog routine shown here is from [Clocksin & Mellish 84]. Its coding is not necessarily optimal : it is used for demonstration purposes only.

The "connection" clauses describe the elementary connections. They correspond to a two-way connection between two cities. The other clauses describe the concept of route. Different and dynamically variable definitions of this concept (e.g. introducing distance management, etc.) can be conceived.

Prolog source of the ROUTE deductive bubble

```
/* list reverse */

reverse ([], L, L).
reverse ([X|L], L2, L3) :- reverse (L, [X|L2], L3).

/* list member */

member (X, [X|_]).
member (X, [_,|L]) :- member (X, L).

/* search out all the possible routes between two points */

route (Start, Dest, Route) :-
  route_int (Start, Dest, [], R),
  reverse (R, [], Route).

route_int (Dest, Dest, Route, [Dest|Route]).
route_int (Here, Dest, Route1, Route2) :-
 (connection (Stopover, Here) ; connection (Here, Stopover)),
 not (member (Stopover), Route1)),
  route_int (Stopover, Dest, [Here|Route1], Route2).

/* elementary connections */

connection (brest, lille).
connection (lille, paris).
connection (nancy, paris).
connection (bordeaux, brest).
connection (nancy, lille).
```

From this Prolog source, the AdLog compiler generates an Ada package whose body includes the Ada form of the clauses; its interface only exports a value used by query operations to denote this bubble :

```
with ADLOG;
package ROUTE is
  BUBBLE: constant ADLOG.BUBBLE_TYPE := ADLOG.NEW_BUBBLE;
end ROUTE;
```

Exploiting the knowledge base in Ada

The interface of the run-time (ADLOG package) supplies the type TERM_TYPE

```
type TERM_KIND  is  (COMPOUND_TERM, VAR_TERM, INT_TERM,
FLOAT_TERM) ;
```

```
type TERM_TYPE is (KIND : TERM_KIND := VAR_TERM) is limited private;
```

and the operations which are used to build or analyze Prolog terms. Likewise, it supplies the operations used to initiate and control a resolution.

```
with ADLOG, ROUTE, TEXT_IO;
procedure ROUTE_DEMO is
  use ADLOG;
  ROUTE : TERM_TYPE;                    -- uninstantiated Prolog variable.
begin

  SET_BUBBLE (ROUTE.BUBBLE);

  -- Add an air connection between Paris and Bordeaux
  --   connection (paris, bordeaux).
  -- The TERM function is used to build structured Prolog terms.
  -- The & function is used to build structured Prolog terms.

  ASSERTZ (TERM (ATOM ("connection"), ATOM ("paris") & (ATOM ("bordeaux"))));

  -- Goal evaluation : search out all the routes connecting Brest and Nancy
  --    route (brest, nancy, Route).
  --The Prolog variable ROUTE is used to store the result.

  if EVALUATE (TERM (ATOM("route"),
                     ATOM ("brest")&ATOM ("nancy")&ROUTE))) then
    loop

      -- The result is written for each route found.
      -- The INSTANCE function is used to retrieve the result term of the evaluation.

      TEXT_IO.PUT_LINE (IMAGE (INSTANCE (ROUTE)));

      -- Continue to retrieve other possible solutions, if any.
      -- Stop when all the possibilities are exhausted.

      exit when not RE_EVALUATE;
    end loop;
  else
    TEXT_IO.PUT_LINE ("No possible route ...");
  end if;

end ROUTE_DEMO;
```

To illustrate the contribution of AdLog, it may be interesting to imagine what could be a version of this simple example entirely written in Ada when considering the possibility of modifying dynamically not only the list of elementary connections but also the definition of what a route is (the contents of the "route" predicate).

5 INSIDE ADLOG

Overview

The choices made to develop AdLog followed three major guiding principles :

- the total portability of an AdLog application;
- the preservation of all the features of Prolog (particulary its dynamic aspects) ;
- the highest possible efficiency.

Clearly, a Prolog clause base cannot be transformed into a set of Ada subprograms :

- the control flow in a Prolog program follows a backtracking model which is incompatible with the call-return model of Ada subprograms,

- Ada is based on an entirely static compilation model incompatible with the dynamic change features of the Prolog clause base.

Traditional Prolog implementations can be broken down into two classes :

- *interpreters*, which consist in a kernel working on data representing the clauses of the program in a form very close to that of the source. This technique promotes higher dynamicity but induces some slowing down. Most deductive language developments in an Ada environment rely on this technique and code the interpreter in Ada [Attali & Franchi 87].

- *compilers*, which transform Prolog clauses into series of instructions for the machine. This technique [Warren 77] relies on the procedural semantics of Prolog and, thanks to static analysis, generates for each clause code that is more specialized than the general-purpose internal loop of an interpreter. So, a compiler can increase efficiency 10 to 20 times compared to an interpreter, but may sometimes induce some restrictions in the dynamicity of the Prolog programs processed.

The solution adopted by AdLog consists in emulating a Prolog-oriented abstract machine in Ada and compiling the Prolog clauses to produce code executable by this machine. Within this framework, the abstract codes representing the Prolog clauses are stored in form of Ada data. Then, this data constitutes programs that can be executed by the abstract machine.

This method combines the advantages of interpretation (emulation of the abstract machine) and of compilation (production of machine-dedicated code) :

- since the Prolog programs are represented in form of Ada data, they feature all the desirable dynamic characteristics ;

- the compilation phase carries out the analysis required to specialize the resulting code, and makes it possible to take advantage of all the gains in efficiency offered by compiled code.

The abstract machine is derived from the WAM [Warren 83]. It was added to and modified in order to facilitate its implementation in Ada. Its emulator constitutes the true inference engine contained in the AdLog run-time.

The body of the package generated by the *compiler* from the source of a Prolog bubble only contains instructions which are executed at elaboration time and induce the creation of the data representing the corresponding clause base (abstract programs, ...).

```
package body ROUTE is

   -- nothing

begin

   -- code to create the clause base

end ROUTE;
```

Selected aspects of the Implementation of AdLog In Ada

It may be worth looking into the combined effects of the nature of Prolog with AdLog's objectives of efficiency and portability on the Ada style used in the abstract machine emulation. Two fundamental domains involved in emulating an abstract machine are treated : control flow management and memory (data) management.

Control

The backtracking control mechanism has no equivalent in Ada. Accordingly, it must be fully emulated (ordinal counter management, control stack management, variable range management) without recourse to any of Ada's similar mechanism.

To this effect, [Muller 87] uses the capabilities offered by Modula2 subroutine variables (non existant in Ada), but it is still difficult to evaluate whether this technique is ultimately more efficient. Ada multitask mechanisms may also offer capabilities more flexible than those of subroutines [Bobbie 87] but they probably can offer efficient solutions on multiprocessor architectures only.

Memory

By nature, the data used by a Prolog implementation, both for the clause base itself and for the resolvent or the execution control during an evaluation, is dynamic and polymorphic. Moreover, the appearance and disappearance regimen of blocks of this data (resolvent and control) is somewhat akin to managing a stack.

The Ada mechanisms for managing dynamically allocated objects are not linked to a specific allocation-deallocation policy. They guaranty the allocation (new) but not the deallocation (UNCHECKED_DEALLOCATION), and afford a large degree of freedom to their implementation. They are thus too general, and therefore too costly to be used fully in such a context. Adlog is then forced to manage itself some of the areas in its abstract machine memory.

Because of the strong typing of the language, it is very difficult to code in Ada a specific management that is both highly efficient and portable for a memory area where different types of data are stored. As a matter of fact, only objects of the same type can be manipulated in this case. The Ada mechanisms that can be used to overcome this difficulty (variant-part records or UNCHECKED_CONVERSION) are either costly, or eminently non portable.

In the emulator of the abstract machine, data of different logical nature are then untyped (in Ada, this means that they are all defined by the same type) in order to be manipulated in one and the same memory area . When this is impossible (some data cannot be defined on the same type as others), the memory areas defined in the WAM are carved out into several differently typed areas.

This technique is used to represent the resolvent and the control information (the stack and heap of conventional Prolog implementations). Because the data types of the information processed in this way are very different (e.g. atoms, variables, arithmetic values or code addresses), this technique greatly affects the solutions adopted in the entire emulation.

Likewise, the Prolog terms are not represented in the same way inside the machine as with the TERM_TYPE supplied to the using application. The required conversions are carried out by the run-time operations (in the INSTANCE function, for example).

However, the management of the clause base itself (the programs submitted to the abstract machine) use Ada allocation mechanisms since its management is not predictable and less performance sensitive .

Comments

On first examination, the adopted solutions do not seem to be the results of the encapsulation of abstractions simulating the real world (that would be Prolog), as it is recommended for using Ada correctly [Booch 83]. It should be noted however that, in this context, the real world is rather the emulation of an abstract machine. It is therefore logical to have sometimes to model very low-level concepts such as the shared memory block.

6 THE EFFICIENCY OF ADA APPLICATIONS USING ADLOG

The true efficiency of AdLog should be measured in terms of the structure, and thus of the global efficiency, of the Ada applications exhibiting deductive requirements. One should then compare applications entirely developed in Ada using and not using the facilities offered by AdLog.

Such an experiment has not yet been conducted, and the only test results available today only bear on Prolog mechanisms measured in a very isolated manner. Lacking precise information on the performance of other deductive tools developed with Ada, the only possible comparison is made with the best conventional Prolog implementations, while keeping in mind what differentiates them from AdLog.

With the very first operating version of Adlog available today, developed on MicroVax-II with VaxAda 1.4, the NAIVE REVERSE benchmark is executed 4.6 times more slowly than with Poplog's Prolog compiler [Poplog] on the same machine.

The ratio observed is much smaller that usually found between compilers and interpreters. This shows that, without recourse to any external software or Prolog specific systems, a good efficiency can be obtained in a full Ada context. Finally, this ratio can be compared with the traditionnal cost of an abstract machine software emulation.

7 A FEW PORTABILITY EXPERIMENTS

AdLog was developed using the VaxAda 1.4 compiler on MicroVax-II under Vax/VMS 4.6. Portability experiments were carried out using various commercially available Ada compilers, purchased by CR2A or lent by their producer, or on third-party sites. These tests were not conducted within the framework of a systematic testing campaign, but merely when the occasion did arise.

In addition to the development compiler, these tests were performed on the following compilers :

- RATIONAL on R1000,
- DATA GENERAL ADE 2.50 on MV20000 under AOS/VS,
- Alsys Ada Aslsycomp004 3.0 on APOLLO DN 300 under AEGIS D3M,
- GOULD APLEX Ada Compiler 1.0 Telesoft on PN6040 under UTX/32,
- VERDIX 5.2 on MicroVax-II under VAX/VMS 4.6,
- Karlsruhe Ada System 1.61 on MicroVax-II under Vax/VMS 4.6,
- MERIDIAN AdaVantage 2.0 on Compaq 2 under MS/DOS 3.10.

Today (late 1987), AdLog only operates fully on VaxAda 1.4 and on RATIONAL.

AdLog was transported to RATIONAL in less than two days, as expected from a software written in a language as standardized as Ada. In addition, AdLog is entirely compiled on the DATA GENERAL compiler, and the search for the source of its misexecution is under way. The other compiler do not even compile entirely the Ada source of the AdLog components.

Detailing all the problems encountered is beyond the scope of this paper. Suffice it to say that problems occur at different levels, and that they may be broken down into several categories, some of which are :

- the limitations attributable to certain compilers with respect to the use of certain Ada constructions :

  Size of the aggregates
  Size of source lines limited to 80 characters !

- detection of errors in perfectly legal uses of certain constructions :

  Generic instantiations, admittedly tricky at times but quite legal
  Using private types
  Static universal expressions
  Ambiguities caused by overloadings and the USE clause

- compiler internal errors.

Many errors were difficult to reproduce and thus difficult to identify. They seem to occur only in complex combinations of Ada constructions, or when reaching a certain program size.

The problems reported here only occurred in strictly legal Ada sources. For a producer of Ada components, these results are somewhat disappointing and call for a few comments :

- The language standard gives implementations the freedom to set certain limits on the use of constructions.

Quite obviously, a software developed with portability as a goal must generally adopt a profile low enough to run on a maximum number of implementations. But the restrictions placed by the latter must remain reasonable. In the future, a large number of Ada sources will be generated by automatic tools. Very often, this kind of code uses unwieldily precise constructions of the language. However, such sources will have to be accepted by Ada compilers. For example, AdLog uses aggregates in a very cumbersome way. In particular, the syntax analyzer contained in the AdLog compiler is built with a generator developed by CR2A and called YACCA (a brother of YACC for Ada). The aggregate which initializes the analysis table of this analyzer is not accepted by all compilers. And yet, the grammar of Prolog seems simple (in comparaison with Ada's one for example).

- Validated Ada compilers (some validated recently) exhibit serious bugs as soon as they are fed a good-sized Ada application.

Validating Ada compilers is certainly not an easy task. But an industry offering reusable software components, as it is promoted by Ada, is heavily dependent on the reliability of portability vectors. In order to develop genuinely reusable components, one must be ensured that all the compilers will process all the language idiosyncrasies correctly, particularly the mechanisms promoting abstraction and parametrization (genericity, private types, and so on).

As a result of these experiments, some modifications of AdLog are scheduled or were already made to ensure maximum portability. These modifications try to lessen the awkwardness involved in using certain Ada constructions to postpone the time when compiler limits are reached. Other problems bordering on the possible interpretations of the standard were circumvented by modifying the sources. As for problems involving actual bugs in compilers, it was deemed preferable not to apply side-stepping solutions and to wait for improvements in the quality of the compilers incriminated. Indeed, when they are possible, such solutions generally weaken the quality of the corresponding Ada sources.

8 WORKS TO COME

The present version of AdLog puts in concrete form the ideas expounded above, but its use will give rise to additional developments. Works along two main directions are already scheduled : fine-tuning AdLog to make it fit better the requirements of future applications ; and improving its performance.

Communication from Prolog toward Ada

Today, AdLog does not provide for any type of communication from Prolog toward Ada. Introducing a few twists to this rule may be benefical to applications. Their number should however remain very limited and not call AdLog tenets into question again, e.g. the standard feature of Prolog bubble sources, and the capability to develop these sources in external Prolog environments.

For example, the possibility of writing certain predicates in Ada should be viewed only as a means to improve the efficiency of a few sensitive predicates (list handling utilities). Likewise, means for manipulating global variables avoiding the awkwardness of standard assertion mechanisms could be developed in the future.

Partial evaluation

Prolog is the most widely used deductive programming language today. Yet, its specific problem-solving stategy may not always be the best for solving all deductive problems. This is one of the reasons why a large number of extensions and changes have been developed, each one incompatible with the others.

Other approaches adjust to applications by constructing on top of Prolog facilities that are better suited to their specific requirements. Meta-programming [Bowen & Kowalski 83], an increasingly popular technique, defines new strategies using meta-rules which are embedded in an interpretation layer itself written in Prolog. In such approaches, Prolog is used as a low-level deductive standard bringing with it a certain level of portability toward higher-level languages.

The cost of such meta-interpretation can be lowered using a partial evaluation of the entire Prolog program assembled in this way (meta-program + meta-interpreter). The application of partial evaluation to Prolog was studied by [Komorowski 81]. Its use was experimented by [Venken 84] in the field of interfacing with databases, and by [Takeuchi & Furukawa 85] in the field of meta-programming.

A partial evaluator relies on the description of a Prolog program to execute the maximum possible number of inferences based on the data statically known. Accordingly, it acts as a tool for source-source transformation of Prolog programs with a view to improving their efficiency without changing their semantics. It can be applied to Prolog programs of all sorts.

Implementing such a tool is planned for in the AdLog project. It should widen AdLog scope by contributing an additional source of efficiency, both in uses of meta-programming and in simpler Prolog bubble sources.

9 CONCLUSION

AdLog is not a new implementation of Prolog usable to develop Prolog application. This is a set of Ada components enabling applications to access all the power of standard deductive programming facility, while fully maintaining the portability allowed by the use of Ada.

Its allows developers to describe in Prolog, with all the flexibility inherent to this language, components that can be inserted in the application in an Ada form.

Thanks to a structure combining the compilation of Prolog and the emulation of a Prolog oriented abstract machine, AdLog provides good performance in comparaison with purely interpretative structures which are the only ones possible within the framework of Ada.

History has shown that Prolog could be used to code applications that it had not originally intended for. Similarly, it may still be prematurate to set any limits on the scope of AdLog today.

10 ACKNOWLEDGMENTS

The AdLog project was financed in part by the Agence Nationale pour la Valorisation de la Recherche (ANVAR). It came to fruition thanks to the combined efforts of a team including, in addition to the author, Gilles DARONDEAU, Laurence FIDON, and Thierry LELEGARD.

We are also greatly indebted to the companies which granted us access to the compilers and/or machines used to carry out some portability experiments reported here : RATIONAL Europe, DATA GENERAL France, SYSTEAM KG, and THOMSON-SDC.

11 REFERENCES

[Attali & Franchi 87] I. Attali & P. Franchi-Zanettacci,
Inference system environment for Ada,
Ada components : libraries and tools, Proceedings of the Ada-Europe International Conference 1987
Ed S. Tafvelin, pp 3-18, Cambridge University Press, 1987.

[BIM_Prolog] BIM,
BIM_Prolog Manual on VAX/VMS, Version 1.0, February 87.

[Bobbie 87] P. Bobbie,
Ada-PROLOG: An Ada System for Parallel Interpretation of Prolog Programs,
Proceedings of AIDA-87, Washington 87, pp 102-123

[Booch 83] G. Booch,
Software Engineering with Ada,
The Benjamin/Cummings Publishing Co., 1983

[Bowen & Kowalski 83] K. Bowen & R. Kowalski,
Amalgamating Language and Metalanguage in Logic Programing,
Logic Programming, Clark and Tarnlund (ed), 153-172,1983

[Buhr et al. 85] R.J.A. Buhr, G.M. Karam, C.M. Woodside,
An Overview and Example of Application of CAEDE : A New, Experimental Design Environment for Ada,
Ada in use, Proceedings of the Ada International Conference1985,
Ed J.G.P. Barnes & G.A. Fisher, pp 3-18, Cambridge University Press, 1985.

[Clocksin & Mellish 84] W.F. Clocksin & C.S. Mellish,
Programming in Prolog, Second Edition, Berlin : Springer Verlag, 1984.

[Dobbins et al. 87] G.L. Dobbins, V.E. Szarek, W.H. Webster,
An Ada/Prolog Database Management System For Ada Source Code,
Proceedings of AIDA-87, Washington 87, pp 23-39

[Hendler & Wong 87] J. Hendler & Y. Wong,
        An Al-Based Ada Reuse Tool, Proceedings of AIDA-87, Washington 87, pp 1-22

[Ice et al. 87]   S. Ice, G. Blair, G Finnegan, R. Yoshii,
        Raising ALLAN: Ada Logic-Based Language,
        Proceedings of AIDA-87, Washington 87, pp 155-165

[Komorowski 81]   H.J. Komorowski,
        A specification of an abstract Prolog machine and its application to partial evaluation,
        Linköping Studies in Sciences and Technologies Dissertations, n 69, 1981.

[Ledoux & Parker 85] C.H. Ledoux & D. Stott Parker,
        Saving Traces For Ada Debugging,
        Ada in use, Proceedings of the Ada International Conference 1985,
        Ed J.G.P. Barnes & G.A. Fisher, pp 3-18, Cambridge University Press, 1985.

[Mellish 85]   C.S. Mellish,
        Some global optimizations for a Prolog compiler,
        Journal of Logic Programming, 1985, n1, pp 43-66.

[Muller 86]   C. Müller,
        Modula-Prolog : a software development tool, IEEE Software, 39-45, 1986.

[Poplog]   Systems Designers,
        Poplog User Guide, Z1/00-00/21, Issue 1.0, June 86.

[Quintus]   Quintus Computer Sytems,
        Quintus Prolog User Guide,   Version 6, April 86.

[Takeuchi & Furakawa 85]   A. Takeuchi & K. Furakawa,
        Partial Evaluation of Prolog programs   and its application to Meta-Programming,
        ICOT Research Center, Institute for New Generation Computer Technology, 1-4-28, Mita,
        Minato-ku, Tokyo 108 Japan.

[Venken 84]   R. Venken,
        A Prolog Meta-Interpreter for Partial Evaluation and its application to source-to-source
        transformation and query optimisation,
        in Proc. of ECAI'84, North Holland, pp 91-100, 1984

[VM/PROLOG]   IBM,
        VM/Programming in Logic,   Program Description/Operator Manual,
        Program number 5785/ABH, first edition, September 85.

[Warren 77]   D.H.D.Warren,
        Implementing Prolog - compiling predicate logic program,
        D.A.I. research report n 39 & 40,   University of Edinburgh, Scotland, 1977.

[Warren 83]   D.H.D. Warren,
        An Abstract Prolog Instruction Set, TR 309, SRI International, 1983

A PILOT IMPLEMENTATION OF BASIC MODULES FOR A PORTABLE NUMERICAL LIBRARY

L.M. Delves
Centre for Mathematical Software Research, University of Liverpool, UK

B. Ford
G.S. Hodgson
L. Steenman-Clark
Numerical Algorithms Group Ltd, Mayfield House, 256 Banbury Road, Oxford, UK

Abstract MAP 750: "Pilot Implementations of Basic Modules for Large Portable Numerical Libraries in Ada" was an EEC funded project under the Multi-Annual Programme (MAP) to develop design criteria for producing a serial numerical library in Ada, and to produce a core library and a range of library modules in selected applications areas. Participants in the project were the Numerical Algorithms Group (prime contractor); Centrum voor Wiskunde en Informatica, Amsterdam; National Physical Laboratory, UK; National Institute for Higher Education, Dublin (for Trinity College, Dublin); and the University of Liverpool, UK (subcontractors to NAG). The project was successfully completed in April 1987; NAG has now announced the first release of a fully supported Ada library based on this work. This paper attempts to give an overview of the aims, the methodology, and the results of the work.

1. INTRODUCTION

In 1985 the Commission for the European Communities, as part of the CEC Multi-Annual Programme (MAP), provided funds for project MAP 750: Pilot Implementations of Basic Modules for Large Portable Numerical Libraries in Ada, as part of a wider effort to investigate ways of using the facilities provided by Ada, and of producing basic software facilities for the emerging Ada community. The aims of the project, which became known as PIA, were to develop design criteria for producing a serial numerical library in Ada, and to produce a core library and a range of library modules in selected applications areas. Participants in the project were the Numerical Algorithms Group (prime contractor); Centrum voor Wiskunde en Informatica, Amsterdam; National Physical Laboratory, UK; National Institute for Higher Education, Dublin (for Trinity College, Dublin); and the University of Liverpool, UK (subcontractors to NAG). Funding available amounted to 7 man years, although in practice the total effort expended by the partners was rather more than this. The project was successfully completed in April 1987, with the submission to the CEC of a detailed project report describing the implementation, documentation and testing of a set of Ada packages demonstrating the methodology developed (referred to here as the Pilot Library). NAG has now announced the first release of a fully supported Ada library based on this work. This paper attempts to give an overview of the aims, the methodology, and the results of the work of PIA.

In more detail the major aims of the project were:

a)   to investigate the ways in which the advanced language facilities of Ada could best
      be used to provide library facilities for the scientific/engineering programmer,

b)   to demonstrate the feasibility of the methodology developed, by designing and
      constructing a pilot library on which a later full scale library effort might build.

The work was able to build upon the earlier MAP funded "guidelines" project (Symm et al
1984), but has gone beyond the recommendations given there in a number of ways.

The Guidelines, and our own initial work, identified the following Ada language features as
being of especial importance, in that they provide facilities at a higher level than those available in previous
languages:

a)   The ability to define *new types*, to overload operator and procedure names, and to
      return a value of arbitrary type from a function. These features potentially allow
      major improvements in the user interface, compared with a Fortran library.

b)   The *package* facility, which not only provides a well defined and safe extension of the
      (de facto) Fortran Library mechanism, but via the distinction between package
      specification and package body, and via the *private* mechanism, allows the hiding of
      inessential information and the guarding of essential information from misuse.

c)   The *generic* facility, which provides direct support for abstract data types and
      potentially allows the provision of facilities much more general than those
      expressible in Fortran or indeed any other widely available language.

d)   The *tasking* mechanism, which allows the expression of parallel and real-time
      programs with arbitrary synchronisation needs.

We set as a major design goal the study of the effective use of features a), b) and c); in this
paper the way in which these language facilities have been used is described in outline. It was not part of the
project to develop or design individual algorithms which would be efficient on parallel architectures; the
underlying expression of the algorithms is serial. However, we were at pains to ensure that the library will
function correctly in a real-time or parallel environment, and the tasking mechanism has been required to
ensure this within the treatment developed for handling errors.

A second major aim was the production of a *portable* library. The language Ada itself
strives for portability; and provides a number of constructs: *attributes* in particular, which aid the attainment
of genuine portability. We tried to make full use of these facilities, which were familiar already from our
experience with Algol68, and from the library substitutes provided in the NAG Fortran library. However, it
is inevitable that, either for efficiency reasons or because of system peculiarities, there are places at which it
is not feasible to provide total portability of a single source code. Difficulties typically occur in the portable
provision of the most basic facilities; a common example, familiar to all Fortran library builders, is that of
providing double-length accumulation of inner-products on machines which do not support two lengths of
real arithmetic. The library design we have produced consists of a *core* of basic facilities: type declarations,

elementary functions, simple vector/matrix arithmetic etc.; and a set of application packages containing higher level routines. We have taken great pains to ensure that the places where potential lack of portability might be encountered, are few and well localised within the core library; then the more extensive applications areas can be totally portable, while we strive to make the core at least *transportable*.

2. OVERALL LIBRARY STRUCTURE

The library has been partitioned into two parts:

a)   core packages

b)   applications packages

The *core* provides the basic facilities which will be widely used by many library packages; it is essentially the foundation on which a uniform library of *applications* packages can be constructed. This core is directly available to a user although its primary purpose is to provide the most common auxiliary facilities for re-use by other packages. Because of this wide re-use, and particularly at lower levels in the library, efficiency of the core packages is an essential requirement.

Portability across different compilation systems is a prime aim of the library. With this partitioning of the library into core and applications packages, the interface between the core and the applications can be at a relatively high level. The applications packages can therefore be made totally portable across different compilation systems; any systems dependencies can be restricted to the core packages, some of which may only be transportable - that is portable with a strictly limited number of modifications for different systems.

2.1 Core packages

The *chapters* of the library which form the core are as follows:

A01, A04   -   Standard Types and Operations

A02   -   Input/Output for such Standard Types

F06   -   Basic Vector and Matrix Operations

G05   -   Basic Random Number Generator

P01   -   Error Reporting Mechanism

S01   -   Elementary Functions.

Because Ada defines different declarations of a type to be distinct types, we must define some standard types globally so as to ensure uniformity across the library.

To try to ensure uniformity of this library with other library developments, these standard types closely follow the joint standardisation activities of the SIGAda Numerics and Ada Europe Numerics Working Groups, and in particular the proposals by Kok and Hodgson (see Kok 1987). This also applies to the design of the Elementary Functions and the Basic Random Number Generator.

2.2 Applications packages

The *chapters* of the library which form the applications packages of this *Pilot Library* are as follows:

D01 - Quadrature
D02 - Ordinary Differential Equations
D03 - Partial Differential Equations
F04 - Solution of Linear Equations.

These applications areas were chosen to demonstrate that the core/application partition does indeed provide a suitable interface to ensure portability of these applications packages. No system dependencies are included in these packages.

These applications packages have substantial source code bodies and a prime aim is therefore to re-use these packages as widely as possible. Much effort has therefore been spent in designing them to make maximum use of the Ada *generic* facilities.

2.3 Error mechanism

The error mechanism is a particularly important part of the core library, since it is used by nearly all other modules in the library, and its design affects almost all users. A full description of the mechanism is given elsewhere (Hodgson & Gardner 1987); we note here that our design aims have been:

a) The mechanism should provide satisfactory default information without effort on the part of the user.

b) Information should be in terms relevant to the module which the user called, even when an error is detected by a lower level library routine.

c) Users wishing to have control over the treatment of errors, perhaps to attempt recovery from them, should be able to do so.

d) The mechanism should make minimal assumptions about the environment; in particular, it should perform safely in a real-time environment.

e) The overheads associated with using the mechanism should be small for those programs which do not yield errors.

We believe that all of these design aims have been met.

3. OVERVIEW OF DESIGN DECISIONS

In this section we discuss briefly the most important of the design decisions which have been reached. Some of these represent the concensus reached by the participants on the best way to use the various features of Ada; others refer to areas in which we have found Ada restrictive, and the ways which we have used to minimise the effect of these restrictions on the user.

3.1 Generic packages

Ada encourages the re-use of software in two ways:

a)   packaging software so as to encourage the sharing of code where possible

b)   providing variants of generic packages (or templates)

By designing the library to use generic packages where possible, we can minimise the amount of distinct library code which needs to be written and maintained.

3.2 Generic formal types

We have chosen to define many of the library packages to be generic with respect to the precision of the floating-point type used. Thus a typical library package has the form:

```
generic
   type FLOAT_TYPE is digits <>;
package VARIABLE_PRECISION_LIBRARY_PACKAGE is
   -- (related) library subprograms
end VARIABLE_PRECISION_LIBRARY_PACKAGE;
```

We can then instantiate with each of the floating-point types (or derivations of them) which are supported by an implementation. For example, on DEC Vax VMS three precisions of floating-point types are supported: FLOAT, LONG_FLOAT, LONG_LONG_FLOAT. Hence we can produce three instances of VARIABLE_PRECISION_ LIBRARY_PACKAGE:

```
package VARIABLE_PRECISION_LIBRARY_PACKAGE_REAL
        is new VARIABLE_PRECISION_LIBRARY_PACKAGE (FLOAT);
package VARIABLE_PRECISION_LIBRARY_PACKAGE_LONGREAL
        is new VARIABLE_PRECISION_LIBRARY_PACKAGE (LONG_FLOAT);
package VARIABLE_PRECISION_LIBRARY_PACKAGE_LONGLONGREAL
        is new VARIABLE_PRECISION_LIBRARY_PACKAGE (LONG_LONG_FLOAT);
```

Floating point types are special generic parameters; predefined operations are implicitly imported with the type. Hence we do not need to explicitly include further generic subprogram parameters for the arithmetic operations +, -, * etc.

If we choose to implement extended precision types, not as floating-point types because a sufficiently precise type is not supported by the compilation system, but as a software type then the extended precision type must be imported by the generic package as a private type.

This means that no implicit operations are imported, and the list of generic parameters grows dramatically. We would then have library packages of the form:

```
generic
    type SOFTWARE_TYPE is private;
    with function "+" (X,Y: SOFTWARE_TYPE)
                            return SOFTWARE_TYPE is <>;
    with function "-" (X,Y: SOFTWARE_TYPE)
                            return SOFTWARE_TYPE is <>;
    with function "*" (X,Y: SOFTWARE_TYPE)
                            return SOFTWARE_TYPE is <>;

    -- etc.
package LIBRARY_PACKAGE is
    -- library subprograms
end LIBRARY_PACKAGE;
```

We have chosen in this library to restrict REAL_TYPES to floating-point types and not to require that all generic library packages will accept both floating-point types and software implemented types as above. Software implemented real types are inherently inefficient, and we have therefore chosen not to penalise the simplicity of library packages generic with respect to floating-point precision for a somewhat dubious gain.

3.3 Generic formal types

Nevertheless, if we are to exploit generic packages fully, library packages should in many cases be generic with respect to a SCALAR_TYPE which may be instantiated with REAL_TYPEs, COMPLEX_TYPEs or perhaps some user defined type, for example a RATIONAL_TYPE. The Ada language can be extended by the definition of new types, and by providing generic library packages (generic with respect to a general SCALAR_TYPE) the library itself can be extended by user instantiation. Hence:

```
generic
    type SCALAR_TYPE is private;
    with function "+" (X,Y : SCALAR_TYPE)
                            return SCALAR_TYPE is <>;
    -- other operations on SCALAR_TYPES
package GENERAL_LIBRARY_PACKAGE
    -- library subprograms
end GENERAL_LIBRARY_PACKAGE;
```

can be instantiated with most types; there are few restrictions on such substitutions. The inclusion of the default symbol <> for the generic subprograms (operations) means that those operations need not be explicitly supplied if a matching subprogram is visible to the instantiation.

Hence by defining:

```
type COMPLEX is record RE, IM : FLOAT; end record;
function "+" (C,D : COMPLEX) return COMPLEX;
-- other operations
package LIBRARY_PACKAGE_COMPLEX
                is new GENERAL_LIBRARY_PACKAGE (COMPLEX);
```

the instantiation is relatively straightforward. Whilst the number of generic formal parameters may be large, the number of generic actual parameters can be minimised.

3.4 Standard instances

Before a generic unit can be used it must first be instantiated - that is substitutions must be made for its generic formal parameters. There is therefore the potential for several identical instances of generic library templates to be made by users. Such instances will in general be large and there is no guarantee that compilers will recognise identical instances. Indeed the process of instantiation is likely to be time consuming.

For both reasons, we wish to avoid user instantiation where possible and provide standard instances of generic library units. Having provided standard types and operations on such types in the core, we are then able to provide standard instances of library units, especially for large applications packages.

We have therefore provided standard instances with respect to REAL (a floating-point type) and where appropriate COMPLEX (in cartesian form). Where there is a choice of precision on a compilation system, the precision chosen for REAL (and COMPLEX) is IEEE standard 754, 32-bit precision (or the closest available to that). In due course, other standard instances for LONG_REAL (IEEE standard 754, 64-bit precision) and LONG_COMPLEX will be provided.

3.5 Subprogram parameters

The Ada language does not permit subprograms to be parameters of other subprograms. This is particularly restrictive in a library environment: many numerical applications require a function or procedure to be passed to a library unit, for example the integrand in numerical integration. This also impacts on the error reporting mechanism, whose flexibility in recovery actions is achieved by supplying a recovery procedure to define the action to be taken after an error has been detected.

To overcome this omission from the language, we have had to use the generic facility.

Hence the general form of a library unit, which includes some error recovery action, is as follows:

```
generic
   with procedure FAIL_HANDLER(FAIL : ERROR_RECORD) is DEFAULT_HANDLER;
procedure GENERIC_LIBRARY_SUBPROGRAM(...;
                              FAIL : ERROR_RECORD := DEFAULT_RECORD);
```

or if packaged it takes the form:

```
generic
   with procedure FAIL_HANDLER(FAIL : ERROR_RECORD) is DEFAULT_HANDLER;
package GENERIC_LIBRARY_PACKAGE is
   procedure LIBRARY_SUBPROGRAM( ... ;
                              FAIL : ERROR_RECORD := DEFAULT_RECORD);
   ...
end GENERIC_LIBRARY_PACKAGE;
```

3.6 Parameter defaults

We have already seen how defaults can be provided for generic formal subprograms in order to reduce the number of (generic actual) parameters which need to be supplied by a user. This also applies to the formal parameters of subprograms.

Hence a particular effort has been made to supply suitable defaults where possible for the parameters of library subprograms. An example of this can be found in the general form of a generic library package:

```
generic
   with procedure FAIL_HANDLER(FAIL : ERROR_RECORD) is DEFAULT_HANDLER;
package GENERIC_LIBRARY_PACKAGE is
   procedure LIBRARY_SUBPROGRAM( ... ;
                              FAIL : ERROR_RECORD := DEFAULT_RECORD);
   ...
end GENERIC_LIBRARY_PACKAGE;
```

The existence of the default FAIL_HANDLER means that the instantiation of the library-package is simplified for a user:

```
package NEW_LIBRARY_PACKAGE is new GENERIC_LIBRARY_PACKAGE;
         -- no generic parameter need be supplied
```

and also a call of the library-subprogram is simplified

```
LIBRARY_SUBPROGRAM ( ...;);
         -- the final parameter need not be supplied.
```

The existence of such defaults means that a user need not be aware of many details of the error mechanism; he can ignore such parameters in library units for simplicity, yet the sophisticated user has the flexibility to supply particular parameters to tailor the error recovery action to his own requirements.

Unfortunately, defaults cannot always be supplied even though a suitable value can be defined. This is because the Ada language insists that defaults can only be supplied for *in* parameters - i.e. parameters which are not modified by the library subprogram. Hence *in out* parameters cannot be defaulted - an inconvenient restriction.

3.7 Overloading of operators and subprograms

The Ada language allows the same subprogram name or operator token to have a number of (overloaded) meanings. Indeed since we cannot define new operator tokens, we are encouraged to overload operators.

This use of the same subprogram name (operator token) significantly improves the readability of the library. For example, the names PUT and GET have analogous meanings to their built-in TEXT_IO equivalents but are defined for each of the new standard types used in the library. Other examples of overloading will be found in many library packages.

Overloading is needed also to alleviate the problem caused by the lack of slicing and trimming of two-dimensional arrays in Ada. By slicing we mean a reduction in dimensionality, in this case the extraction of rows or columns; by trimming we mean a reduction in bounds, i.e. the extraction of a submatrix. In a language which provides slicing and trimming, a single procedure expecting a vector argument may be called with a one dimensional array, or with a row or column from a higher dimensional array (e.g. a matrix). This is not possible in Ada; we must provide different variants of a subprogram to cover operations upon vectors, rows and columns (or parts thereof). But inconvenience to the user is minimised by using the same program name for each variant.

Of course this means that the library code and documentation size grows considerably, but we have found it necessary to make up for this important omission from the language. The solution we have used ensures that the impact on readability of the user interface is minimised.

3.8 Data types

The Ada language can be extended by the definition of new data types, COMPLEX is an obvious example. We have therefore taken the opportunity to define new data types within the library. However, we have not been able to define as many new data types as we would like because of language restrictions.

We make much use of unconstrained arrays in a numeric environment, indeed little use is made of constrained arrays. But we cannot directly include unconstrained arrays in a record type. A fudge exists in the language: we can include a discriminated record containing just the unconstrained array, where the discriminant(s) is (are) the size of the array. Thus by defining

```
type ERROR_STRING (N : POSITIVE := 1) is
   record TEXT : STRING (1 .. N); end record;
```

we can include ERROR_STRINGs in other records, whereas we could not include STRINGs directly.

Such discriminated records are used in the error mechanism, but we have avoided too liberal a use within the library. There is no guarantee that a compiler will implement such a construct by reserving space for exactly the length of the actual STRING - the compiler may choose always to reserve the maximum possible, hence the unconstrained array may in reality become constrained. Further, the introduction of the discriminant(s) has in effect introduced extra parameters (to define the bounds of the array); extra parameters which a user would justifiably regard as unnecessary. Our experience of large parameter lists suggests that as the number of parameters grows so does the likelihood of user error in constructing the calling sequence of the library subprogram. Hence for both of the above reasons, we have in general avoided the use of discriminated records in this way.

Another candidate for a method of including unconstrained arrays in records is via an access type, i.e. a pointer to the array. The drawback is that such pointers can only point to objects on the heap (such objects must have been declared by an allocator). However, users may well have already declared the array on the stack and, without expensive copying into newly allocated space on the heap, we cannot point to such arrays. Indeed we have been cautious of extensive use of the heap since there is no guarantee in the language that a garbage collector (compacting or otherwise) will be provided by the compilation system. Hence we also in general avoid pointers to unconstrained arrays.

3.9 Private and limited private types

However, Ada does provide some features for data types which are very valuable additions to what is provided by other languages. We have found the private (and/or limited private) type very useful, particularly in ensuring the integrity of internal data-structures. By making a type limited private, the library has complete control over how objects of that type may be accessed by the user. If such objects are to be shared in a parallel environment, we can protect against simultaneous updating of such global variables. An example of such protection can be found in the library error mechanism.

Further, by making a type private we can simplify the user interface by including implementation dependencies (in the internal representation of objects of that type) in the non-visible private part of a library package. Thus we can clearly separate the user specification from the implementation specification; the documentation of the user specification is then much simplified. An example of such clarity of specification can be found in the random number generator - a user need not be aware of how many integers we need to store the seed of the generator.

3.10 Enumeration types

We have also found that the use of enumeration types can improve the clarity of the user interface. Even in the case where there are only two values for such a type, the use of an enumeration type with well chosen literals rather than a BOOLEAN type can reduce the risk of error, especially when the two values are not opposite in meaning (if they are, TRUE and FALSE may be appropriate literals).

4. DOCUMENTATION

Documentation of the library is an essential aspect of the work we have carried out. The design of the documentation standards has not been easy, despite considerable experience within the project of documenting large libraries. Two important aims, which tend to conflict, are to make the documentation:

a) complete and unambiguous for the user wanting full details

b) concise and clear for the casual user.

Achieving both of these aims has proved to be particularly difficult for the generic modules which we have designed, because of the need to fully document their greater generality. The documentation standards adhered to have evolved over the project life; the documentation of the library is in two forms:

a) reference manual

b) (simplified) user manual.

The reference manual gives the fullest documentation, giving all variants (i.e. instances) together with the generic template of the generic library packages; the user manual gives just the common instances.

By extensively genericising the library, we have provided the sophisticated user with a very flexible (and extendable) library (something not provided by other languages); but we also wish to retain the simplicity for other users.

Hence, the two forms of documentation. Indeed, the reference manual documentation is further partitioned into:

      A.   package specification

      B.   standard instances (and examples of use)

      C.   subprograms

      D.   generic template (and examples of instantiation)

to reinforce this difference in the use of the library and its documentation.

5. ENVIRONMENT

We have taken a particularly broad view of the environments in which we expect that the library can be used; we recognise three forms of user environments:

      a)   sequential environment

      b)   parallel environment

      c)   real-time environment.

The provision of a library whose design is applicable to all three environments is an exciting challenge which the project has by intent only partly met. The library we have designed is essentially serial in its nature. It is however safe in a parallel or real time environment; and as noted earlier, the error mechanism in particular has been designed specifically to ensure this. This design, and the rules adhered to within the applications packages, reflect in particular two potential problems in trying to use a single library in both a parallel and a serial environment.

      a)   The protection needed for shared variables in a parallel environment, may well be very expensive in a sequential environment (for example a rendezvous may be inefficient in a sequential environment). This has influenced both the design and implementation of the library as will be seen from the variants provided in for example the error mechanism.

      b)   If we are also to cater for a real-time environment, we must try to prevent system overheads (such as a garbage collector) from becoming a significant proportion of the execution of a particular algorithm. Therefore, great care has been needed in, for example, our use of storage to prevent dangerous accumulation of garbage in the library.

While we are confident that the library design we have developed is effective in a real-time environment, we note that the challenging problem of developing a library of numerical algorithms in Ada which will take advantage of parallel hardware, remains to be tackled.

6. TESTING STANDARDS

No library can be developed without testing. Following the established practice with the NAG Fortran and Algol68 libraries, we have considered the provision of test programs to be an integral part of the library development process. Two test programs are associated with a library module:

a) An "Example Program": a model of the use of the facility, which may be used directly to form a skeletal program utilising the module. The example program, and its results, form part of the documentation of the library.

b) A "Certification Test" program: a much more extensive program intended to test all aspects of the implementation of the relevant algorithm, and in particular its handling of errors and of algorithmic branches. This set of programs is intended to be run whenever the library is ported to a new machine, operating system, or compiler version.

Manpower limitations have set limits on the effort available to develop comprehensive Certification Test programs. However, preliminary test programs, which will form part of a certification suite, have been developed for every unit, in order to establish both the principle and the size of the effort needed.

7. CONCLUSIONS

By April 1987, we had available firm design guidelines for Ada numerical software, and a substantial body of implemented, tested, and documented algorithms forming a pilot library which we believe makes good use of the unique features of Ada, while minimising the impact of its odd rough edges. We also have experience of the difficulties in documenting generic packages in a manner which is both concise and easy to follow; this is an area in which we expect to experiment further. The overall success of the project can be assessed, we feel, by the following:

a) the stimulation of further collaborative work in numerical libraries, particularly in the areas of international standardisation (of type packages and elementary functions) and also in other collaborative work outside the European Community, for example in the area of curve and surface fitting in Sweden,

b) the implementation of many parts of the pilot library on different partner's compilation systems has demonstrated the portability of the design,

c) the announcement by NAG of a fully supported library based on this work.

We believe that this pilot library will form a sound basis for future collaborative effort in numerical libraries, and that with suitable further projects in this area Ada scientific and engineering users will have available library environments more advanced than those currently enjoyed by the Fortran community.

8. ACKNOWLEDGEMENTS

This work was made possible by funds provided from the Multi-Annual Programme of the CEC. The work described here represents the collaborative efforts of many people; we wish to thank all of our colleagues in PIA both for their contributions to the work and for the friendly atmosphere in which it was carried out.

9. REFERENCES

Hodgson G.S., and Gardner P.P. (1987)

A Proposed Ada Library Error Mechanism.

Proceeding of the Ada-Europe International Conference, Stockholm, May 1987.

Ed. S. Tafvelin, Ada Companion Series, Cambridge University Press.

Kok, J

Proposal for Standard Mathematical Packages in Ada.

CWI Report NM-R8718, November 1987.

Centre for Mathematics and Computer Science, Amsterdam.

Symm, G.T., Wichmann, B.A., Kok, J. and Winter, D.T. (1984)

Guidelines for the Design of Large Modular Scientific Libraries in Ada.

NPL Report DITC 37/84 and CWI Note NM-N8401.

AdaVIEW: A DATA SUBLANGUAGE FOR Ada

D.A.Leonte
D S N, BP 2185, L-1021 Luxembourg, G-D de Luxembourg

Abstract. A data sublanguage is presented which provides data
definition, query, manipulation and control facilities for
applications written in Ada. Data definition is supported at
two levels: conceptual and representation. Two forms of
queries are supported: query blocks (given as statements) and
views (given as declarations). Manipulation operations are
available in the basic form (create, modify, remove objects)
and in the form of data subprograms (application - defined
operations given as subprogram units). The control aspects
covered include transactions, integrity constraints and user
authorizations. Advanced sublanguage features include generic
data declarations and instantiations which allow dynamic data
definition, query and manipulation.

INTRODUCTION

In spite of its advanced features, well suited for the
management of large scale on-going system development activity, Ada has
been slow in penetrating the world of business data processing, which,
paradoxically, requires just this kind of features. This is apparent
particularly well in the case of large, and very large businesses whose
reliance upon massive own development efforts is crucial to their
activities e.g. banks and insurance companies, manufacturing companies and
others.

Our explanation for this state of things is two fold. First,
we believe that Ada has been too much identified, from its beginnings,
with a modern solution for the development of real time systems only, in
spite of enormous similarities that exist between the two kinds of system
development activities, particularly in the areas of management and
control of the development process itself. Second, we believe that the
scarcity of means to support Ada in a database application development
environment (on which the business data processing relies heavily) has
played an important part.

Our contribution to these Proceedings tries to address this second cause in presenting the results of an effort to define and develop a data sublanguage for Ada.

Objectives

The objectives of our effort have been as follows. First, the proven architecture of the relational data sublanguages such as SQL should form the skeleton of AdaVIEW, our data sublanguage. The pillars of this architecture consist of the capabilities to define, query, manipulate and control the application's data. It is quite clear that these architectural elements can exist independently of the characteristics of the database environment (whether relational or not). However the analytical nature of the relational way of looking at data allowed a better understanding of the functions within the database environment hence a better definition of the tool to handle this environment, the data sublanguage. Second, key architectural elements of the Ada language particularly well suited for the management and control of large scale system development activity should be directly inherited and extended by the data sublanguage. These architectural elements are type, package, generic units, context clauses, libraries and the capability to separate the specification of an operation from its implementation. Third, it has become clear that the relational database environment, in spite of its present commercial success, displays limitations in several important aspects. One of these aspects is the use of application-defined values to implement relationships. This may limit severely some applications that require to modify these values since the structure of their data is dependent on its contents. Another limiting aspect is the lack of capability to express but in a limited way the semantic contents of a data structure. Current developments in areas such as expert systems, CASE tools and others, suggest that this capability will become important for the next generation of data systems. Our third objective was to insure that the data sublanguage is capable of handling a database environment that goes beyond the limits of the relational one. Fourth, in line with our motivation of advancing the use of Ada in business applications, the data sublanguage must be capable of handling database environments, besides its own one, created and maintained by "guest" database management systems (dbms's) already in use.

System Architecture

AdaVIEW is the data sublanguage component of AdaVIEW/DS, an integrated application development system which supports the development of database/data communication applications in Ada. The AdaVIEW database environment is created and maintained by another AdaVIEW/DS component called the Data System Nucleus (DSN). Two kinds of functions are supported by DSN: definition functions and processing functions. The DSN components that support these functions are called respectively the Definition Support System (DSS) and the Processing Support System (PSS). Figure 1 gives a functional view of the DSN architecture.

Figure 1. Functional view of the DSN architecture

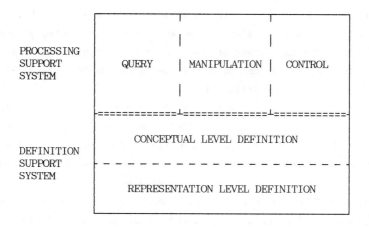

The DSS supports the definition of the properties and the structure of an application's data, a process generally known as data definition. It organizes the database environment in two levels: conceptual (or logical) and representation (or physical). The PSS consists of three functional groups supporting respectively data query, manipulation and control.

The DSN functions are available to the application program through AdaVIEW facilities for data definition, query, manipulation and control respectively. These facilities are presented in their basic form in the following sections. The last section presents, rather more briefly, generic and other sublanguage facilities which allow dynamic data definition, query and manipulation.

DATA DEFINITION FACILITIES

Data definition occurs at two levels: conceptual and representation. At the conceptual level data is organized in collections of objects called databases. The objects of a database can be grouped together in classes according to their properties. A class is a collection of objects characterized by a set of properties and represents the database counterpart of the type. The members of a class have composite value, similar to a record value. Its components, called attributes, are characterized by a type and an operation modifier. The latter allows the specification of access and control options during the query or manipulation operations with the attribute.

Data properties can be defined at three levels: member, class and database. The basic properties of a member are its attributes; additional member properties may be described by the values of other members from the same class or several other classes. The described and the describing members are connected through a one-to-one logical link called a descriptive relationship.

Class properties include the properties of all the class members and properties that are either common to all the class members or are characteristic of the class as a whole. (An important class property, common to all the class members, is the set of operations available with the class members.) Some or all the properties of a class can be inherited from another class or several other classes. Such a class is called a subclass of its parent class(es) and is connected to the latter through a logical link called an inheritance relationship. A class whose properties are entirely defined (rather than inherited) is called a base class. Base classes together with their subclasses form disjoint families of classes organized in a hierarchy whose root is a base class. The descriptive and the inheritance relationships are the means for the definition of data structures at the conceptual level.

The properties of a database include the properties of its constituent classes and properties that are either common to all the database objects or characteristic of the database as a whole.

Figure 2 illustrates the conceptual diagram of a database whose objects represent the personnel members of an organization. There are six classes of which four (EMPLOYEES, DEPARTMENTS, PROJECTS and DEPARTMENT_PROJECTS) are base classes and two (PROJECT_MANAGERS and PROJECT_WORKERS) are subclasses of class EMPLOYEES.

Several descriptive relationships exist: Dept_where_employed (describes an employee), Manager (describes a project), Project (describes a project worker), Project_where_involved (describes a department involved in a project) and Participating_dept (describes a project shared among several departments). The descriptive relationships are indicated with arrows from the described to the describing class. Two inheritance relationships exist: (PROJECT_MANAGERS, EMPLOYEES) and (PROJECT_WORKERS, EMPLOYEES); they are indicated by letters A and B respectively.

Figure 2. Conceptual diagram of database PERSONNEL.

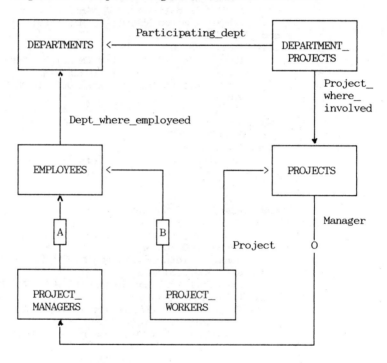

A: Job = PROJECT_MANAGER
B: EMPLOYEES **not in** PROJECT_MANAGERS
   where Job /= PERSONNEL_OFFICER

In AdaVIEW, data definition is achieved through operations with database definitions as entities of the database environment. One way of creating a database definition is through the elaboration of a database declaration (the specification part of this declaration is called schema). Figure 3 illustrates the declaration of database PERSONNEL; the package PERSONNEL_TYPES, on which it depends, is sketched in figure 4.

With reference to figure 3 the following remarks are made. First, there is a close and simple correspondence between the conceptual database diagram (in figure 2) and the database schema, which allows the developer to control the database design process using simple graphical means.

Figure 3. Schema of database PERSONNEL.

```
with PERSONNEL_TYPES; use PERSONNEL_TYPES;
schema PERSONNEL is
        class DEPARTMENTS is
                Dno:    key DEPARTMENT_NUMBERS;
                Dname: DEPARTMENT_NAMES;
                Dloc:   letnull LOCATION_NAMES;
                Nemps: limited NUMBER_OF_EMPLOYEES;
        end class DEPARTMENTS;
        class EMPLOYEES is
                Eno:                    key EMPLOYEE_NUMBERS;
                Ename:                  EMPLOYEE_NAMES;
                Dept_where_employed: access DEPARTMENTS;
                Job:                    JOBS;
                Salary:                 SALARIES;
        end class;
        with class EMPLOYEES
        class PROJECT_MANAGERS is
                Management_experience: letnull NATURAL;
                Appointment_date:      DATES;
        where
                Job = PROJECT_MANAGER
        end class PROJECT_MANAGERS;
        class PROJECTS is
                Pno:    key PROJECT_NUMBERS;
                Pname: PROJECT_NAMES;
                Manager: letnull access PROJECT_MANAGERS;
        end class PROJECTS;
        with class EMPLOYEES not in PROJECT_MANAGERS
        class PROJECT_WORKERS is
                Project:       limited access PROJECTS;
                Date_joined: DATES;
                Hours_worked: NATURAL := 0;   -- default allowed
        where
                Job /= PERSONNEL_OFFICER
        end class PROJECT_WORKERS;
        class DEPARTMENT_PROJECTS is
                Project_where_involved: key access PROJECTS;
                Participating_dept:     key access DEPARTMENTS;
        end class DEPARTMENT_PROJECTS;
    end PERSONNEL;
```

Second, the declaration of a class entails, in its basic form, the declaration of its member attributes and the indication of its relationships. A descriptive relationship is indicated by declaring an attribute called a descriptor; for example class EMPLOYEES contains

the descriptor declaration Dept_where_employeed. A descriptor is an object
of an implicitly declared type whose values implement descriptive
relationships. A descriptor attribute is declared using the operation
modifier **access** and the name of the describing class.

The indication of an inheritance relationship is achieved
through class context clauses and optional where clauses. A class context
clause indicates the class context of the subclass. This includes the
indication of the parent class(es) and the constraints, if any, governing
the inheritance of the parent's (or parents') properties and
membership(s). A where clause can be used, in addition to the class
context clause, to refine the membership constraints therein. For example
subclass PROJECT_MANAGERS inherits all the properties of class EMPLOYEES
and a certain part of the membership (those employees for whom the
predicat of the where clause is true). Similarly, subclass PROJECT_WORKERS
inherits all the properties of class EMPLOYEES and part of its membership
as indicated by the predicat given in the class context clause and refined
by the predicat of the where clause.

Figure 4. Token specification of package PERSONNEL_TYPES.

```
package PERSONNEL_TYPES is
        type DEPARTMENT_NUMBERS is range 1..50;
        subtype DEPARTMENT_NAMES is STRING (1..30);
            .
            .
            .
        type JOBS is (PROJECT_MANAGER, ENGINEER, SECRETARY,
                      PERSONNEL_OFFICER, WORKMAN);
            .
end PERSONNEL_TYPES;
```

A somehow more complex inheritance relationship can be
indicated as follows:

```
with class PROJECT_MANAGERS or PROJECT_WORKERS
class PROJECT_MEMBERS is
      Date_joined: DATES renames
            Appointment_date of PROJECT_MANAGERS,
            Date_joined of PROJECT_WORKERS;
      end class;
```

Subclass PROJECT_MEMBERS inherits the properties and the membership of
both PROJECT_MANAGERS and PROJECT_WORKERS; two of the inherited properties

are renamed for programming convenience: Appointment_date (of
PROJECT_MANAGERS) and Date_joined (of PROJECT_WORKERS).

Finally, with reference to figure 3, a few remarks concerning
the operation modifiers. A **key** operation modifier has several meanings:
(a) attribute values are unique within the class, (b) class members are
ordered in collating attribute value and (c) an attribute value must exist
at all times during the lifetime of the member (from its creation till its
removal). A **key** attribute corresponds, partially, to the primary key
domain of the relational data model where its role is to identify the
tuples of a relation. In AdaVIEW, a similar approach is taken however with
the remark that there are two aspects of the identification role: external
(that is in the application environment hence external to the database
environment) and internal (inside the database environment). **Key**
attributes are only used to support the external identification of the
data objects whereas the internal identification is achieved through
descriptor values. As a result a **key** attribute can be modified freely
without impact on the data structure.

A **letnull** operation modifier allows the attribute value to be,
or become, null (undefined) during the member's lifetime. Its absence
enforces the existence of an attribute value at all the times during the
member's lifetime. A default attribute value can be indicated through an
expression on the attribute declaration, for use at the creation time.

Finally, two operation modifiers are available to control the
visibility of an attribute in query and manipulation operations: **limited**
(usual visibility in queries, modification only through views) and **private**
(visibility for both query and modification only in view bodies); their
utility will become apparent in the following sections of the
presentation.

A database definition can be modified by editing its schema
and elaborating its modified database declaration; the old definition
is replaced providing the database is empty. A new database definition
(following either creation or modification) is always temporary. In order
for it to become permanent the program must issue a keep statement. For
example:

```
with schema PERSONNEL;
procedure CREATE_DB_PERSONNEL is
begin
      keep schema PERSONNEL;
end CREATE_DB_PERSONNEL;
```

Database defintions can be removed from the database
environment with a remove statement (as below) or by manipulating the
definition cursors presented in the last section:

remove schema PERSONNEL;

The elaboration of a database declaration for a database whose
definition is permanent results only in the logical connection of the
program to the database definition; this logical connection allows the
program to use the database definition on behalf of its active user and is
subject to authorization. Similar authorizations are also enforced on the
use of the data definition facilities themselves since this implies usage
of the database environment resources.

The means presented here for creating and modifying database
definitions are based on database declarations which must be prepared
before the execution of the program. The dynamic facilities presented in
the last section represent means to perform the creation and the
modification operations using information obtained dynamically i.e. at
program execution time.

At the representation (or physical) level data is organized in
arrays of record structures of objects. Operations with the definitions of
these arrays constitute the data definition facilities at the
representation level. These operations include creation, modification,
removal, space allocation / deallocation and access path definition (
create, modify, remove). The creation and the modification operations are
implicit in the elaboration of data representation and access path
clauses given as part of a database declaration. For example figure 5
illustrates an IMS representation of the conceptual diagram of database
PERSONNEL and gives the corresponding AdaVIEW coding of the data
representation and access path clauses (normally given as part of the
schema). The creation and the modification operations as well as the
remaining operations at the representation level can also be given
explicitly using statements.

The capabilities which the representation level facilities
offer to a database application developer are several. (a) True data
independence can be achieved: conceptual structures can be mapped onto the
most efficient physical structures and the latter can be changed in time
without affecting the former (hence the programs).

(b) Conceptual structures (and the programs) can be ported from one database environment to another without change. (c) The management and control of the storage space, a valuable resource in any database environment, can be achieved in a straightforward manner.

Figure 5. IMS representation of database PERSONNEL.

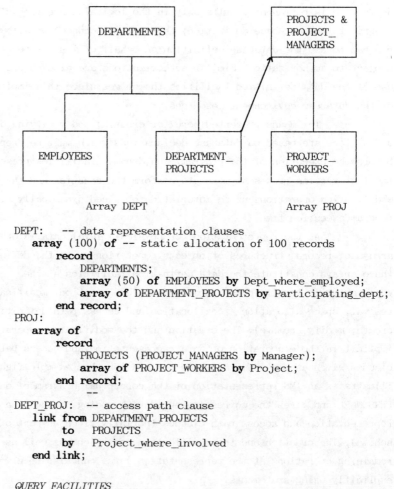

```
                    Array DEPT                          Array PROJ

DEPT:    -- data representation clauses
    array (100) of -- static allocation of 100 records
        record
            DEPARTMENTS;
            array (50) of EMPLOYEES by Dept_where_employed;
            array of DEPARTMENT_PROJECTS by Participating_dept;
        end record;
PROJ:
    array of
        record
            PROJECTS (PROJECT_MANAGERS by Manager);
            array of PROJECT_WORKERS by Project;
        end record;
            --
DEPT_PROJ:   -- access path clause
    link from DEPARTMENT_PROJECTS
        to    PROJECTS
        by    Project_where_involved
    end link;
```

QUERY FACILITIES

A query is a process whereby values obtained from one or more databases are made available to the program. The result of a query is in general a sequence of query objects that can be either processed by the program or input to another query. A query object has a composite value whose components can be attribute values or values derived from these.

AdaVIEW query facilities consist of query blocks and views. A query block is a statement that describes a query and causes its execution. It consists of two parts: a descriptive part and an imperative part. The descriptive part describes the query object and the constraints defining the query set. The imperative part contains the processing instructions to be applied to each (or only) object of the query set. For example the following query block obtains from database PERSONNEL (figure 3) a list of names of projects and project workers for a department given by its number (In_Dno):

```
declare
      P:  Pname from PROJECTS;
      Pw: Ename from PROJECT_WORKERS;   -- Ename is inherited
      ...
begin
      ...
      obtain P; Pw
      where
            P'Desc, In_Dno =
                Project_where_involved, Participating_dept.Dno
                from DEPARTMENT_PROJECTS
          and
                Pw.Project = P'Desc
      order by
            Pname, Ename
      loop
      ...
      end loop;
      ...
```

The descriptive part of this query block (delimited by the reserved words **obtain** and **where**) refers to two cursors (P, Pw) that describe the query object. A cursor is an entity that represents (or is a view of) an active object, or part thereof, of a query set.It has name, processing intent, list of components (attributes + descriptor) and query set. The processing intent is an indication of what form of processing will be applied to the actual object and is similar to the mode of a formal parameter: **in** (fetch only), **in out** (modify / remove), **out** (create). The cursor query set can be a class, a class restriction or the query set defined by a view.

The processing intent, the component list and the query set of a cursor represent together its specification. Cursor specifications can be used either in cursor declarations (given in declarative parts) or as query object descriptions (or parts thereof) in query blocks.

For example the previous query block can be rewritten:

```
obtain Project, Project.Pname, Ename from PROJECT_WORKERS;
        Pn: PROJECT_NAMES renames Project.Pname
where
        Project, In_Dno =
            Project_where_involved, Participating_dept.Dno
                from DEPARTMENT_PROJECTS
    order by
        Pn, Ename
```

The descriptive part of a query block may include simple expressions
using some of the components of the query object. For example the
following query block obtains a list of project numbers (Pno), name, hours
worked and salary of the project workers with a pay rate greater than a
standard value (Standard_pay_rate):

```
declare
        Pay_rate: NATURAL;
begin
        obtain Ename, Project.Pno, Hours_worked, Salary
                            from PROJECT_WORKERS;
                Hours_worked / Salary into Pay_rate
        where
                Pay_rate > Standard_pay_rate
        order by
                Project.Pno, Ename
        loop
        ...
```

For more complex queries there is a factoring facility which improves the
clarity of the coding. For example, if in the previous query we are
interested only in the project numbers (Pno) of the projects with a pay
rate higher than standard pay rate then the following query block can be
given:

```
obtain distinct Pno from PROJECTS
where
        let X: Project, Hours_worked, Salary
                        from PROJECT_WORKERS;
                Hours_worked / Salary into Pay_rate;
                where Pay_rate > Standard_pay_rate
            end X;
        in
            Pno = X.Project.Pno
    order by
    Pno reverse
```

Predefined attributes can be used to specify derivations such as averages,
minima, maxima and others.

For example the following query obtains the average salary of the project
workers of a project given by its number (Pno):

obtain Salary'Average, Project **from** PROJECT_WORKERS
where
      Project.Pno = Pno

The imperative part of a query block can be used to process
either the entire query set or only the first (which may be the only)
object of the query set. In the first case the descriptive part of the
query block forms the iteration scheme of a loop statement (otherwise said
the imperative part of the query block is a loop). In the second case the
query block can be embedded in a block statement or used in conjuction
with a data manipulation statement (presented in the following section).
The following example illustrates a procedure using a query block with a
loop imperative part:

```
with schema PERSONNEL;
procedure LIST_ALL is
        E: Ename, Dept_where_employed from EMPLOYEES;
        procedure NEW_PAGE (...) is separate;
        procedure PRINT (..) is separate;
begin
        obtain Dno, Dname from DEPARTMENTS; E
        where
                Dno = E.Dept_where_employed.Dno
        order by
                Dno, E.Ename
        when Dno'Break => NEW_PAGE (Dno, Dname);
        loop
                PRINT (E.Ename);
        end loop;
end LIST_ALL;
```

The descriptive part of the query block can be followed with event
handlers (introduced by the reserved word **when**) to perform special
processing in connection with certain events occurring during the query.
An event handler is a statement executed when a condition, normally
associated with a query event, becomes true. Examples of query events
include breaks in the sequence of query entries, end of data, no data
found, unavailable data (when locked by another user) and others. If more
than one event handler is associated with an event they are executed in
the sequence in which they are given. Following the execution of the event
handler(s), the program execution resumes with the remaining statements of
the loop, if any.

A view is a package of specifications which allows a program to query and manipulate databases in a previously established way. Like an Ada package, a view consists of a specification and a body. The view specification has a declarative part, a query constraint and a discriminant part. The items of the declarative part can be cursor, variable or subprogram declarations. The query constraint is identical to that of a query block. The discriminant part can be used to vary dynamically its declarative part. The view body is identical to a package body and is required when subprogram declarations are given in the declarative part or when event handlers need to be provided with the view. View declarations can be given as library units only (like the database declarations). Unlike a query block, a view can allow both query and manipulation operations to be performed. Figure 7 illustrates a view which allows both query and modifications depending on a discriminant. The use for modification will be presented in the following section. Here the interest is focused on the query side and we give below an example procedure using the view to print a list of employees with their names, salaries and tax deductions (obtained by the view):

```
with view PAYROLL;
procedure LIST_PAYROLL is
     Query_only: constant := 1;
     procedure PRINT (...) is ...
begin
     use view PAYROLL (Query_only)
     loop
          PRINT (Ename, Salary, Tax_deduction);
     end loop;
end LIST_PAYROLL;
```

DATA MANIPULATION FACILITIES

Data manipulation facilities allow the programs to operate with, or upon, database objects. The manipulation operations are class properties common to all the class members; their classification consists of two groups: basic manipulation operations and data subprograms. The basic manipulation operations include the operations inherent in the member creation, modification or removal from a class, inclusion or removal from a subclass. For example the procedure in figure 6 creates an employee object for an employee in a department given by its number (Emp_Dno). Two cursors are declared in the declarative part of this procedure: D and E. D is an input (fetch only) cursor without component list, which receives the descriptor of a DEPARTMENTS object (the latter representing the property "Dept_where_employed" of the EMPLOYEES member to be created). E is an output cursor which represents the EMPLOYEES object to be created (the component list of this cursor is given implicitly by the schema to which it refers - in this case PERSONNEL, see figure 3).

Figure 6. Example procedure for member creation.

```
with schema PERSONNEL;
procedure CREATE_EMPLOYEE (
        Emp_Dno:        DEPARTMENT_NUMBERS;
        Emp_details: EMPLOYEES'RECORD)
is
        D: DEPARTMENTS (Emp_Dno); -- class restriction using a
        E: out EMPLOYEES;          --            key constraint
        .
begin
        .
        set E := (Emp_details, Dept_where_employeed => D'Desc);
        .
end CREATE_EMPLOYEE;
```

A set statement is used to create the object and assign its value to cursor E. The creation becomes persistent at the end of the transaction in which the procedure is called (transactions are presented in the following section). A class attribute (RECORD) is used to indicate a record type implicitly defined by the class declaration with a component list consisting of all non-descriptor attributes of the class member (inclusive the inheritted ones in the case of a subclass member).

In order to modify the Job and the Salary attributes of an EMPLOYEES object (given by Emp_details.Eno) one can code as follows:

```
        E: in out Job, Salary from EMPLOYEES;
        New_job: JOBS;
        New_sal: SALARIES;
        .
begin
        .
        obtain E
        where  E.Eno = Emp_details.Eno
        set    E := (Job => New_job, Salary => New_sal);
        .
```

The removal of an EMPLOYEES member can be coded as follows (E is an in out cursor, with or without components) :

```
        set E := null;
```

The inclusion of an EMPLOYEES member in PROJECT_MANAGERS can be coded as follows:

```
E:    EMPLOYEES (Emp_details.Eno);
Pm:   out PROJECT_MANAGERS;
Today: DATES := Current_date;
            .
begin
            .
     with E set Pm := (Appointment_date => Today);
            .
```

The removal of a PROJECT_MANAGERS member can happen in two ways: removal from the subclass only and removal from both class and subclass. For the first case the coding is as follows:

```
Pm:   in out PROJECT_MANAGERS (Emp_details.Eno);
            .
begin
            .
     set Pm := null;
            .
```

For the second case the member (of the base class e.g. EMPLOYEES) must first be removed from all subclasses, if any, then removed from the base class itself. A special form of the statement **set**, the inverse of **with ... set** form, is useful in such cases to decompose a subclass member into its constituents. For example:

```
E:    in out EMPLOYEES;
Pm:   in out PROJECT_MANAGERS (Emp_details.Eno);
            .
begin
            .
     set E from Pm;
     set E, Pm := null;
```

The basic manipulation operations can be used to operate upon single objects (as in the previous examples) or sequences of objects within implicit or explicit data loops. In the following example view PAYROLL (see figure 7) is used to increase by 5 % the salary of all the employees whose tax deduction is greater than 20 % of their current salary (an implicit form of data loop is used):

```
set Salary := old Salary * 1.05
when Tax_deduction > 0.2 * Salary
in view PAYROLL (0);
```

An explicit form of data loop can be given, for the previous example, as follows:

```
use view PAYROLL (0)
loop
    if Tax_deduction > 0.2 * Salary then
        set Salary := old Salary * 1.05;
    end if;
end loop;
```

A data subprogram is an application-defined manipulation operation which can involve several objects (or parts thereof) at a time. A data subprogram is declared in a view and is visible at all the places where all other view declarative items are visible. In figure 7 view PAYROLL declares data function Tax_deduction whose body is given later in the body of the view.

Figure 7. Example view declared with a discriminant part.

```
with schema PERSONNEL;
view PAYROLL (Usage: NATURAL) is
        Ename, Dept_where_employed from EMPLOYEES;
        case Usage is
            when 0 => in out Salary from EMPLOYEES;
            when others => Salary from EMPLOYEES;
        end case;
        function Tax_deduction return SALARIES;
where all
group by Dept_where_employed
order by Ename
end PAYROLL;

view body PAYROLL is
        No_of_dependents from EMPLOYEES;
        function Tax_deduction return SALARIES is
            .
            .
        end Tax_deduction;
end PAYROLL;
```

The entities visible within the data function declaration include the view declarative items given before it, the class declarations of the schema(s) given in the view's context clause(s) together with all the other entities made visible via the usual mechanism of context and use clauses. Private attributes of visible classes can also be used as cursor components given in the view body. For example, figure 7 illustrates a cursor that uses a private attribute (No_of_dependents) and it is given in the view body where it is used by the data function Tax_deduction.

The private attribute declaration (normally given as part of the declaration of class EMPLOYEES in schema PERSONNEL) would be:

No_of_dependents: **private** NATURAL;

Note that the declarative part of the view body is but a continuation of the view declarative part and so the cursors declared therein are obtained from the same objects selected by the query constraint of the view.

The private attributes can only be manipulated through data subprograms or event handlers given in view bodies. For example in order to manipulate No_of_dependents one requires a view and a data procedure as follows:

```
with schema PERSONNEL;
view CREATE_EMPLOYEE (In_Dno: DEPARTMENT_NUMBERS) is
     D: DEPARTMENTS (In_Dno);
     E: out EMPLOYEES enforce Dept_where_employeed => D'Desc;
     procedure SET_NO_OF_DEPENDENTS;
end CREATE_EMPLOYEE;

view body CREATE_EMPLOYEE is
     function Input_nod (
             Eno: EMPLOYEE_NUMBERS) return NATURAL is
         .
         .
     end Input_nod;
     procedure SET_NO_OF_DEPENDENTS (
             In_Eno: EMPLOYEE_NUMBERS) is
         .
     begin
         .
         set E.No_of_dependents := Input_nod (In_Eno);
         .
     end SET_NO_OF_DEPENDENTS;
end CREATE_EMPLOYEE;
```

This view can be used in the following block statement to create an employee object:

```
use view CREATE_EMPLOYEE (Emp_Dno) -- see figure 6 for Emp_Dno
begin
     set E := Emp_details; -- see figure 6 for Emp_details
     SET_NO_OF_DEPENDENTS (Emp_details.Eno);
end;
```

Note that the declaration of No_of_employees does not provide a default value which forces the creation program to issue a call to procedure SET_NO_OF_DEPENDENTS before the end of the create transaction (whenever this occurs).

Views and **limited** attributes can be used to manipulate objects related through complex relationships that are neither descriptive nor inheritance relationships. For example the project on which a project worker works must be one of the projects in which his (her) department is involved. In order to implement this relationship one could limit the visibility of the attribute Project (of class PROJECT_WORKERS) and provide one (or several) view(s) to manipulate it. For example, the following view can be used to create a member of PROJECT_WORKERS:

```
with schema PERSONNEL;
view CREATE_PROJECT_WORKER (
     In_Eno: EMPLOYEE_NUMBERS;
     In_Pno: PROJECT_NUMBERS)
is
     E: in out EMPLOYEES (In_Eno); -- forces object locking
     P: in out PROJECTS (In_Pno);  -- same
     Pw: out PROJECT_WORKERS enforce Project => P'Desc;
assert
     P'Desc, E.Dept_where_employeed.Dno =
     Project_where_involved, Participating_dept.Dno
                          from DEPARTMENT_PROJECTS
end CREATE_PROJECT_WORKER;
```

The view can be used as in the following set statement:

```
use view CREATE_PROJECT_WORKER (Given_Eno, Given_Pno)
with E set Pw := (Date_joined => Current_date);
```

Note that the other manipulation aspects of a PROJECT_WORKERS member can be dealt with freely by the program; the only other provision that could be necessary in this case would be a view to allow a project worker to change projects, if the application requires it.

DATA CONTROL FACILITIES

AdaVIEW distinguishes two aspects of the data control: data integrity and authorizations. Data integrity means the existence of certain relational constraints among objects, which must be enforced during, or at the end of, the time the objects are active. (Active objects are those upon which the program performs query and manipulation operations). The period of time in which the objects are active is called a transaction. The data control facilities for the enforcement and the preservation of data integrity are transactions, relationships, operation modifiers and views. A transaction consists of a chain of transaction steps each consisting of the execution of a subprogram.

A transaction step is indicated by the reserved word **step** following
immediately the reserved word **begin**. For example:

>   **with schema** PERSONNEL;
>   **procedure** CREATE **is**
>
>   .
>   .
>
>   **begin step**
>
>   .
>   .
>
>   **end** CREATE;

The beginning of a transaction step acquires all the resources required in
connection with the cursors declared in its declarative part. The end of a
transaction step (caused by the end of the subprogram) may release some of
the resources acquired at its beginning that are no longer necessary e.g.
resources for **in out** cursors that have not been modified or otherwise
used. (A similar process takes place when a query block is executed; this
time however the resources are in connection only with the cursors
becoming visible in the corresponding context). The end of the outermost
transaction step saves the modifications to the active objects made during
its course and the course of any nested transaction steps, if any. This
allows the restarting (or the continuation) of a long transaction
following the last completed transaction step. Finally, a transaction is
ended by issuing a **commit** statement either from whithin its outermost step
or after its last step has ended. The **commit** statement causes the end-of-
transaction integrity constraints to be applied and makes persistent the
modifications to the active objects. (Note that the persistent
modifications may be kept in the environment or discarded according to
whether the corresponding data definitions are permanent or temporary
respectively). Violations of the integrity constraints terminate the
execution of the **commit** statement and raise exceptions. A **backout**
statement is available to backout all the modifications up to and
including the modifications of a given transaction step, e.g.

>   **backout to** FIRST_UPDATE;

The **backout** statement can be given within or outside a transaction step.
        The end-of-transaction integrity constraints are those in
connection with attributes whose operation modifiers enforce the presence
of a value, operation modifier **key**, descriptive and inheritance
relationships.

For example key values are checked for unicity, descriptive relationships are enforced such that the describing objects cannot be removed from the environment as long as there are described objects, and others. The end-of-transaction integrity constraints can be applied sooner in the transaction by using an **enforce** statement.

The remaining facilities for the enforcement of data integrity have an immediate nature in that they provide at the same time both the modification and the enforcement means. These are the **private** and **limited** operation modifiers, views using the **assert** and **enforce** options, data subprograms and the event handlers given in view bodies. A **private** operation modifiers prevents the program from directly quering and manipulating the attribute which can be used only in data subprograms. A **limited** operation modifer allows the attribute to be used in queries however the program is prevented from its direct manipulation which can be done only through views. The latter can use **assert** and **enforce** clauses to control the values of such attributes. Event handlers can be associated with views in order to implement more complex relational constraints among the data objects hence a tighter data control. Such event handlers can be given in the bodies of the associated views as in the following example of a view designed for the manipulation of the attribute Dept_where_employeed of class EMPLOYEES when an eployee changes departments:

```
with schema PERSONNEL;
view CHANGE_DEPARTMENT (In_Eno: EMPLOYEE_NUMBERS) is
      E: in out Dept_where_employeed from EMPLOYEES (In_Eno);
end CHANGE_DEPARTMENT;

view body CHANGE_DEPARTMENT is
      when Dept_where_employeed'New =>
            declare
                  Old_dept: in out Nemps from DEPARTMENTS (
                             old Dept_where_employeed.Dno);
                  New_dept: in out Nemps from DEPARTMENTS (
                             Dept_where_employeed.Dno);
            begin
                  set Old_dept.Nemps := old Old_dept.Nemps - 1;
                  set New_dept.Nemps := old New_dept.Nemps + 1;
            end;
end CHANGE_DEPARTMENT;
```

The event handler of the previous view body maintains the attribute Nemps (number of employees) of class DEPARTMENTS (see figure 3).

Authorizations refer to the rights of the users to use the resources of the database environment in certain ways and to pass these

rights onto, or revoke them from, other users. These resources include
storage space, database definitions, data objects, libraries, predefined
databases, and others. The authorization facilities consist of predefined
databases of users, libraries and application-defined database definitions
(SYS_USE, SYS_LIB and SYS_DEF respectively) and operations (available
through statements) to allow access links and rights to be created,
modifed or removed from, among the corresponding objects of the predefined
databases.

DYNAMIC FACILITIES

A data definition is an entity of the database environment
which describes the properties of collections of data objects, an
individual data object or a part thereof. Such an entity is called a
definition object and can be a database definition, a class definition, a
member definition or an attribute definition. The properties of the
definition objects themselves are described by generic data definition
units which are sublanguage entites declared by generic data declarations.
The instantiation of a generic data declaration (which happens
dynamically) creates a definition object. The instantiation of generic
data declarations and the elaboration of database declarations (presented
in the first section) are the two means for creating definition objects in
AdaVIEW. The latter method of specifying data properties is static (it has
to be prepared before the execution of the program), the former is
dynamic.

The definition objects of a database environment exist in the
predefined database SYS_DEF. The program can manipulate the definition
objects by using a special kind of cursors called definition cursors. For
example:

```
with schema SYS_DEF;
procedure REMOVE_CLASS (
        Library_name, Schema_name, Class_name: STRING)
is
        S: schema (Library_name, Schema_name);
        C: in out class (S, Class_name);

begin step

        set C := null;

end REMOVE_CLASS;
```

The AdaVIEW dynamic facilities consist of generic data declarations and instantiations, definition cursors, the predefined database SYS_DEF (for data definition) and generic view declarations and instantiations (for query and manipulation).

CONCLUSION

We have presented the architecture and the basic facilities of a data sublanguage for Ada. The sublanguage architecture is drawn from three different sources, namely the architecture of the relational systems (Astrahan et al. 1976), the semantic data model (Hammer & McLeod 1981) and the architecture of the Ada language.

The sublanguage facilities for data definition allow a compact and economic way of specifying complex data models that would require significant more effort and system resources using other means, notably SQL-based data systems.

Data definition facilities exist at two levels, conceptual and representation. This separation insures that the programs depend only upon the conceptual definitions and remain portabil accross a wide range of supported representations.

The conceptual level definition facilities equal the power of their relational counterparts (class = table) and present important advantages over them, in particular the protected use of object descriptors (equivalent to tuple identifiers), which eliminates the problem of modifications to key attributes, and the existence of inheritance relationships, which increases the semantic expressiveness of a data model.

The representation level definition facilities include means for the specification of both access paths and physical storage structures. The latter facilities are not generally available in the relational systems, or are available in some only in a form that serves the performance of their own management system (for example cluster definitions in some SQL implementations). The AdaVIEW representation level facilities allow a finer mapping of the conceptual structures onto both the sublanguage own database environment and "guest" database environments that can be relational or non-relational.

The query blocks and the views represent the two forms of query facilities present in the sublanguage. Queries can be structured in a manner compatible with the SQL query block.

In addition, AdaVIEW provides factoring features that allow complex queries to be expressed more clearly.

The view mechanism represents a veritable extension of the concept of package to a data sublanguage. It provides integrated facilities for query, manipulation and control, which reduces the programming effort, provides ample scope for the standardization of the development process and represents a valuable source of information for the optimization of the access paths by the optimizer component of a data system.

The existence of predefined databases allows a flexible implementation of important sublanguage features such as authorizations and dynamic facilities for definition, query and manipulation.

The generic facilities, inherited from the architecture of the Ada language, offer the possibility to create, modify and use complex data definitions dynamically. They can also be used statically to specify generic data structures that may represent the common parts of a range of similar application databases with the advantage of reducing the development effort and increasing the reusability of the application software.

ACKNOWLEDGEMENTS

We wish to thank Mr. Georges Schmit from the Government of the Grand Duchy of Luxembourg for his interest and support towards our effort. We also wish to thank Mrs. Françoise Le Bris of Alsys SA (France) for her interest in our work and support in obtaining the Alsys Ada compiling system which is being used on our project.

REFERENCES

Astrahan, M.M., et al. (1976). System R: Relational approach to database management. ACM Trans. Database Syst., 1, 2, June.

Bancilhon, F. (1986). A logic-programming/object-orientated cocktail, ACM SIGMOD RECORD, 15, 3, September.

Banerjee, J., et al. (1987). Data model issues for object-oriented applications. ACM Trans. Office Inf. Syst., 5, 1, January.

Blasgen, M.W. & Eswaran, K.P. (1977). Storage and access in relational data bases. IBM Syst. Journal, 16, 4.

Chamberlin, D.D., et al. (1981). A history and evaluation of System R. Comm. ACM, 24, 10, October.

Chen, P.P. (1976). The entity-relationship model - Toward a unified view of data. ACM Trans. Database Syst., 1, 1, March.

Claybrook, B.G., et al. (1985). Defining database views as data abstractions. IEEE Trans. Software Eng., SE-11, 1, January.

Codd, E.F. (1970). A relational model of data for large shared
        data banks. Comm. ACM, 13, 6, June.
Dittrich, K.R., et al. (1986). An event/trigger mechanism to enforce
        complex consistency constraints in design databases.
        ACM SIGMOD RECORD, 15, 3, September.
Fishman, D.H., et al. (1987). Iris: An object oriented database management
        system. ACM Trans. Office Inf. Syst., 5, 1, January.
Hammer, M. & McLeod, D. (1981). Database description with SDM: A semantic
        database model. ACM Trans. Database Syst., 6, 3, September.
Hardwick, M. & Spooner, D.L. (1987). Comparison of some data models for
        engineering objects. IEEE Comp. Graphics, 7, 3, March.
Purdy, A., et al. (1987). Integrating an object server with other worlds.
        ACM Trans. Office Inf. Syst., 5, 1, January.
Smith, J.M., et al. (1985). A tool kit for database programming in Ada.
        Proceedings Ada Int. Conference, Paris, 14-16 May

ADA IN SAFETY CRITICAL APPLICATIONS

R. Holzapfel
G. Winterstein
SYSTEAM KG, Am Rüppurrer Schloß 7, D-7500 Karlsruhe

Abstract. Starting from a standardized safety definition, a definition of safe programs is developed. This definition is specialized for the programming language Ada and programming rules for Ada are derived from this definition. These rules support the writing of safe Ada programs, i.e. if the programmer obeys them when writing an Ada program, it is significantly more likely that the resulting program is safe than otherwise. It is our conclusion that the programming language Ada is suitable for writing safety critical software if these programming rules are obeyed. The results of this paper and the method for their derivation is compared with two other studies that deal with the same or a similar subject.

1   INTRODUCTION

Our aim is to use the programming language Ada for the implementation of embedded real time systems with special emphasis on the requirements for safety critical software. At the time being most real time systems are implemented in assembler, with all its well-known drawbacks. It is not necessary to repeat here the benefits of a high-order language that is well-defined and standardized.

In this study we shall concentrate our efforts on the question: How can Ada support the implementation of safety critical real time systems? And furthermore: Are special programming guidelines necessary to increase confidence in the safety of the programs?

There are several other studies which deal with these or similar questions. One of them is "SPARK — The SPADE Ada Kernel" by Carre & Jennings (1987). It defines a safe subset of Ada that is quite small, similar to Modula-2.

The aim of this study was "to produce a simple, verifiable language, better suited to systematic program development, which sits inside Ada." They say "that the development of a safe sublanguage of Ada has to be mainly 'constructive', i.e. that it must proceed by gradual enlargement of a 'safe kernel', rather than by successively excising unsatisfactory constructs." Although it was intended to "gradually extend the language" in the future we have to ask whether SPARK can truely be addressed as Ada because SPARK is an extremely curtailed Ada subset for formal verification purposes.

Another study was done by Aeronautical Radio (1987). Its title is "Guidance for Using the Ada Programming Language in Avionic Systems". The base of their examination is their experience with software for avionic systems. It contains a detailed examination of most Ada features resulting in a categorization of the examined features in one of five categories:

1. "The features are commonly used in avionics software."

2. "They have a specific preferred implementation."

3. "They should be supported by the selected compiler."

4. "They should be used only after careful cost/benefit analysis."

5. "They are inappropriate for avionics equipment."

In contrast to these studies we are using an alternative approach: Our first step is to find a definition of what we call a safe program in general. Then we have to specialize that definition so that it can be applied to Ada programs. We shall set up a number of programming rules that support the writing of safe programs.

The whole investigation was carried out by SYSTEAM KG under contract from MBB for a recent project (Holzapfel & Winterstein (1987 a, b)). We are grateful for the permission to present our findings in public.

2   THE TERM SAFETY

The Military Standard MIL-STD-882B (1984) gives a definition of the term safety:

"3.1.12 Safety. Freedom from those conditions that can cause death, injury, occupational illness, or damage to or loss of equipment or property".

Safety is different from reliability, from security, and from correctness. Leveson (1986) gives good hints to these delimitations: "In general, reliability requirements are concerned with making a system *failure free*, whereas safety requirements are concerned with making it *mishap free*. ... Reliability is concerned with every possible software error, whereas safety is only concerned with those that result in actual system hazards. ... Even if all failures cannot be prevented, it may be possible to ensure that the failures that do occur are of minor consequence or that, even if a potentially serious failure does occur, the system will 'fail safe'. ... Unfortunately, in many complex systems, safety and reliability may imply conflicting requirements, and thus the system cannot be built to maximize both. ... In fact, the safest system is sometimes one that does not work at all." Mishap is another word for the situations that are named in the MIL-STD-882B safety definition.

Leveson (1986) explains the difference between safety and security: "There are differences, however, between safety and traditional security research. Security has focused on malicious actions, whereas safety is also concerned with inadvertent actions. Furthermore, the primary emphasis in security research has been on preventing unauthorized access to classified information, as opposed to preventing more general malicious actions."

A system (or a program) is correct if it conforms to its (formal) specification. But there may be an error in the specification so that a hazard will occur although the software is correct.

So we can say that a system (or a program as a special case) can be correct, reliable, and secure but *not* safe. Consequently Leveson demands treatment of safety as a special topic in system design.

Since the software in embedded real time systems has at least partial control over the state of the whole system, precautions must be taken so that the software does not lead the system into a hazardous state. A typical example is the software for avionic systems: It must never cause the aeroplane to get out of control or to crash.

Note that often hardware failure tolerance does not prevent a software error from leading to a hazardous state of the whole system, because in most cases of hardware failure tolerance is achieved by hardware redundancy in form of several equivalent processors which all execute the same program. The program which is executed by these parallel processors may contain a programming error that may lead to a mishap of the system — possibly followed by a crash of the aeroplane for example.

Leveson (1986) formulates two further definitions concerning safety critical software:

"Safety critical software functions. Functions that can directly or indirectly cause or allow a hazardous system state to exist."

"Safety critical software. Software that contains safety critical functions."

The term safety has been sufficiently clarified so that we can devote our efforts to the definition of safe programs now.

2   DEFINITION OF SAFE PROGRAMS

We have seen that in general safety is not a topic that can be dealt with when designing a component of a system independently of the rest of the system. However, a system can not be called safe if one of its components is unsafe. If software is a system's component it has to be safe. For a safety requirements analysis we have to know what hazardous effects may occur when the program takes wrong steps. But we do not want to determine specific safety requirements for a specific application; rather, we want to lay down general properties that characterize each safety critical program, no matter what the application.

We think that there are indeed some properties which are common to all safety critical programs. The major principle behind them is that a safe program must never get out of control, i.e. the program must never be aborted and must never do unpredictable things. Furthermore — but with lower priority — the program must be written so that other persons are able to read and to understand it in order to approve or to maintain it. Maintainance must never lead to a program that violates our major principle.

Now we give our definition of safe programs that is considered consistent with both our theoretical findings and with accepted software engineering practice for current implementations of safety critical software.

A program is called *safe* if it has the following four properties:

1. The memory requirements of the program are known before run time.

2. The program contains no action that has an unpredictable overhead in execution time.

3. The program and all its components have a deterministic behaviour for every possible set of input data. All branches in the program are explicit. The program is verifiable so that no error can occur at run time — no matter whether it is detectable or not.

4. The program is source level transparent. That means it is written in a consistent and readable way. The program does not make use of different features to express the same thing. All actions are visible.

Property 1 guarantees that the program's memory will suffice whatever the input of the program. Memory requirements are determined before run time and enough memory space is made available to meet these requirements. If memory exhausts at run time the program may be aborted and might no longer control the surrounding system. This may lead to a mishap.

Property 2 prevents actions that consume an unpredictable amount of time that cannot be influenced by the programmer. However, this does not include constructs whose time consumption can be influenced by the programmer, such as loops. An embedded real time system normally has strict time constraints to guarantee maximal reaction times. If the reaction time for a safety critical function is longer than required a mishap may be the result.

Property 3 guarantees that there are no errors in the program (errors in the sense of the programming language that is used to write the program). Furthermore, all program components have to behave deterministically. Run time errors and indeterminisms may also lead to hazardous situations.

Property 4 supports checking of the correctness of the program. For this purpose it must be easily readable for a person who is not the author of the program.

Because our aim is a safe programming language and not only safe programs we need a further definition:

Safe programming language. A programming language is safe if every program written in that language is safe.

3   SAFE ADA PROGRAMS

To get a safe Ada program it would be sufficient in general to demand the four properties of safety of the program. For instance, program verification may be a method to guarantee that the program's space will not exhaust at run time. Inspection of the program by a person other than its author may support source level transparency. So restrictions of language features are not absolutely necessary to achieve safe Ada programs.

In practice, however, it is rather difficult to check for the four properties even for a given program. Formal verification, for instance, is not possible for all programs. So it is desirable to have a set of rules that support and restrict the programmer of an embedded real time system. If he obeys the rules when writing the programs, then it is likely that the program will be safe than if he disregards the rules.

In order to support the writing of Ada programs which are safe in the sense of the definition given above, all Ada features are examined with regard to whether or not their use may have an impact on the safety of a particular program. The result of this examination is a list of 35 rules that restrict some language features. Obeyance of these rules can be checked for each program, maybe by automatic tools.

Choosing the programming rules is a difficult undertaking because the following needs must be taken into consideration:

- The rules must be simple to allow simple checking of whether they are observed in a given program.

- The rules must maintain the character of the language in toto — although they restrict the language.

- The rules should reflect the intended application area, i.e. if a feature is known not to be used, then it can be excluded in order to simplify the rules.

Because these needs are partially conflicting requirements, there are a lot of variations possible when choosing the programming rules. This is especially true for the last need. Because the project for which this study was done did not intend to use Ada tasking facilities we could exclude tasking completely. Note that this exclusion is not a direct (or indirect) consequence of our definition of safe programs. Rather it is a consequence of the last need and can be expressed as a simple rule (Rule numbering is taken from Holzapfel & Winterstein (1987 a) without change.):

R5.   Tasks and tasking statements shall not be used.

If, in contrast, the application wants to use Ada tasks then several other rules have to be stated, for example not to use dynamic tasks, not to write programs that contain deadlocks and so on. In any case the rules have to guarantee the four properties of safe programs.

There were many reasons for the exclusion of Ada tasking in the project which the study was written for. First, there were no tasks in the programs that had been written up to that time. Second, the project members estimated an intolerable time overhead for a typical rendezvous. Third, the delay statement in Ada only guarantees a minimum delay time but not a maximum time. Fourth, scheduling is a 'hidden' job that is not transparent to the programmer.

The first reason results from the power of habit and so does the fourth, and so we think time will fade this habit and future projects will use Ada tasking. The second reason — the time overhead of rendezvous — will disappear with growing efficiency of Ada task implementations. Furthermore, it is possible that there will be task implementations in the future that allow the user to select specific scheduling mechanisms that have to conform to Ada semantics. The problems with the delay statements are also problems of the tasking implementation.

So we are convinced that this general restriction on Ada tasking will vanish in the future.

The following list gives an overview of the most important Ada features that shall not be used in safe Ada:

- Access types
- Dynamic constraints
- Recursive subprograms
- Tasks
- Predefined exceptions
- Unchecked type conversions
- Default values
- Derived types
- Choice **others**
- Anonymous types

In contrast, the following Ada features are also part of safe Ada. They can not be found in simpler high-order programming languages as Pascal or Modula-2:

- Based literals
- Fixed point types
- Limited types
- Private types
- Aggregates
- Operations for boolean arrays
- Overloading
- Operator declarations
- Subunits
- User defined exceptions
- Generic Units
- Representation clauses

Safe Ada is an abbreviation for Ada restricted by the programming rules. Safe Ada is considered to be a safe programming language with respect to the definitions above.

The following four chapters show the derivation of programming rules for safe Ada from the four properties of safety. Only a few examples for those rules are given.

4 STATIC MEMORY REQUIREMENTS (PROPERTY 1)

All the situations in which memory space is requested within an Ada program are listed in the description of the predefined exception STORAGE_ERROR:

STORAGE_ERROR

"This exception is raised in any of the following situations: when the dynamic storage allocated to a task is exceeded; during the evaluation of an allocator, if the space available for the collection of allocated objects is exhausted; or during the elaboration of a declarative item, or during the execution of a subprogram call, if storage is not sufficient." (LRM 11.1/8)

If we can

1. determine the memory requirements $M(A)$ of each memory consuming action A within the program at compile time and

2. assure at compile time that each such action *A* will be executed at run time only a statically fixed number of times, say *N(A)*

then an upper limit of the program's memory requirements can be determined before run time. This upper limit is the

sum M(A) * N(A) over all memory consuming actions *A*.

The following subchapter examines allocator calls as an example for a memory consuming action. Tasks which are addressed in the description of STORAGE_ERROR are no problem in safe Ada because they are excluded due to other reasons.

4.1   Allocator call
Storage for an object of type T on a collection is requested by NEW T. Because an allocator can be called within a loop it is impossible to determine *N(NEW T)* statically. So allocator calls are considered unsafe. R1 embraces the exclusion of allocator calls:

R1.   Access types shall not be used.

5   LIMITED EXECUTION TIME (PROPERTY 2)
Actions that consume an unpredictable amount of time are:

– Exception handling

– Allocator call

– Waiting for a rendezvous

As an example, we shall consider exception handling:

5.1   Exception handling
After raising an exception E (e.g. by **raise** E) the dynamic subprogram call chain must be searched backward in order to find an exception handler for E.

The maximum number of steps within this search is the maximum number of nested subprogram calls that can occur in the program at run time. The nesting depth is limited by excluding recursive subprogram calls from safe Ada. So here is no need to exclude exceptions from safe Ada if we obey R3:

R3. Subprograms shall not be called recursively.

6 DETERMINISTIC AND PREDICTABLE BEHAVIOUR (PROPERTY 3)

In order to guarantee deterministic and predictable behaviour and the absence of run time errors all errors of the following classes defined in LRM (1983) 1.6/(b)-(d) have to be avoided:

- Errors that must be detected at run time by the execution of an Ada program

- Erroneous execution

- Incorrect order dependences

The absence of errors of the first class can only be guaranteed by program verification or complete testing. Each run time check within a program must become superfluous. One possibility to make run time checks superfluous is by explicit condition testing in the form of **if** and **case** statements wherever necessary for verification. (Note that the absence of such errors can never be achieved by simply suppressing all run time checks. This would only turn off the detection of the errors but not their existence and result in an erroneous program!)

The Ada Language Reference Manual LRM enumerates all the erroneous situations which are possible in Ada. Each situation can be avoided by a certain rule that imposes a specific restriction. Subchapter 6.1 contains an example for the avoidance of an erroneous situation in which an uninitialized object is used.

Furthermore, all kinds of incorrect order dependences must be avoided. These will not occur if specific features are eliminated. One typical example of an incorrect order dependence can be found in subchapter 6.2.

In order to guarantee that all branches in a program are explicit predefined exceptions must not be raised implicitly (for example by run time checks):

R8. Actions shall not raise a predefined exception.

Furthermore, indeterministic features must be excluded, e.g. select statements (which in our case is also a consequence of R5).

6.1   Undefined values

Using the value of an object that is not assigned a legal value previously might lead to an erroneous situation:

"The execution of a program is erroneous if it attempts to evaluate a scalar variable with an undefined value. Similarly, the execution of a program is erroneous if it attempts to apply a predefined operator to a variable that has a scalar subcomponent with an undefined value." (LRM 3.2.1/18)

A similar situation might occur when parameters are passed:

"The following constraint checks are performed for parameters of scalar and access types:
- Before the call: for a parameter of mode **in** or **in out**, it is checked that the value of the actual parameter belongs to the subtype of the formal parameter.
- After (normal) completion of the subprogram body: for a parameter of mode **in out** or **out**, it is checked that the value of the formal parameter belongs to the subtype of the actual variable. In the case of a type conversion, the value of the formal parameter is converted back and the check applies to the result of the conversion.

In each of the above cases, the execution of the program is erroneous if the checked value is undefined." (LRM 6.4.1/5-8)

It must therefore be guaranteed that:

1. every object that is used within an expression or as an actual parameter of a subprogram whose corresponding formal parameter has mode **in** or mode **in out** has been assigned a value before the first usage

2. and that a subprogram assigns a value to every parameter of mode **out** before returning.

The following two rules guarantee these conditions:

R9.   Objects shall have program defined values before they are used.

An object obtains a program defined value either by an initialization at its declaration or by an assignment or by being passed as an actual parameter where the corresponding formal parameter has mode **out**.

R10. Subprograms shall assign a value to all parameters of mode **out** before returning.

6.2   Expression Evaluation

The LRM (1983) says the following about the order in which operands within an expression are evaluated:

"The operands of a factor, of a term, of a simple expression, or of a relation, and the operands of an expression that does not contain a short-circuit control form, are evaluated in some order that is not defined by the language." (LRM 4.5/5)

An incorrect order dependence can occur only if a function within an expression E is called that changes one of the operands of E. So a rule is necessary to avoid this:

R11. Functions shall not change (directly or indirectly) non-local objects, i.e. functions shall have no side effects.

A function with a side effect is a function that changes the value of a non-local object either by an explicit assignment, or by calling a procedure that does the change, or by calling a procedure with a non-local object as an **out** or as an **in out** parameter.

7   SOURCE LEVEL TRANSPARENCY (PROPERTY 4)

To gain source level transparent programs we have to avoid:

– Aliasing,

– Default and implicit actions, and

– Features that are difficult to survey.

Property 4 leaves much freedom to state further programming rules. Nissen & Wallis (1984) for example give very good stylistic guidelines for Ada programs in the second part of their book "Portability and style in Ada". It makes recommendations for the manner of writing for nearly every Ada feature.

The following subchapter deals with aliasing as an example for source level transparency.

7.1   Aliasing

Aliasing means that an entity in the program has more than one name. The following kinds of aliasing are possible in Ada:

1. An object allocated on a collection can be accessed by two different pointers.

2. Within the scope of a renaming declaration or a subtype declaration without a constraint two different names exist for the same entity.

3. If an object X that is global to a subprogram S is associated with a formal parameter of S in a call of S then S can gain access to X either by the parameter or by directly naming X.

4. One object can be associated with two different formal parameters in a subprogram call. So within the subprogram this object has two different names, the names of the two formal parameters.

Kind 1 of aliasing is excluded from safe Ada by R1:

R1.   Access types shall not be used.

If a new name is introduced by a renaming declaration instead of an old name then only the new name shall be used within the scope of the renaming declaration (kind 2 of aliasing):

R21.   If an entity is declared by a renaming declaration then within the scope of this declaration only the new name shall be used and not the old one.

Kind 3 of aliasing is avoided by forbidding subprograms to use the same object by direct naming and by a formal parameter:

R13. A subprogram shall not be called with an object as an actual parameter that is also used within the subprogram (directly or indirectly) other than via the corresponding formal parameter.

R14 prevents kind 4 of aliasing:

R14. If the same object is associated with two different formal parameters in a procedure call then both shall have mode in.

8   CONCLUSION

The previous chapters have given examples of the programming rules for safe Ada. They meet the following requirements:

- They support the writing of safe Ada programs (with respect to our definition).

- They are simple enough to make it easy to check whether they are obeyed in a given program.

- They maintain the character of the language.

In contrast to SPARK (see Carre & Jennings (1987)), which defines a very curtailed Ada subset, safe Ada includes many more features. SPARK is a subset of safe Ada. Features included in safe Ada but not in SPARK are:

- Exceptions
- Generic Units
- Discriminants
- Variant Records
- Renaming
- Declare blocks
- Goto Statements
- Initial values in object declarations
- Packages containing object declarations

The study done by Aeronautical Radio Inc. (1987) is the opposite of SPARK: It excludes only a few features of Ada completely, e.g. dynamically allocated tasks. The study gives a lot of recommendations how Ada features should be used. It searches through all features and judges them by the special requirements of software for avionic systems. Checking whether all these recommendations were obeyed in a given program does not seem to be simple.

We think that the safe Ada programming rules are applicable in programming practice for the average programmer with only little effort. It is our conclusion that the programming language Ada is suitable for writing safety critical software.

9   REFERENCES

Aeronautical Radio Inc. (1987). Guidance for Using the Ada Programming Language in Avionic Systems. Annapolis, Maryland.

Carre, B. & Jennings, T. (1987). SPARK - The Spade Ada Kernel. Department of Electronics and Computer Sciene, University of Southampton.

Holzapfel, R. & Winterstein, G. (1987 a). Safe Ada Language Study. SYSTEAM KG, Karlsruhe.

Holzapfel, R. & Winterstein, G. (1987 b). Safe Ada Compiler Study. SYSTEAM KG, Karlsruhe.

Leveson, N.G. (1986). Software Safety: What, Why, and How. In acm computing surveys, Vol. 18, No.2.

LRM. (1983). The Programming Language Ada. Reference Manual. ANSI/MIL-STD-1815A-1983. Springer-Verlag.

Maule, R.A. (1986). Run-Time Implementation Issues for Real-Time Embedded Ada. In Proceedings of the First International Conference on Ada Programming Languages for the NASA Space Station.

MIL-STD 882B. (1984). Military Standard. System Safety Program Requirements.

Nissen, J. & Wallis, P. (1984). Portability and style in Ada. Cambridge: Cambridge University Press.

Part 6 Interfaces for Ada

EVALUATING TOOL SUPPORT INTERFACES

F.W. Long,

M.D. Tedd,

Department of Computer Science, University College of Wales, Aberystwyth.

Abstract. This paper describes a method of evaluating tool support interfaces and reports on our experiences of using this method to evaluate CAIS and PCTE.

1 INTRODUCTION

The new generation of tool support interfaces such as the Portable Common Tool Environment (PCTE) (PCTE 1986) and the Common APSE Interface Set (CAIS) (DoD 1986) is seen as a step forward in Software Engineering (Lyons & Tedd 1987 a,b) but very little has been done to evaluate these interfaces.

In evaluating interfaces one needs to consider two main areas: the impact on the tool writer, and the cost and behaviour of implementations of the interface. As discussed below, we refine this further to have four main criteria in mind when evaluating particular facilities: level, appropriateness, implementability, and performance. Where possible, we intend to make quantitative measurements, but much of our experience, especially in the area of the impact on the toolwriter, has to be subjective.

Evaluation projects like ours are hard, and the results have to be treated with care. However we do feel that limited evaluation is better than none, and greatly needed by the communities defining these interfaces.

2 DISCUSSION

There are four general criteria that we distinguish in evaluating the facilities of an interface.

2.1 Level

A "low level" facility is one that corresponds fairly directly to the facilities of an underlying operating system, such as the 'signal' facilities for inter-process communication found in PCTE, or the node and object locks found in CAIS and PCTE respectively. A "high level" facility is one that provides a more abstract function which probably maps onto a sequence of more primitive functions; examples of higher level facilities are the transactions of PCTE and the mimic queues of CAIS.

High level facilities are generally more desirable than low level ones, so long as they are appropriate in the sense described below. The tool writer is able to design with more abstract, more application-oriented concepts; this raises productivity and removes the opportunity to make various kinds of error. The implementer of the interface has more freedom in the mapping of higher level constructs, which may allow more overall efficiency than would arise from the individual mappings of a sequence of lower level constructs. Indeed, the very fact that there are less calls made, to an appropriate high-level interface, should allow for reduction in total system overheads.

To some extent, the level of a function can be measured objectively by looking to see how many primitive operations of the underlying system are needed to implement it. Judgement is needed to avoid classifying functions as high-level when the operations arise from mismatch of functions rather than difference of level.

2.2 Appropriateness

We use the word 'appropriate' to indicate that the facility provided is, in some sense, what the tool writer needs. Any lack of appropriateness, or mismatch of function, will lead to extra work by the toolwriter, and probably to inefficiency in the running system. In our sense, appropriateness is a different criterion from level, but there is an increased chance that high level facilities will be found inappropriate for a given tool; there is greater flexibility in designing a tool to use low level facilities.

Appropriateness of an interface's functions can really only be measured subjectively. However, it is a major factor in the overall cost of running tools - inappropriateness causes extra overheads.

2.3 Implementability

To be useful, a tool support interface must be implementable
on a range of underlying architectures, and with a reasonable
development cost. This implementability can be demonstrated by the
simple, but costly, exercise of doing it, and studying the problems that
arise.

2.4 Performance

By studying a well-instrumented implementation of a tool
support interface, the cost of using each function of the interface can
be measured and dissected. Crude measurements of the resource (cpu,
disc traffic) demands of the functions are worth making, but not
sufficient. To produce meaningful results on the intrinsic performance
of the interface one needs to examine the causes of these resource
demands and use ones best judgement to separate them into:
- characteristics of the hardware and software underlying the
  implementation
- avoidable characteristics of the implementation being
  studied
- intrinsic characteristics of the interface.

3 OUR PROJECT

In 1985 we started our implementation of a well-instrumented
prototype of CAIS. This is now operational.

As the basis of our evaluation, we have designed, at an
abstract level, a number of typical "scenarios" which exercise the
various aspects and features of a tool support interface. These
scenarios were first designed in application terms without reference to
any particular tool support interface and then mapped onto CAIS and,
later, onto PCTE.

The five scenarios chosen were a configuration management
system, an edit-compile-link-test cycle, a conference management system,
a window manager and a design editor.

When mapped onto actual interfaces these were not
implemented in full but their actions were simulated. For example, we
did not write a compiler but instead wrote a tool which accessed a
typical collection of files and structured libraries and soaked up

processing power for a typical length of time.

By studying the designs of the scenarios on the two
interfaces we have been able to make subjective judgements of the level
and appropriateness of the function of the interfaces. At the time of
writing this paper four of the scenarios are implemented and running on
our CAIS prototype, we are about to start measuring these, and we hope
to report more quantitative results at the conference.

4 CAIS EVALUATION

We implemented most of CAIS on a SUN, in three man years.
Our implementation omits a few of the less interesting packages, and was
never intended to approach production quality. Nevertheless, our
experience does show that a quality implementation could be achieved for
a reasonable cost (20 man years?). No aspects of the CAIS interface
presented substantial problems to the implementation.

Our implementation is about 30,600 statements of source
code, including instrumentation; 98% of this is Ada (we used the Verdix
Ada Development System). A lot of space is used: each tool carries an
overhead of 950KB, and there are four "daemons" (separately running
processes) totalling 1840KB. Removing instrumentation, improved
compilers, or lower-level implementation languages would all reduce
these sizes.

All our scenarios mapped quite easily onto CAIS, which feels
like a nice "clean" interface to the toolwriter. We found no glaring
omissions, and the different facilities are certainly appropriate in the
sense described above.

The node model of CAIS supported the design of the tools'
data structures in a natural way, although it is clearly lower level
than PCTE in the area of integrity control. The integration of the node
and process models was of particular help to the tool writer where data
needed to be associated with particular processes.

The inter-process communication mechanisms (queues) provided
by CAIS are quite high-level, so it was a pleasure to discover that
these facilities were totally appropriate for our purposes.

5 PCTE EVALUATION

A major difference between CAIS and PCTE is that PCTE supports typing of its objects whereas there is no typing of nodes available in CAIS (apart from the distinction between the three basic kinds of node).

The typing in PCTE does cause the designer work to make the data design more explicit, which is probably a good thing: certainly we have not found this onerous in developing our scenarios on PCTE. Indeed, the typing introduces more structure into the tool which can be of help to the tool writer. It also enables more checking to be done by the interface so there is less need to write other code.

The PCTE interface was not felt to be as "clean" as that of CAIS. Some of the calls are overloaded, for example sdsscan carries out several quite different functions on schema definition sets. In contrast, there may be several different calls to carry out very similar functions, for example starta, startl and startp are slightly different ways of starting another process.

Experience elsewhere has shown that PCTE can be implemented, but the development cost is greater than that for CAIS. (Implementing CAIS-A which also has typing and transactions will presumably be comparable with PCTE).

We have an early version of Emeraude, the implementation of PCTE from our colleagues in the Sapphire project; each release improves the robustness, and the quality of documentation, but there is certainly scope for further improvements.

The separation of the object model and the process model in PCTE made the mapping of the conference system and window manager scenarios onto PCTE more difficult than their mapping onto CAIS. In both these scenarios there are objects (files) associated with processes. PCTE provides no natural place in which to put these objects and care must be taken in naming them to ensure that there is no possibility of name clashes with objects associated with different processes.

6 FUTURE WORK

Our work on PCTE is continuing and we will be making further comparisons of CAIS and PCTE. We are hoping that our scenarios will be mapped onto Unix*, VMS and MS-DOS which will enable us to compare the modern tool support interfaces with more traditional operating systems.

Also, we have a Ph.D. student working on the novel Flex system developed at RSRE (Malvern) and at least one of our scenarios will be mapped onto this.

Both CAIS and PCTE are being further developed, as CAIS-A and PCTE+ respectively. We are contributing to both developments and hope to apply our evaluation techniques to the new versions at an appropriate moment.

7   ACKNOWLEDGEMENTS

The work on the evaluation of CAIS was carried out under the KITE project and supported by the Ministry of Defence (RSRE, Malvern). The work on the evaluation of PCTE and the comparisons between CAIS and PCTE were carried out as part of the Sapphire project (Tedd 1987) and supported by the ESPRIT programme of the Commission of the European Communities.

8   REFERENCES

PCTE (1986). PCTE. A Basis for a Portable Common Tool Environment. Functional Specifications. Fourth edition.

DoD (1986). Common Ada Programming Support Environment (APSE) Interface Set (CAIS). DOD-STD-1838, 9 October 1986.

Lyons T.G. & Tedd M.D. (1987a). Recent Developments in Tool Support Interfaces, CAIS and PCTE, Ada UK Conference, York, January 1987.

Lyons T.G. & Tedd M.D. (1987b). Technical Overview of PCTE and CAIS, Ada UK Conference, York, January 1987.

Tedd M.D. (1987). The Sapphire Project : Building Confidence in PCTE, ESPRIT Conference, Brussels, September 1987.

*Unix is a registered trademark of Bell Laboratories

A STANDARD INTERFACE TO PROGRAMMING ENVIRONMENT INFORMATION

Thomas Smith
Helen Gill
Annelle Harrison
David Hough
Charles Howell
Teresa Reed
The MITRE Corporation, McLean, Virginia 22102

Abstract. There have been several investigations of the use of intermediate representations as a communications mechanism for language-based tools in an Ada® Programming Support Environment (APSE). The Descriptive Intermediate Attributed Notation for Ada (DIANA) is the most widely used intermediate representation for Ada. In 1986 a new draft definition of DIANA was released. However, all implementations of DIANA to date are based on the 1983 draft definition. The MITRE Corporation has implemented a prototype DIANA generator and Ada interface based on the 1986 revision. This prototype provides an opportunity to evaluate the revised definition as a possible standard for the representation of programming environment information. The purpose of this paper is to report the results of this work. We provide an introduction to intermediate representations, an overview of DIANA, and a description of the MITRE project. Finally, we present our observations, recommendations, and conclusions.

1 INTRODUCTION

A **Programming Support Environment** (PSE) consists of software tools and data that assist in the task of constructing, testing, and validating software. The data that are used and produced by these software tools include the source program code, information derived from the source program text (program compilation information), and information derived outside source program text. Symbol tables, graphs of subprogram calls, data flow graphs, and various syntactic and semantic attributes are all examples of program compilation information. Information that is derived outside source program text includes requirements, design decisions, software configuration status, and testing status.

Interfaces among software tools are called **inter-tool interfaces**. These interfaces provide the mechanism for the communication of data among software tools. The mechanism must consist of (abstract) data structures (describing the form of the data) and subprograms (providing the protocol for access and manipulation of the data). An **integrated (software) toolset** is a collection of software tools having a precise and consistent definition of the data structures and subprograms used to communicate data via inter-tool interfaces. A **language-based environment** is a PSE that is based on a single programming language and consists of an integrated toolset.

An **intermediate representation** defines abstract data structures that can represent the syntactic and semantic information about a source program. Primarily, intermediate representations decoupled the front end (syntactic/semantic recognition) and back end (code generation/optimization) of language compilers. This enabled the production of compilers with multiple back ends, one for each computer hardware on which programs written in the language are to execute. Intermediate representations coincidentally provided software tools with information derived from the source program text. In addition to information derived from source program text some intermediate representations capture other programming environment information such as requirements, design decisions, software configuration status, and testing status. Therefore, an intermediate representation can serve as the basis for an integrated toolset.

The constituents of a programming environment can be classified into four categories (Luckham et al., 1987):
- Components: A reusable package which accepts input or delivers output in an internal representation (e.g., a parser).
- Support Tools: Tools used to build components (e.g., scanner and parser generators).
- Integration Mechanisms: Components whose role is to connect tools together.
- Application Tools: Tools built out of components which use the integration mechanisms, and provide a specific capability to the environment user.

For the purpose of this paper, an interface that provides access to the intermediate representation is considered to be an integration mechanism. It defines a realization of the intermediate representation data structures and the subprograms that access these structures.

Two intermediate representations currently under investigation in the Ada community are DIANA and Internal Representation Including Semantics (IRIS), a notation under development by the Arcadia consortium (Taylor et al., 1986; Clarke et al., 1986). However, since the IRIS intermediate representation is under development and several versions of DIANA are currently in use, DIANA has received the majority of industry attention.

2 OVERVIEW OF DIANA

2.1 History

DIANA was developed in 1981 (Butler, 1984; Evans et al., 1983), as the result of the merger of two intermediate representation languages defined for Ada (TCOL Ada and AIDA). The Ada Joint Program Office (AJPO) funded the maintenance and revision of a draft DIANA definition in 1982 and 1983. Despite the absence of an AJPO standard interface for DIANA, DIANA has been used in several commercial Ada compiler developments (e.g., Intermetrics (ACS Compiler), Rational®, SYSTEAM, VERDIX™ (VADS™)). Ada compiler vendors conform to the draft DIANA definition to varying degrees (Heroz, 1986) and there is little coordination among vendors. As a result, DIANA interfaces and tools are very vendor-specific. A revised draft DIANA definition was prepared by Intermetrics in May 1986, under a contract to the Naval Research Laboratories in Washington, DC (McKinley and Schaefer, 1986). This document is titled, "DIANA Reference Manual" (DRM). The DRM involved significant restructuring of DIANA but did not include an Ada interface to DIANA. However, the majority of DIANA implementations are based on the 1983 draft definition.

2.2 Interface Description Language (IDL)

Concurrent with the first draft definition of DIANA, a notation was developed for expressing the DIANA definition. This notation is called the Interface Description Language (Lamb, 1987; Nestor et al., 1982). IDL provides the means to describe abstract data structures as typed, attributed, directed graphs. Each node has a set of attribute values that reference other nodes. A group of nodes called a **class** may be defined. All nodes belonging to a class inherit the set of attributes defined by the class. This allows attribute definitions to be factored to a class. The SoftLab Project of the University of North Carolina (UNC) at Chapel Hill has developed tools to support the use of IDL, called the UNC IDL Toolkit (Warren et al., 1985; Snodgrass and Shannon, 1986). This toolkit supports IDL translation to C and Pascal.

2.3 Draft DIANA definition

The IDL specification for DIANA captures the structure of an Ada source program, but does not fully capture the static semantic information of the Ada source program. In the DRM the DIANA semantic information is presented in English text.

DIANA attributes are only distinguished by a naming convention. DIANA attributes pertaining to structure, lexical content, semantic analysis, and code information are designated by the prefixes as_, lx_, sm_, and cd_, respectively. The IDL description of DIANA may be extended to include additional attributes for the capture of other information.

The following illustration is extracted from the DRM corresponding to a portion of section 10.1 of the Ada Reference Manual (ARM) (U.S. DoD, 1983):

```
pragma_s => as_list : Seq Of pragma;
compilation_unit => as_context_elem_s : context_elem_s,
        as_all_decl : ALL_DECL,
      as_pragma_s : pragma_s;
CONTEXT_ELEM ::= context_pragma;
context_pragma => as_pragma : pragma;
```

In this notation, classes are represented with all capitals. The notation for node definition consists of a node name followed by "=>" and a list of node attribute definitions. This notation also serves for defining attributes of a class. Attribute definitions consists of an attribute name followed by ":" and a type name. A class definition consists of a class name followed by "::=" and a list of member names. Note the suffix _s denotes a sequence of items.

2.4   Use of DIANA in an APSE

In an ideal APSE, all software tools would be completely vendor-independent and 'plug-compatible' (Butler, 1984). For example, in an APSE based on a standard DIANA interface, a system manager could select a specific software tool from any available DIANA-compatible toolset. In such an environment, an obsolete software tool could be upgraded by simply replacing that software tool with a different software tool that also uses a DIANA intermediate representation. The advantages of this capability are significant, especially for government procurements where a wide variety of vendors may be used. However, substantial problems must be solved before such an environment can exist. Vendors of those tools that create and use DIANA must agree on a DIANA definition. Without a standard DIANA definition and a standard Ada interface or interfaces to DIANA, there will continue to be a wide range of vendor DIANA implementations. The variety of vendor-specific implementations is a real obstacle to the use of DIANA as a common inter-tool interface for Ada-based software tools.

Despite the lack of a standard DIANA definition, several Ada tool vendors have made use of DIANA for their integrated environments. DIANA is the basis of a programming environment and hardware offered by Rational® computers (Archer and Devlin, 1986). Other Ada tool vendors, such as SYSTEAM and VERDIX™, have also used variants of DIANA as the basis for their inter-tool interfaces.

Other tool efforts involving DIANA include the work of Besson (Besson and Queyras, 1987) whose Test Environment Generator (GET) tool is based on DIANA. GET is a unit level testing tool providing the generation of test drivers and skeletal bodies associated with the testing of components. Chesi (Chesi et al., 1984) is developing an experimental program development environment based on an internal representation language such as DIANA for source programs. Luckham (Luckham et al., 1987) is also working on a prototype environment for the development of Ada programs that is based on Annotated Ada (ANNA) and Task Sequencing Language. One of the underpinnings of this environment is a variant of DIANA that has been extended to support ANNA. Finally, Rosenblum (Rosenblum, 1985) describes a methodology for the design of source to source transformation tools based on DIANA.

The potential benefits of a standard Ada intermediate representation are considerable. Standardization would reduce duplication of effort, encourage a third-party market for language-based tools, encourage open systems, and provide a manageable standard for integrated toolsets as a step toward an eventual standard for an APSE. DIANA is an attractive candidate for standardization because it is the only widely used Ada intermediate representation.

There is a tension between the benefits of standardization and the costs. On the negative side, adoption of a standard would make existing software obsolete, and perhaps preclude vendor specific optimizations and implementation strategies. Premature standardization inhibits further research. The Rational® Environment is an "existence proof" that DIANA can be useful as the communications vehicle for language-based environments. However the approach taken by Digital Equipment Corporation (DEC™) is a good example of an implementation strategy for an Ada compiler that would not benefit by a standard Ada intermediate representation. DEC's Ada compiler and debugger use a proprietary intermediate representation that is essentially the same for DEC's entire family of languages for the VAX™.

3 PROJECT DESCRIPTION

The objective of the MITRE research was to assess the adequacy of the DRM as a foundation for inter-tool interfaces among Ada-based tools. This assessment included an analysis of the DIANA specification itself with respect to its structure, completeness, and correctness. Also, we assessed the usability of the abstract data structure defined by DIANA. Because an Ada interface to access DIANA was not defined in the DRM, we investigated the issues involved in defining one.

Initially, we built a parser, and integrated it with the software produced by the IDL Toolkit. The result was an Ada parser capable of translating Ada source code into an equivalent DIANA graph with only the lexical and syntactic attributes evaluated. A set of semanticization packages was then provided for the purpose of adding semantic information to the DIANA graph. Two Ada interfaces to DIANA were developed. One interface was based on the Ada variant record data structure, and the other was constructed from graph components reused from Grady Booch's *Software Components with Ada* (Booch, 1987). The latter interface was used in the semanticization packages. Several tools were created for reading and writing the of DIANA graphs produced by the parser. A source code formatter developed by the project was used to exercise the variant record interface to DIANA and for testing the DIANA readers and writers.

We investigated the use of an interface using Ada variant records to represent different classes of nodes in the IDL specification of DIANA. The variant records show the entire node-attribute structure for the main classes in DIANA, where the record discriminants represent class values and the record components represent node values. Seven variant record types constitute the fundamental structures: compilation unit information, declarations, defining occurrences, type specifications, type definition, expressions, and statements. Thirteen other record types support these structures. The compilation unit structure combines several DIANA classes to provide a top level view of an Ada program unit. A shortcoming of the variant record interface is that it does not provide a simple mechanism for traversing all attributes of a node without regard to the type of an attribute. The use of a variant record interface for tree traversal requires many specific procedures to handle each node structure, since Ada does not have a mechanism to discover all the components of a record type and traverse them.

We also investigated an untyped graph interface to DIANA data structures. This approach allows the DIANA syntax tree to be "walked" recursively. However, the untyped graph interface is not sufficient by itself for accessing DIANA because it does not present the DIANA type structure to the user.

4   OBSERVATIONS AND RECOMMENDATIONS

The observations and recommendations for the DRM are discussed in three categories: suitability for capturing Ada syntax and semantics, ability to support derived and other environment information, and ability to support an Ada interface.

4.1   Ada semantics

The IDL specification of DIANA does not fully capture the static semantics of Ada. We considered this a drawback, since this information is not inherent in the DIANA structure and thus not available in machine processible form. Butler (Butler, 1984) indicates that one of the challenges for DIANA is to provide a more formal definition of DIANA semantics.

The presentation of the IDL class structure and the order of the node attribute relationships in the DRM obscures the structure of DIANA. The DRM includes hierarchy charts that show the relationships among the classes and nodes. The charts are useful in clarifying the DIANA structure.

Some restructuring was required because the DIANA definition required a special "Void" node that, unlike other IDL nodes, does not inherit attributes. IDL does not have a provision for a special node such as that, so the Void node accumulated the attributes of all the classes to which it belonged. This is erroneous, since the Void node should not have any attributes. The solution adopted was the creation of special classes above the normal DIANA classes to include the Void node. These classes are out of the main derivation sequence of DIANA classes and bear no attributes of their own, so the Void node has no unwanted attributes.

Even though the ARM defines enumeration literals to be equivalent to parameterless functions and treats them as such, the DRM does not reflect this. The only information stored for an enumeration literal is its lexical value and position number. The DRM treats enumeration literals as a special case and not as part of subprograms, especially with respect to visibility, renaming, and type derivation. We believe the DRM should incorporate the functional aspect of enumeration literals into its definition of DIANA.

We believe that there are errors in the description of the DERIVABLE_SPEC class. Since only certain Ada types can be anonymous (i.e., have no simple name) according to the ARM, the semantic attribute sm_is_anonymous associated with this class can never be true for Ada subtypes. That is, Ada subtypes always have simple names. The DRM implies that an Ada subtype may not have a simple name. Also, the DRM indicates that there are circumstances under which the derived type of a derived type definition is not anonymous. Since the ARM specifically indicates that all derived types are anonymous, this contradicts the DRM. The concept of derived types in the DRM needs to be reworked to bring it into conformance with the ARM.

We found the presentation of normalization of parameter and component sequences (i.e., the attributes sm_normalized_param_s, sm_normalized_comp_s) to be inadequate. The concept of normalization is defined, partly by example, for component sequences but not for parameter sequences. Further, no cross references are given in the DRM to locate the point of definition for normalization of sequences. It is not clear whether other sequences such as the as_alternative_s attribute need to be normalized also. The presentation of normalization in the DRM needs clarification.

The English text description of the DIANA semantics is difficult to use. The factorization into a class of commonly named attributes with respect to Ada syntax (e.g., sm_exp_type attribute of the NAME_EXP class) is one reason for this difficulty. Such factored attributes can have different meanings across the nodes of the class. For example, sm_exp_type may indicate the subtype of an entity, the subtype of a designated object, or may be void in the case of an entry call. Such overloaded meanings for a name reduces the clarity of the semantic descriptions. Since attributes can only be differentiated within IDL by name, some of these factored attributes that do not have invariant meaning across the nodes of an class should be unfactored to the nodes and renamed to convey their true meaning.

In order to use the existing DIANA definition, several small changes were required. These did not alter the substance of the definition. Problems included name conflicts with C and Ada reserved words (solved by adding the prefix "Di_"). During the implementation of the prototype DIANA translator, we also encountered a number of minor typographical errors and omissions. Because there is no index furnished with the DRM, we found it difficult to locate information. We realize that these are common problems associated with draft definitions.

4.2 Derived and other environment information

There are a number of areas not addressed in the DRM that should be. The definition does not specify how the predefined Ada environment is to be incorporated into DIANA. The predefined environment includes package STANDARD, the predefined operators of the predefined types, and universal integer. In the context of a DIANA library of separately compiled Ada program units, there is a need to maintain the table of symbols defined and used in each program unit as part of DIANA. This capability is desirable because defining and used occurrences of symbols of a given program unit need to be externally referenced by other units and because the associated referencing mechanism should be efficient.

According to the DRM, derived information that can be "easily computed" is not included in DIANA. "Easily computed" in this context means that information can be computed in a single traversal of a DIANA graph that visits a small number of nodes. We do not believe that this is necessarily a valid criterion for deciding whether certain kinds of information should be excluded from DIANA. Examples of information that tools need to have readily accessible include: defining and used occurrences of symbols, (potentially) visible symbols, potentially overloaded operators, derivable subprograms associated with an Ada type, and predefined operators associated with a type. In particular, the DRM does provide for the inclusion of derived subprograms for a derived type. However, the efficient identification of derivable subprograms for a given type is not addressed. Addressing this identification of subprograms would make the former process of inclusion more efficient and make the DRM more symmetric with respect to derived and derivable types.

Even though the DRM allows extensions to the original DIANA definition, it does not provide a standard mechanism for the incorporation of such extensions into DIANA in a manner that does not affect tools not using these extensions. Currently, extensions can only be made in an ad hoc manner. Rational® has incorporated a flexible extension mechanism into the 1983 draft DIANA definition in order to support the capture of additional environment information. Such a mechanism is needed for the DRM.

The DIANA structure has been oriented toward the front end of compilers. That is, the DIANA class structure has been designed to factor commonly named attributes with respect to the Ada syntax. This essentially provides a bottom up description of the DIANA structure. This structure may not be the appropriate one for other tools. On the other hand, restructuring DIANA to accommodate a large class of tools may introduce a number of inefficiencies for compilers. Additional implementation and evaluation of DIANA based tools is required in order to better assess these tradeoffs.

4.3   Ada interface

If the DIANA interface is not reasonably efficient, then it will not be usable for high-quality software development tools. So far, both prototype Ada interfaces seem fairly efficient. The biggest efficiency problem occurs in reading and writing DIANA graphs. Lamb (Lamb, 1987) indicates that the ASCII external representation for storing DIANA graphs is not so inefficient as to prohibit it from being used in production quality DIANA implementations. However, others such as Rational® and VERDIX™ claim that to produce efficient compilers some sort of fast binary form for storing DIANA graphs is necessary. What is the best stored form for DIANA is still an open question.

The IDL specification of DIANA has taken advantage of IDL's support for classes and type inheritance. For example, DIANA is a hierarchical decomposition of classes with a number of attributes being factored to classes. However, this class and inheritance structure is not readily expressed in Ada. One approach uses Ada records with discriminants. However, an Ada interface to DIANA requires the ability to traverse over nodes of possibly different types and at any point to determine for a given node what are the discriminants and the value of each discriminant associated with the Ada record object representing the node. Ada does not support the capability to determine for a given record object its discriminants and the value of each discrminant. The development of an Ada interface for DIANA is an important area for further investigation. The ultimate Ada interface may consist of a two level interface: one level based on fundamental operations on nodes and attributes and the other based on traversal. Moreover, DIANA may also need significant restructuring to accommodate such an interface.

5   CONCLUSIONS

The DRM is not ready for standardization. Work needs to be done in the following areas: definition of an Ada interface, restructuring of the DIANA specification, correction of errors, and specification of the Ada predefined environment. The usability of the DRM as the foundation for an inter-tool interface for Ada-based tools is still an open question.

6 ACKNOWLEDGEMENTS

The authors wish to thank John Summers, Roger Duncan, and Rebecca Bowerman at MITRE for supporting this project. We also wish to thank John Nestor, Grady Booch, Richard Snodgrass, and his students at UNC for stimulating technical discussions and insights during the course of this project. Finally, the views expressed in this paper are strictly those of the authors.

7 REFERENCES

Archer Jr., J. E. and M. T. Devlin (1986), "Rational's Experience Using Ada for Very Large Systems," *Proceedings of the First International Conference on Ada Programming Language Applications for the NASA Space Station*, Houston, TX: University of Houston-Clear Lake, pp. B.2.5.1-B.2.5.12.

Besson, M. and B. Queyras (1987), "GET: A Test Environment Generator for Ada," in *Ada Components: Libraries and Tools, Proceedings of the Ada-Europe International Conference*, The Ada Companion Series, pp.237-250, Cambridge England: Cambridge University Press.

Booch, G. (1987), *Software Components with Ada*, Menlo Park, CA: The Benjamin Cummings Publishing Company, Incorporated.

Butler, K. J. (1984) "DIANA Past, Present, and Future," in *Ada Software Tools Interfaces*, pp. 3-22 New York: Springer-Verlag, LNCS 180.

Chesi, M. et al. (1984), "ISDE: An Interactive Software Development Environment," in *ACM SIGSOFT Software Engineering Notes*, IX:3, pp. 81-88.

Clarke, L. A., J. C. Wileden, and A. L. Wolf (1986), *GRAPHITE: A Meta-Tool for Ada Environment Development*, COINS Technical Report 85-44, Amherst, MA: University of Massachusetts.

Evans Jr., A., K. J. Butler, G. Goos, and W. A. Wulf (1983), *DIANA Reference Manual*, Revision 3, TL 83-4, Pittsburgh, PA: Tartan Laboratories, Incorporated.

Heroz, W. (1986), *DIANA, An Intermediate Language for Ada, Modifications and Implementation Decisions*, SYSTEAM KG (Internal).

Lamb, D. A. (1987), "IDL: Sharing Intermediate Representations," in *ACM Transactions on Programming Languages and Systems*, IX:3, pp.297-318.

Luckham, D. C., R. Neff, and D. S. Rosenblum (1987), "An Environment for Ada Software Development Based on Formal Specification," *Ada Letters*, VII:3, pp.94-106.

McKinley, K. L. and C. G. Schaefer (1986), *DIANA Reference Manual*, Draft Revision 4, IR-MD-078, Bethesda, MD: Intermetrics, Incorporated.

Nestor, J. R., W. A. Wolf, and D. A. Lamb (1982), *IDL - Interface Description Language Formal Description*, Draft Revision 2.0, Pittsburgh, PA: Computer Science Department, Carnegie-Mellon University.

Rosenblum, D. S. (1985), *A Methodology for the Design of Ada Transformation Tools in a DIANA Environment*, TR No. 85-269, Stanford, CA: Computer Systems Laboratory, Stanford University.

Snodgrass, R. and K. Shannon (1986), *Supporting Flexible and Efficient Tool Integration*, SoftLab Document No. 25, Chapel Hill, NC: Department of Computer Science, University of North Carolina.

Taylor, R. N. et al. (1986), "Arcadia: A Software Development Environment Research Project,: in *IEEE 2nd International Conference on Ada Applications and Environments*, pp. 137-149.

U.S. Department of Defense (1983), *Reference Manual for the Ada Programming Language*, ANSI/MIL-STD-1815A-1983, Washington, DC.

Warren, W. B., J. Kickenson, and R. Snodgrass (1985), *A Tutorial Introduction to Using IDL*, SoftLab Document No. 1, Chapel Hill, NC: Department of Computer Science, University of North Carolina.